ASIL NADIR

Tim Hindle was born and educated in Britain. He was finance and business editor of *The Economist* and founder editor of *EuroBusiness* magazine. He is also the author of *Pocket Manager* and *Pocket MBA*. Through his Turkish wife he knows the Istanbul business community well, and he provides a unique insight into the two cultures that created Asil Nadir.

ASIL NADIR

FUGITIVE FROM INJUSTICE?

TIM HINDLE

PAN BOOKS
IN ASSOCIATION WITH MACMILLAN LONDON

To my family, all of them, for their support and their love. I can only wish they will be as proud of this as I am of them.

First published 1991 as *The Sultan of Berkeley Square: Asil Nadir and the Thatcher Years*
by Macmillan London Limited

This revised and expanded edition published 1993 by Pan Books Limited
a division of Pan Macmillan Publishers Limited
Cavaye Place London SW10 9PG
and Basingstoke
in association with Macmillan London Limited

Associated companies throughout the world

ISBN 0 330 33155 8

1 3 5 7 9 8 6 4 2

A CIP catalogue record for this book is available from the British Library

Typeset by Pan Macmillan Limited
Printed by Cox and Wyman Ltd, Reading, Berkshire

CONTENTS

PREFACE

THE disturbing story of Asil Nadir and Polly Peck, the company he founded and built up in the 1980s into one of the largest corporations in Britain, will remain among the most bizarre business mysteries of all time. In the three years following Asil Nadir's first arrest in December 1990, enormous resources from the British accounting and legal professions and the newspaper industry were devoted to finding the answers to three main questions:

1) Was the billion-pound Polly Peck in reality just a balloon pumped up by accounting tricks which disguised a small-scale operation that sometimes scarcely made a profit?

2) Was Asil Nadir himself an audacious crook who took the hundreds of millions of pounds raised by the City of London for this artificially swollen corporation and then squirrelled them into offshore accounts for his own benefit?

3) And after he had been first charged with fraud and false accounting, was there a complicated plot designed to pervert the course of justice at his trial? And was Asil Nadir himself the perpetrator or the victim of this plot?

Despite all the time and money spent in investigation, none of these questions has yet received a fully satisfactory answer. For sure, the reported results of Polly Peck's fruit businesses in Turkey and Cyprus were exaggerated by the problems of accounting for inflation in Turkey, and then of converting the accounts into sterling, the currency of Polly Peck's registered head office. But if the accounts were not really what they seemed to be when converted into pounds, then should the highly efficient London stockmarket not have identified the chimera for what it was, and marked down Polly Peck's share price accordingly?

In the early 1990s a book called *Accounting for Growth*, written by investment analyst Terry Smith, attracted a good deal of attention. It described some of the tricks that companies had been using in the 1980s to fluff up their accounts and to help make their claims for growth self-fulfilling. At one point in the book the author says, 'It is difficult to judge whether Polly Peck failed because of malpractice, or because of fundamental flaws in currency mismatching, working capital controls or even just the absolute levels of debt.'

As for whether Asil Nadir was one of the biggest crooks this century, there is a problem with his motive. Why would he want to steal hundreds of millions of pounds for his personal use when he was already worth hundreds of millions of pounds? And if he had stolen them and hidden them away in Switzerland, then surely he would have used them whenever he wanted to buy Polly Peck shares? Yet the company's share price seems to have collapsed on 20 September 1990 partly because banks were selling the Polly Peck shares that they held as security for loans they had given to Asil Nadir. And among other things these loans had enabled him to buy Polly Peck shares. Why borrow tens of millions from one set of banks if you've got hundreds of millions sitting in another?

Another theory has it that the stolen money was being channelled into northern Cyprus to support this isolated piece of land and to remove some of the burden from Turkey, which was virtually its only other economic support. Nadir himself claimed that by the end of the 1980s Polly Peck companies accounted for about 40 per cent of all economic activity in northern Cyprus.

This theory casts Asil Nadir in the role of a modern Robin Hood, a role which many of his fellow countrymen were keen to give him but which did not fit comfortably with his long absences from the island. Alternatively, perhaps the money was no more than a balancing item in double-entry bookkeeping, where every asset has to have an equal and opposite liability. Thus it was balancing non-existent profits from fruit-picking in the Near East, and no more tangible than those profits.

That Asil Nadir never fully separated his personal wealth from that of the company is not in doubt. At one time he was the sole signatory on cheques, and he frequently signed company cheques for his personal expenditure. He shuffled money around the world, in and out of places like Jersey, the Isle of Man and Switzerland, with a dexterity that deceived many a keen-eyed accountant. Why was all this necessary if not for purposes of deceit?

Evidence from the administrators of Polly Peck alleges that Mr Nadir took £371 million of money that the company had raised in various international financial markets. This, they allege, was used to buy Polly Peck shares, newspapers in Turkey, country houses in England, hotels in Cyprus and antiques all over the place.

But by the summer of 1993, after Mr Nadir had fled to Cyprus, his businesses there (which the administrators had unsuccessfully been trying to get their hands on for years) were being repossessed by the northern Cyprus government in settlement for unpaid tax and social security bills amounting in the first instance to less than £100,000. If Mr Nadir had stolen so many millions then surely he would have wanted to use them to maintain good faith with the government of what was effectively the only territory in the world that would take him in?

In the Nadir/Polly Peck story straightforward explanations for events were often ignored. For example, there were periods when Asil Nadir's lifestyle ratcheted up a notch or two without any visibly corresponding improvement in his income. There was never any shortage of colourful explanations for these apparent mismatches: he was trading arms for the Middle East in and out of Cyprus; or he was running brothels and gambling rackets in London's Soho; or he was dealing in heroin before America bought up Turkey's poppies and cut off a major source of the drug.

The reality was probably more prosaic. For instance, in the late 1970s the considerable success of Nadir's garment company Wearwell, against the market trend of the time, enabled him to launch Polly Peck and his cardboard-box business in Famagusta. The mystery of Wearwell's success was based not on superior competitive ability but on Nadir's exploitation of a clever scheme devised by the Turkish government to get round the fact that it then had no foreign exchange.

Nadir was very adept at recognising and taking advantage of opportunities like this, and their complexity often required sailing close to the wind. But his apparent ability again and again to produce rabbits out of his hat – cash-and-carry at Wearwell, the Turkish forex scheme, cardboard boxes in Cyprus, water in central Anatolia – helped create the image of a commercial wizard.

The British media loved the magic of it, and when Polly Peck collapsed they loved it even more. Pages and pages were devoted to revelations about the wizard's tricks and alleged 'proof' that they were just frauds. Eventually this played into the hands of Nadir and his supporters who frequently referred to his 'trial by media' – a process which cast increasing doubt on the ability of any jury in the UK to give him a fair hearing.

Throughout the life and after-life of Polly Peck the interest of the media in the story was always extraordinary. Its role in picking up bits of leaked information and running with them became part of the story itself. From the moment when the press was tipped off about the Serious Fraud Office's raid on Polly Peck in 1990, to the MP Michael Mates's letters to the Attorney General about the Nadir case, leaked to the press in June 1993, the media was used continuously by both sides to manipulate their message.

Following the leak of his letter, Michael Mates was forced to resign. In his resignation speech to the House of Commons he said, 'the only people who had copies of those letters are the Attorney General, Mr Nadir and the SFO. It is a matter perhaps of speculation as to who leaked the letter to the press last week.' In fact the letter was faxed to the *Daily Mail* by a senior tax official. Mr Mates said that he could only have got the letter from an officer of the SFO.

And so to the third question. Was Asil Nadir the victim of an elaborate plot to pervert the course of justice – of which leaks to the press were a significant part? Or was he (or his supporters) the perpetrator of the plot, designed to muddy the waters over his trial and ensure that it never came to court?

The Nadir story aroused such strong passions, both for and against, that it became difficult to separate fact from feeling. In such an atmosphere all sorts of conspiracies were conceivable: that he was a mere pawn in a game of international diplomacy over Cyprus; that he was paymaster to the Conservative party at a time when it could not afford to be too choosy about its friends; there was even an allegation, disclosed in court, that he was involved in a scheme which would have led to a bribe being offered to the judge.

Nadir once said, from the safety of his Cyprus home, that tapes he possessed of meetings with Conservative cabinet ministers would make 'Watergate look like a minor bugging offence'. He also claimed that he had a recording of one minister saying, 'We know there is a conspiracy by the intelligence services, but there is nothing we can do.' But then we know also that in 1992 and 1993 Mr Nadir was suffering from paranoia. A Harley Street doctor wrote in March 1993 that 'the despair which he manifests (anomie) can, in my experience, lead to death'.

In the end Asil Nadir spent two and a half years awaiting trial, two and a half years in which he was deprived of many of his basic liberties: he was not allowed to leave the country, a country that was not his place of birth; he had to report regularly to the police; he was bankrupted and effectively barred from carrying out his profession (as a company director); and in April 1993 his defence documents were confiscated and removed from his home, and the court admitted it was powerless to order that they be returned.

If Asil Nadir had been detained in prison for those two and a half years (which was the wish of the Serious Fraud Office) he would have served a longer sentence than any person found guilty in the big UK fraud cases of the early 1990s . . . and that before he had even come to trial. That it took so long to put together the case against him has at least to raise questions about the whole new mechanism for prosecuting fraud that was introduced in the late 1980s, and of which the Serious Fraud Office was a big part.

The purpose of this book is to help readers to learn something of the history of Polly Peck and to understand something of Asil Nadir, of how he operated and where he came from. Only when armed with this knowledge can readers hope to judge the man and his actions, although there are still many intriguing questions about this case that will have to remain unanswered.

CHAPTER ONE

NOW AND THEN

AT midday on Monday, 17 December 1990 it was freezing cold on the streets of central London. In Number 10 Downing Street, the youngest prime minister this century was settling into an office he had held for less than a month. John Major's predecessor, Margaret Thatcher, was struggling to come to terms with being a mere commoner in the House of Commons after an eleven-year reign which had beaten Britain into a different shape.

Londoners earnestly sought last-minute Christmas bargains before they locked themselves up for their annual hibernation over the week-long holiday. There was little seasonal jollity about: a war in the Persian Gulf seemed increasingly inevitable as Iraq's Saddam Hussein stubbornly refused to get out of Kuwait. And Britain was already in the throes of a recession. Shopping lists were being honed to take account of the fact that there was little sign of interest rates, or mortgage payments, coming down, and every sign of more job losses in the New Year. Granny may have got a video-cassette recorder last year; this year she would be getting a scarf.

In mixed-up Covent Garden, where the expensive London headquarters of the First National Bank of Chicago sits just a few doors from the offices of *Me* magazine and of Lynx, an anti-fur movement run on a shoe-string, the narrow lanes and boutiques were far less busy than shopkeepers had hoped. At lunch-time, office workers hurried past the homeless vagrants who frequented the area by day before returning to their night-time hovels. In one doorway an old lady had chosen to shelter under an umbrella inscribed with a corporate logo and a company's name: Polly Peck International. This was the human detritus that the Thatcher years, the 'Me' decade, had left behind. It was a sight that Londoners used to associate with Paris or New York, not with their own more 'caring' city.

After a decade dedicated to creating a home-owning democracy, there was more homelessness than almost anybody could remember. Cuts in social security payments to the jobless young accounted for some of it, as did a philosophy of caring for the mentally sick 'in the community' instead of in stark Victorian hospitals. For many of these people, however, there was no community other than the streets. Adam Smith's 'invisible hand', the mechanism on which Thatcherite economics relied to pass down wealth from those who made it to those who didn't, seemed too often to be just that – invisible.

Some of the homeless hung around a noisy fairground on the edge of the great glass-roofed arcade which had once housed the famous Covent Garden fruit and vegetable market. Two decades ago, produce came straight from the plantations of the world to this collection of early-morning wholesale stalls. But the market had long since moved to cheaper premises outside the centre of the city. The only fruit now on display was made of soap or bath salts, and it was gift-wrapped for Christmas.

Within earshot of the fairground that Monday lunch-time, two dozen photographers huddled outside Bow Street Magistrates' Court. The temporary barricades holding them back had not been removed since the previous Friday when a financier called Roger Levitt had appeared at the court on charges of stealing money from customers of the financial services group he had founded.

Bow Street, says its street sign, is 'Theatreland'. On it stands the grand Covent Garden Opera House which, that cold December day, was preparing for an evening performance of the Russian ballet *La Bayadère*. Down the road, American tourists were queueing for tickets to *Miss Saigon*, the hottest show in town. But the greatest drama on the street was taking place inside the Victorian magistrates' court. Asil Nadir, one of the richest men in England and chairman of Polly Peck, the most successful company of the Thatcher years, was being charged by the Serious Fraud Office, a zealous new government body set up to look into cases of suspected white-collar crime involving over £1 million, with eighteen alleged offences of theft and false accounting. It would be a huge scandal if he was guilty; the media were making sure it would be a huge scandal if he was not. Even the British tabloid newspapers, which preferred to uncover vice and the female breast, found space for the story on their front pages.

Mr Nadir, a Turkish Cypriot, had been arrested on the previous Saturday. On Monday, 17 December he arrived at the court early – before 7 a.m. – in a modest Vauxhall Astra, to find that he was sixteenth on the list of cases to be heard that day. The others included petty weekend criminals and a former world darts champion, Eric Bristow, who pleaded guilty to being drunk and disorderly.

The darkly handsome Mr Nadir, dressed in a black suit with a red pocket handkerchief and tie, stood calmly in the dock for fifteen minutes while the charges were read out. Although doctors had been called to the police station the previous day when he had complained of chest pains, he looked tanned and well. Then came a sensation. Bail was set at £3.5 million – £2 million in cash and £1.5 million in sureties. Nobody could remember bail ever being higher in English legal history. After frantic calls on mobile telephones by relatives and friends in the court it was clear that Mr Nadir was not going to find the money that day. The assembled photographers grew disgruntled as they realised that the star of the show was going to be driven in a shrouded police van to spend the night at Wormwood Scrubs, a top-security prison some five miles to the west.

When a high van with seven slit windows emerged from the court, spotlights lit up the early evening gloom. Photographers jostled to get a picture, and their cameras, raised like periscopes to the windows, flashed indiscriminately. The van drove off and they waited for the supporting cast to emerge: Barbara Mills, the head of the Serious Fraud Office, wrapped in a beige trench coat; Peter Knight, from Mr Nadir's law firm of Vizards; and Anthony Scrivener, his counsel.

These legal technicians were followed by two well-dressed women, one wrapped in a black shawl, with short-cropped blonde hair and a pert nose, Mr Nadir's English girlfriend. Then came his son Birol, a greyhound enthusiast, in a cashmere coat and a conspicuous wide-brimmed fedora. Finally, in the absence of Mr Nadir, came the co-star of the show, Mrs Nadir. After a tempestuous twenty-eight years of marriage and two divorces from one husband, the glamorous Ayşegül Nadir had offered in court to put up £500,000 of her former husband's bail. If need be, she said, she would raise the money by selling her jewellery and antiques.

Only four months earlier Asil Nadir had been fêted like a

demi-god at the million-dollar opening of a spectacular new Polly Peck hotel on the Turkish Riviera. Now he was reduced to spending three nights in a prison cell because he could not put his hands on less money than it took to furnish his office in Berkeley Square.

Mrs Nadir paused briefly before stepping out of the court and into the waiting flash bulbs. She walked to a nearby silver-grey BMW while photographers, bodyguards and police scuffled and fell about her. The next day, as she would have wished, her photograph duly appeared on the front pages of many of the national daily newspapers.

Despite all his years in England, eighteen of them as chairman of a British quoted company, Mr Nadir's court-house appearance was a very Turkish affair. None of the great and the good of England were standing in the wings with support and bail money. Nor were there any armies of workers from the West Midlands demanding job security. There was only a makeshift poster in a nearby block of council flats, declaring: 'We love Asil.'

It was just a family affair featuring a handsome young man from a village in Cyprus who met and married a pretty girl from Istanbul and came to work in England. It was a fitting end to the Thatcher years, described by the political commentator Hugo Young as 'an individualist age in which the family became the largest unit of mutual assistance'.

Asil Nadir's rise and fall had mirrored that of Polly Peck, the billion-pound company he created and whose name became almost synonymous with his own. In the 1980s Polly Peck had made an unbelievable journey from rags to riches, a journey that took it from the curry and chips of the East End's Commercial Road to the Bentleys and chauffeurs of the West End's Berkeley Square.

Starting out in 1979 as a humble 'penny stock', a quoted company whose shares were worth next to nothing, its value grew by almost 130,000 per cent in the 1980s: £1000 invested in the company in 1980 was worth £1.3 million by 1990. No other share anywhere in the world at that time rose by anything like that amount. Polly Peck became bigger than household British names like Pilkington and Tate & Lyle, companies which had taken generations to reach the size Polly Peck achieved in a few short years.

It was a heady success built on a curious collection of businesses based in northern Cyprus and Turkey. At first Polly Peck's factories made cardboard boxes, then they packaged fruit, then they bottled water, screwed in circuit boards, made televisions, built hotels and then holiday villages . . . the new projects tumbled out from a cornucopia of Mediterranean abundance.

But Polly Peck was the creature of a particular age, the decade of the 1980s, the years when Thatcherite economics put competition before control. That competition spread most fiercely in the City of London where the stock-market and a myriad foreign banks fought for the privilege of backing Mr Nadir's next exciting venture.

While Polly Peck was fed by the Anglo-Saxon financial markets of the City of London, it was run by Mr Nadir in the style of a family company from the eastern Mediterranean. That was fine in the good times, but when one of the longest continuous periods of uninterrupted economic growth ended abruptly in 1990, it all fell apart.

On 20 September 1990 Polly Peck's shares plunged from 245 pence to 108 pence before they were suspended at the company's request. The stock-market had somehow caught wind of the fact that Mr Nadir was to be interviewed by the Serious Fraud Office. The company's shares were dumped as if every one of its products had been instantly contaminated with the guilt that was just as instantly assumed to have attached to its chairman.

From there things deteriorated fast. Banks that had lent money to Polly Peck were like commuters at Waterloo Station in a bomb scare: they almost crushed each other in the rush to get out. On 24 October Polly Peck asked to be put in the hands of administrators, legally appointed accountants who take over the running of troubled companies to save them from bankruptcy. Mr Nadir himself had to face a personal bankruptcy suit from other bankers who had lent him money. Finally, on 15 December he was arrested at Heathrow airport in a style worthy of an out-take from *The Untouchables.*

It all happened so dizzyingly fast that few knew what on earth was going on. People could only wonder why such a huge public company had been brought to its knees because one man was suspected of they knew not what. When, on 17 December, the shareholders learned that their chairman was charged with fourteen counts of theft from their company, they asked themselves why, as alleged victims, they were being punished. It was hard to know whether to be more astonished by the company's rise or by its fall.

It was, however, entirely appropriate that at the same time as the headlines were recording the fall from grace of the most extraordinary industrial Titan of the 1980s, they were also recording the downfall of the extraordinary politician who had done so much to create the environment in which Mr Nadir and Polly Peck had thrived. For, less than a month before Mr Nadir appeared in court, Mrs Thatcher had been unceremoniously removed from Downing Street. Her reign had been almost exactly coterminous with the life of Mr Nadir's Polly Peck.

Mrs Thatcher's nemesis had begun where she was always most vulnerable – abroad. On 28 October she had attended a regular summit meeting of European Community heads of government in Rome. Her less than fulsome support for the European Community, and in particular for its planned fast progress towards economic and monetary union, had made the Continent see her as a latter-day Canute, resisting the irresistible. Moreover, her hostility to European unity had separated her not only from the rest of Europe but also from her own Cabinet.

The Italians, chairing the Rome meeting, determined to outflank her. At the last minute they persuaded all the other member countries of the Community to agree that the second stage of European economic and monetary union should start from January 1994. Mrs Thatcher had not expected to be presented with a timetable. Like a cat cornered, she lashed out. She declared the Italian chairmanship incompetent and stormed back to London. There she informed the British parliament that 'We have surrendered enough', and vowed that she would never put before it a plan for a single European currency, an ultimate aim of monetary union. She was right; she never would.

Two days later her faithful deputy Sir Geoffrey Howe resigned. He had presented her government's first budget back in June 1979 and was the only minister to have remained in her Cabinet all through her premiership. In a memorable resignation speech in the House of Commons nearly two weeks later Sir Geoffrey pointed to the invidious xenophobia never far from the surface of British public life. He also signalled the end of Mrs Thatcher's premiership.

> I have to say that I find Sir Winston Churchill's perception [of the EC as a pooling of sovereignty] a good deal more convincing, and more encouraging for the interests of our nation than the nightmare image sometimes conjured up by the prime minister, who seems sometimes to look out upon a continent that is positively teeming with ill-intentioned people scheming, in her words, 'to extinguish democracy', 'to dissolve our national identities', to lead us 'through the back door into a federal Europe' . . . the prime minister's perceived attitude towards Europe is running increasingly serious risks for the future of our nation . . . the time has come for others to consider their own response to the tragic conflict of loyalty with which I have myself wrestled for perhaps too long.

Others considered their response quickly. The very next day Michael Heseltine, a former minister and heir apparent, announced that he was challenging Mrs Thatcher for the leadership of the Party. In the first ballot of the 372 Conservative members of parliament who decide these things, Mrs Thatcher got 204 votes. Humiliatingly, that was not enough to give her victory outright.

Combined with opinion polls which said that the Conservatives would overtake Labour in the polls if Mr Heseltine replaced Mrs Thatcher, this was enough to persuade her to stand down. In a second ballot John Major, the son of a circus performer and Mrs Thatcher's last chancellor of the exchequer, defeated Mr Heseltine. The Thatcher era was over. And so too, for a while, was the financial and entrepreneurial excess that it gave birth to.

Mr Nadir has claimed that in 1990 he received more column inches in the British press than anyone since Winston Churchill in 1943. If there was another challenger for that honour it was Mrs Thatcher herself in 1990. Like Mr Nadir she fell far and newsworthily fast. On 2 August, the day Saddam Hussein invaded Kuwait, she had still been at the peak of her power, staying at the elegant Colorado ski resort of Aspen where the American president was also staying.

She had escaped briefly to America from a long hot British summer. In Aspen she was to give a speech which had been billed as one of her most powerful statements ever on foreign affairs. She was also to receive the Aspen Institute's prestigious Statesman Award, an award which had been given to only two other people in its forty-year history: the Frenchman Jean Monnet and the German Willi Brandt.

In Aspen, too, she was scheduled to meet President Bush, a man with whom she had yet to establish the same rapport as she had with his predecessor Ronald Reagan. Upon Iraq's invasion of Kuwait Mr Bush hastily called a press conference, and Mrs Thatcher sat at his side. After the event the president said that he had been 'very comforted' by the presence of the prime minister to 'answer the tougher questions'. He had, he said, found the directness and clarity of the victor in the Falklands War of 1982 'useful'.

But for the prime minister, from there on it was downhill. Her speech, which had originally contained some unflattering criticism of the United Nations and some forthright plans for the future of the world, had to be watered down at the last minute. Nobody wanted to offend the United Nations at a delicate moment when it was trying to flex its flaccid muscles over Iraq's invasion of Kuwait. 'We were promised a Churchillian vision on the role of the United Nations,' said Paddy Ashdown, the leader of the Liberal Democrats in the House of Commons. 'All we got [in her Aspen speech] was the same tired old rhetoric, fine phrases but few new ideas.'

IT was hard then to recall how far British industry and finance had travelled from the time when Polly Peck and Prime Minister Thatcher had begun their remarkable careers – a time when the Rover, Austin Reed and the Parker pen could still hold their own against the BMW, Hugo Boss and the Mont Blanc. But at a time when in one year (1979) almost 30 million working days were lost through strikes. The Labour government in power at the beginning of that year was trying to arrest the decline of British manufacturing industry with an industrial strategy which involved heavy intervention by the state. Regional development grants and subsidies for creating jobs were part of the strategy. At best these succeeded in attracting marginal investments in areas which right-minded companies would otherwise have barely considered.

Most of the government's energy, however, had been directed not at future prospects but at past mistakes. For these it had set up an organisation called the National Enterprise Board (NEB), a sort of sick-bay for convalescent companies. On its board sat trade unionists, bankers and industrialists, and in its beds were once-famous names like British Leyland, Rolls-Royce and Ferranti. In other countries, such companies would have been supported by intertwined banking and industrial communities, or simply allowed to go under.

In Britain there was only the state to provide them with a chance to turn their fortunes round. Understandably, once the state had done so it was reluctant to give the benefits of its struggle back to private shareholders by throwing the companies on to the stock-market. The inevitable consequence was that the number of companies in the state sector just grew and grew. Thatcherite policies were to remove the state crutch from British industry. But they never provided an alternative.

At the beginning of 1979 British industry was a continuous story of state-managed corporate rescues, strikes, attempts to stem the tide of manufactured imports, and struggles to control the spending of nationalised industries. It was a process of shoring up the old. There was little time to build up the new.

The only bright spot was oil. In May 1979 the oil producers' monopoly, OPEC, had managed to reassert its control over the oil price, which had been slipping steadily since it had first been explosively hiked up five years earlier. Aberdeen was Britain's boom town. The exploitation of North Sea oil turned the country into a major offshore oil producer which happened to have a bit of tacky onshore manufacturing.

In the City of London, the financial markets were strictly segregated between the tightly controlled domestic markets and the totally disparate free-wheeling offshore markets. For some strange reason these were called Euromarkets, although they had little to do with Europe and a lot to do with mopping up surplus American dollars – dollars that floated around the world like a currency on a diplomatic passport.

In the domestic markets, control was everywhere. Exchange controls kept the flow of sterling in and out of the country on a tight leash; control of the money supply provided Treasury mandarins and financial journalists with their favourite mental gymnastics; and bank lending was controlled by something called 'the corset', which was a wonderfully apt name for the constraints on the entire domestic financial system of the time. The aim of many of these controls was to squeeze inflation out of the economy. But they weren't having much success. Inflation was over 13 per cent in 1979, and by the end of the year minimum lending rate, the benchmark interest rate, was 17 per cent.

The government's voracious appetite for money meant that the market for fixed-interest government securities (called 'gilts') was more lively than the market for equities in those remaining companies not owned by the state or cared for by the NEB. They had not been much interested in making new investments lately. There had been a dearth of new equity issues by British companies over the previous few years.

Nevertheless, there were some glimmers of light in the City. The stock-market index reached all-time highs in the first half of 1979 on the promise of North Sea oil and the hope of a Conservative victory in the general election scheduled for May. In a foretaste of things to come, the police had to be called in to cope with a crowd of unruly investors brandishing cheques outside a City bank in their eagerness to subscribe to a new share issue from a retailer called B&Q.

International markets in the City were thriving. The demand from developing countries for the surplus dollars in the coffers of the City's international banks was bringing in business on an unprecedented scale. Every year the number of foreign banks in the City grew, and the value of their dollar deposits likewise. Many of these dollars came from around the Persian Gulf, and they were soon to be multiplied by the second wave of unspendable oil revenues. The City's international success was about to be celebrated with a number of self-confident architectural extravaganzas. Lloyd's, the international insurance market, had put on display a model of its proposed new modernist building, a Richard Rogers fantasy that rejoiced in wearing its intestines outside its skin.

There were signs, too, that corset-like controls had had their day. Foreign banks in London were calling on top British companies with new-fangled loan proposals. The Bank of England could not monitor these with the same degree of accuracy as it could the activities of its tame poodles, the British clearing banks. More and more lending was squeezing outside the banking system. The use of plastic credit cards was spreading, and retailers like Tesco and Marks and Spencer were launching their own cards, as if they had anticipated the consumer-credit boom that was to become such a dominant feature of Britain in the 1980s.

In Turkey and Cyprus, the other arenas in which the Polly Peck story was to unfold, the picture was also very different from today. Northern Cyprus had been cut off from economic growth since the Turkish army invaded the island in 1974 to safeguard the interests and the lives of the Turkish-speaking minority. Since then Cyprus had been rigorously divided between the Turkish-speaking northern third, protected by the presence of the Turkish army, and the Greek-speaking southern two-thirds.

The government of the northern part of the island was divided over how to inject life into the stagnant economy. In early 1979 two former prime ministers, Necat Konuk and Osman Orek, broke away from the ruling National Unity Party (NUP) to form a new party in favour of the establishment of an 'independent, non-aligned, bi-regional and bi-communal sovereign federal Cyprus Republic purged of all foreign bases'. (All proposed solutions to the Cyprus problem possess an obligatory string of such brain-twisting adjectives. What the two ex-prime ministers meant was that they wanted the north of the island to be reunited with the south.)

Only by re-establishing links with the southern Greek-speaking part of the island, the breakaways believed, could economic growth return to their citizens. Their action put the remaining NUP party under pressure to find an alternative way to develop the limited resources of the Turkish third of the island. One option was to turn for help to the small number of Turkish Cypriots who had made a name for themselves in business communities elsewhere. One of them was Asil Nadir.

The Cypriots could hardly turn to the Turkish mainland for help, because Turkey was close to the brink of civil war. On Christmas Day 1978 martial law had been declared in thirteen eastern provinces of the country, and every day some twenty people were being killed in politically motivated attacks. In June 1979 a young man called Mehmet Ali Ağca was arrested in a café in Istanbul and subsequently confessed to the murder of Abdi Ipekci, the editor of *Milliyet*, a respected Turkish daily newspaper. The murder in February of Mr Ipekci, a brave opponent of all forms of political violence and a friend of the prime minister Bülent Ecevit, had stunned all sober-minded Turks. The mentally unstable Mehmet Ali Ağca escaped from prison and went on to get himself into the history books of the world. In 1981 he attempted to assassinate the Pope.

In March 1979, *The Economist* called Turkey 'The Sick Man of Europe Again'. The economy was lifeless, and its industrialists were paralysed behind bullet-proof glass. Inflation was high, and many of the most able people in the country were buying one-way plane tickets to another life.

Turkey, northern Cyprus and Britain: it was not a promising mix at this time. But enough was to change over the next few years to make it richly fertile soil for the plans that Asil Nadir was already hatching on 4 May 1979, the day that Mrs Thatcher was first elected prime minister of Great Britain and Northern Ireland.

Polly Peck was not then in the Nadir picture. Although quoted on the London Stock Exchange, it was a small clothing company controlled and run by a Jewish couple, Mr and Mrs Raymond Zelker; a typical firm in the rag trade of the time. After good years in the early 1970s, Polly Peck had fallen on hard times. The company was about to report a loss of £2000 on a turnover of just over £1 million for its latest financial year. 'In common with others in the industry,' said Mr Zelker, '[the group] is experiencing extremely difficult trading conditions.'

There were some in the clothing industry, however, who were experiencing better trading conditions. One was a firm called Wearwell, based on the industry's home ground in London's East End. Its 1978/79 accounting year actually ended on the day of Mrs Thatcher's election, 4 May, and the company celebrated by doubling its profits for that year to just over £750,000.

The chairman and managing director of Wearwell was Asil Nadir, and he was already cutting a dash in the East End, where dowdy penny-pinching was commonplace. Wearwell's offices on the Commercial Road, with their black and white marble façade and plush showrooms, stood well out from the crowd.

Mrs Thatcher's economic stamp was first clearly impressed on the nation in the Conservatives' first budget, presented to parliament on 12 June 1979 by the then chancellor of the exchequer, Sir Geoffrey Howe. There were two key elements in the budget. The first was the abolition of the control on dividends which had prevented British companies from giving shareholders the returns that the system demanded for the raising of new capital. 'If industry is to flourish,' said Sir Geoffrey, 'it needs not only adequate profits but a vigorous capital market to provide funds for investment and expansion. The control of dividends has now outlived its purpose and will accordingly come to an end.'

The second key element was the beginning of the removal of exchange controls, a process which was completed by October 1979. 'This,' said Sir Geoffrey, 'should allow the majority of UK firms who invest overseas all the sterling finance they are likely to want.' As it turned out, that meant firms like Polly Peck.

The removal of exchange controls broadened the potential for Britons and British investors to put their sterling overseas. Bankers in the City of London had spent much of the 1970s in aeroplanes and foreign hotels in the course of lending dollars to the governments of countries whose capital they had scarcely heard of until they landed there. This recycling of OPEC's surplus oil revenues had given these bankers a taste for foreign travel. Foreign was fun, or at least a great deal more fun than sitting at a desk in a gloomy office on Cannon Street, or popping up to Birmingham to see yet another metal-basher bash.

By 1980 City investors and bankers were more attuned to things foreign than they had been at any time this century. So much so that had Asil Nadir not existed they might have had to invent him. He suited them perfectly. Although he was undeniably foreign, he knew enough about England to be an ideal bridge between the often xenophobic public schoolboys who ran the City of London, and the suspicious, corner-cutting business minds of the eastern Mediterranean.

What Slater Walker and its chairman Jim Slater were for the 1970s, Polly Peck and its chairman Asil Nadir were set to become for the 1980s – industrial supermen on whom were imposed the get-rich-quick fantasies of thousands of ordinary folk who bought their shares, gave them credit, or merely sidled up to them as they grew richer. The fantasy was that these men had discovered an elixir which could turn base industrial assets into pure commercial gold, almost overnight.

CHAPTER TWO

THE FRUITS OF APHRODITE'S ISLAND

ASIL Nadir was born on 1 May 1941 on the island of Cyprus, a place which has withstood and absorbed so many invaders over time that it has to be surprising that its people are totally polarised as either Turkish or Greek. Mycenaeans, Phoenicians, Romans and Venetians have all mingled their genes with the local population's. But the polarisation between Greek and Turk is now absolute, and at the root of all the island's recent troubles. It was the strongest formative influence on the young Asil Nadir.

The Nadir family was not particularly well-off, but it was ambitious. Asil's parents, Irfan and Safiye Nadir, decided to call their only son Noble (Asil in Turkish). At one time Irfan Nadir was working for one of the biggest farmers on the island. The family lived in Paphos, a coastal town in what is now the Greek part of Cyprus. Asil earned his first pennies working as a newspaper boy to supplement the family income.

Paphos is steeped in history. The capital of the island under the Ptolemies, the Greek rulers of Egypt, it was also the island capital of the Romans and a grand metropolis when St Paul visited it in AD 46. In more recent times it was a stronghold of the Eoka movement, the terrorist group led by George Grivas which in the 1950s and 1960s pushed ruthlessly and fatally for Enosis, union of the island with Greece. Enosis had little geographical validity (Greece is a lot further from Cyprus than is Turkey or, for that matter, Syria), even less historical validity, and no constitutional validity at all.

When Grivas first landed on the island in 1954 to begin his campaign of terror he came ashore on the deserted beaches north of Paphos. Asil Nadir was thirteen years old.

At one stage in the 1950s Irfan Nadir became an auxiliary policeman, a member of a special force of local people formed by the British, who ruled the island at the time, to contain the rising tide of Eoka terrorism. Since the terrorists were Greek Cypriots the auxiliary force was made up almost entirely of Turkish Cypriots. It did nothing to help inter-community relationships. Hundreds of people from both communities were murdered between 1955 and 1958. Anybody who was not in favour of Enosis, from whatever community, was fair game.

Irfan Nadir left the police force and moved to Famagusta on the opposite side of the island. Young Asil went to the secondary school in the city and his father built up a number of small businesses. At one stage Irfan Nadir was importing London buses for the island's first public transport service.

East-facing Famagusta is very different from west-facing Paphos, a mix of different ages and cultures. In particular, it marks the apogee of the European medieval presence on the island. In the fourteenth century the Lusignan monarchs, of Italian descent, were crowned in the high Gothic splendour of the city's St Nicholas Cathedral. While they were about it, the Lusignans also crowned themselves Kings of Jerusalem, Famagusta being the nearest Christian place to the Holy City. The cathedral's remains still rest amid fragments of Greek Orthodox, Armenian, and a hundred other Christian faiths.

At that time Famagusta was one of the busiest trading posts in the world. The wealth of the Lusignan merchants was legendary throughout Christendom. The jewels on the wedding head-dress of one of their daughters were said to be more precious than 'all the ornaments of the Queen of France'. Another Lusignan ground up a jewel to serve as spice for his food.

Almost as fast as it came this magnificence disappeared, remaining only as a proud memory. In Renaissance Europe Cyprus shifted from a position at the centre of the known world to that of a mere dot at the end of a maritime cul-de-sac. When the Ottomans invaded the island in 1570 much of Famagusta was already in ruins. The Ottomans sacked it, then left it to rot while they pursued their sybaritic pleasures in Istanbul.

In the following centuries Cyprus was cut off from the rest of the world. The local people withdrew into the mysticism and mythology that had always proliferated on the island. In Cyprus – indeed, out of the waters of a bay near Paphos – had been born Aphrodite, goddess of love and daughter of Zeus. Throughout the centuries countless religions and their abstractions had washed across the island's shores.

Monasteries, mosques and evidence of strange rites could be found everywhere. Overlooking Kyrenia stands the crag-clinging fortress of St Hilarion, said to have been the model for Walt Disney's film of *Snow White and the Seven Dwarfs*. On a clear night the monastery's lights merge with the stars to resemble another galaxy. Everywhere the sea beats loudly on deserted rocks and in hidden bays to throw forth whatever the imagination fancies. It might be Aphrodite, or a satyr, or maybe just the barrel of a gun.

Down-to-earth mainland Turks say that the trouble with the Cypriots is that they cannot separate all this myth from reality. And indeed the two do mingle. At some stage in the island's history Aphrodite became a real person with a real grave in Paphos. The so-called 'Tomb of Venus' was later carried in triumph to Famagusta. There it lay in state in front of the cathedral until in Queen Victoria's time a no-nonsense British High Commissioner commandeered it for himself.

Not until the Suez Canal was opened in 1869 did Cyprus re-appear as a place of any strategic significance. Then the British turned their beady eyes on it as a means of protecting their new route to the riches of India. In 1877 they signed an agreement with the Ottoman sultan to occupy the island. 'If the sultan does not consent to the arrangement,' wrote the British prime minister of the time in the tone of voice of the time, 'the capture of Constantinople and the partition of the Ottoman Empire will be the immediate result.' After the First World War Turkey gave up its claims to Cyprus, and the British governed the island until 1960.

In Cyprus Christianity had long met and mingled with Islam; now it also became the place where Turkey met Britain. Throughout Asil Nadir's childhood the British influence was strong. 'All through my childhood,' he has said, 'I was told how humane the English were. We were brainwashed about the British, about how they looked you in the eye.' Cars on the island still drive on the left-hand side of the road, as they do in Britain (in both Greece and Turkey they drive on the right). The best schools on the island were British – Cypriots value education highly, claiming that they have more graduates for the size of their population than any country outside North America. Many of the more educated

Turkish community speak English at least as well as they do Turkish. They also speak Greek.

Asil Nadir was always embarrassed by his spoken Turkish, instantly recognisable as not from the mainland. Even when talking to Turkish ministers he would fumble for the right words. It is not just a question of accent. For example, a mainland Turk will not say 'Manchester United beat Chelsea', because the only use of the verb 'beat' is the literal use, as in 'to beat over the head'. A Turk will say 'Chelsea lost to Manchester United', or some such phrase. A Cypriot Turk, however, will translate literally from the English, adding a new dimension to football hooliganism for the mainlander.

The high standard of education on the island, combined with the lack of job opportunities, has resulted in a continual stream of emigrants that has impoverished the country – much as has happened in Ireland. In the 1950s there was another pressure to emigrate: 'encouragement' – both physical and material – to the Turkish minority to leave in order to ease the process of Enosis. In 1959 the Nadir family decided they too would go. Like many others before them they chose the most obvious destination – London, the capital of the country which had governed the island for nearly a century. More than twenty years were to pass before Asil Nadir returned to Cyprus.

It was as well the family left. In 1960 Cyprus became an independent republic, and its first president, the bearded, black-cowled Greek Archbishop Makarios, became a familiar figure on the televisions found increasingly in the living-rooms of western Europe. Makarios made little secret of the fact that he supported Enosis, even though the new republic's constitution set up a bi-communal sovereign state whose independence was guaranteed by Britain, Greece and Turkey.

Eoka made Cyprus an unpleasant place to be in the 1960s. Turkish Cypriots were slaughtered and forcibly moved around in large numbers with, it sometimes seemed, the tacit approval of the president – although just before he died Makarios did seem to show some signs of repentance for what had happened. In an interview with a Danish journalist in 1977 he said, 'I must say that I am not happy, looking back, with how I acted in some cases . . . it is in the name of Enosis that Cyprus has been destroyed.'

Enosis and Eoka were the source of most of the island's problems, and of the unsettled scores and suspicion that still fester between the two communities. The occasional statements by Asil Nadir about Greek Cypriot plots to bring him down sounded to the ears of the comfortable English like paranoia. And the bull-necked bodyguards who were rarely far away from him wherever he went were the target of much mockery. (Even in the early 1980s he would go shopping in London at weekends accompanied by two bodyguards.) But only those brought up in a divided community like Northern Ireland or Lebanon can hope to understand what living with constant sectarian violence can do to a child.

The destruction of the republic of Cyprus was completed in 1974 when the Turkish army invaded the island and took control of the northern part after a former Eoka terrorist called Nicos Sampson had overthrown Makarios and declared Cyprus a Hellenic republic to be duly annexed to Greece. It was internationally recognised that the Turks were perfectly within their rights to invade under the agreements guaranteeing the island's independence. That they have stayed there ever since is a reflection of the intransigence of the island's problem.

By separating the northern third of the island from the rest, the Turkish invasion created a land in limbo – a territory which was not part of a sovereign state, not recognised internationally, and cut off completely from the rest of the island. Travel between north and south became virtually impossible. When the Greek Cypriots effectively prevented international flights from using airports in the unrecognised north, the territory became even more isolated.

The Turkish section of now-divided Cyprus occupies some 37 per cent of the island. Here live 18 per cent of the island's population, some 170,000 people. They are as cut off from the Greek Cypriots as if they were in Australia. Flights and boats head northwards to the Turkish mainland. A tightly guarded border keeps people away from the villages where they were born as surely as if they had emigrated to the other side of the earth.

This almost universal dispossession is underlined by the wholesale change of place-names that has been imposed on the northern part of the island. What was Kyrenia is now Girne; Morfou has become Güzelyurt. And anybody looking for the way to Nicosia, the divided capital of the island, will do so in vain. The Turks call it Lefkoşa.

For as long as the Turkish- and Greek-speaking communities lived side by side it was the Greeks who dominated the island's commercial life. The Turks of yore saw themselves as soldiers and rulers, not tradesmen, following the example of their Ottoman overlords in Istanbul who left their empire's economic life in the hands of non-Muslim minorities: Greeks, Armenians or Jews.

Many of the productive assets in the north of Cyprus – citrus trees and hotels, for example – were once owned by Greek Cypriots. Of the 105,000 *dönüms* of citrus plantations recorded in the northern part of the island in 1972, the Greek Cypriots claim they owned 93 per cent. (A *dönüm* is equal to about one-third of an acre. So the citrus plantations covered an area about ten times the size of the London borough of Kensington and Chelsea.)

Since 1974 the status of property in the north has been a constant thorn in the flesh of Greek Cypriots to the south. For as soon as the Turkish Cypriots saw that the division of the island was more than temporary, they took steps to work these deserted assets. To do so they effectively created three distinct property markets:

1 For property whose title-deeds have been held by Turkish Cypriots since before 1974. This type of property is the most expensive.
2 For property owned by Greek Cypriots who fled. The government has given leases on this to Turkish Cypriots, typically for forty-nine years. The leases can be sold or inherited, but the status of the title remains unchanged. Much of the property on the island owned by Polly Peck is of this type.
3 For property which was also Greek, but which has been set aside by the northern Cyprus government for settlers from the Turkish mainland. The rights to this property are more limited then those in the second category, but owners of property in both the second and third categories are free to improve and develop it as they wish.

With the departure of the Greek Cypriots, the northern part of the island lost its more commercially-minded people. So at the end of the 1970s Rauf Denktash, the long-serving leader of the

Turkish Cypriot community, cast around for someone to help him work the assets in the north and to build on the territory's minimalist economy. His eyes fell on Asil Nadir who was by then a millionaire from the successful clothing business which he had started in London's East End. His company, Wearwell, was already known on the island because it was shipping out garments to be sewn cheaply in villages there before being returned to London for finishing.

Mr Nadir was persuaded to set up a number of local businesses in packaging and fruit, and Polly Peck was first bought specifically as a vehicle to own and develop these businesses.

But the commitment to Cyprus was not just commercial, it was also from the beginning political. For what would happen to Polly Peck should one of the many attempts to reunite the island prove successful, and the Greeks reclaim their property? And what would then happen economically to the Turkish Cypriots, many of whom soon became directly or indirectly employed by Polly Peck?

The best way to secure the future of its existing investments in Cyprus (which, although limited, were of vital importance to the company and to the region) was always for Polly Peck to invest even more on the island. Increased investment would further weaken the political pressure in the north for reunion with the south. And it would prevent northern Cyprus from becoming no more than a sort of Jersey to mainland Turkey. Turkey is said to have given over $500 million in official aid to the region between 1974 and 1988 ($3000 for every man, woman and child) – a figure which does not include the spending of the Turkish armed forces who live on the island.

With more Polly Peck investment, the little local economy would come closer to self-sufficiency. The people could 'lead a better life and hold their heads high', as Asil Nadir had always sincerely wished. But economic self-sufficiency in the north was the last thing the Greek Cypriots wanted to see. They knew that it could only lengthen the time until the island was reunited and their property returned to them.

What Polly Peck came to mean for northern Cyprus was clearly demonstrated by the impact of its collapse. By the second half of the 1980s the company had decided to enter what was for it an entirely new industrial sector: hotels and leisure. It could not have chosen anything better suited to northern Cyprus, where half-built hotels were almost as abundant as rotting grapefruit had once been. In 1986 the company bought a number of leases from the government on run-down hotels and potential hotel sites. These included a forty-nine-year lease on Jasmine Court, which had sat half-finished on the edge of Kyrenia since being parted from its owner (a company called Pharos Estates) in 1974. The lavishly renovated Jasmine Court was officially opened in September 1990.

The bundle of hotels also included the (completed) Palm Beach in Famagusta and the Salamis Bay which, from nearby Famagusta, looks like a deserted cement factory. The Salamis Bay was bought from the British construction company Leonard Fairclough for either £4 million or £6 million, and was sold on to the Turkish Cypriot government in 1990 for $12 million. But the showpiece of all these hotels was to be the Crystal Cove, a five-star de luxe effort on the coast west of Kyrenia. It is still unfinished.

Very large sums of money went into the hotels. Polly Peck's marketing men described Crystal Cove as being for the 'world-class affluent traveller who flies first-class and expects to be chauffeur-driven'. At one stage Mr Nadir envisaged overcoming the fact that Crystal Cove's beach had no sand by flying the stuff in. Jasmine Court too was an ambitious property with no beach. It is set around a courtyard with marble rotunda, streams and wooden bridges.

All the designs were the responsibility of Armağan Tekvar, Polly Peck's architect and a close Nadir associate for many years. A charismatic Turk with great taste, he could turn the most humble Polly Peck building into a visual delight. His wife Gülderen was responsible for assembling the stunning collection of antiques which graced Polly Peck's London headquarters at 42 Berkeley Square when the company was at its peak.

The hundreds of millions of pounds going into these hotels made it look as if Polly Peck was trying to create a Mediterranean Barbados overnight, with Crystal Cove as its Sandy Lane. And why not? After all, Barbados retains its economic independence on little more than a single strand of expensive hotels and a few fruit trees. Mr Nadir once said that Crystal Cove or Jasmine Court would fetch $50 million if sold on the open market – and they might, had they been located in Barbados or Hawaii. But, for as long as they had only a trickle of tourists paying less than £30 a night their value was nothing like that.

Even in the final days before it was taken over by the administrators Polly Peck was said to be pouring vast amounts of money into more tourism projects in northern Cyprus. Between June and October 1990 over £220 million of the company's recorded cash was reported to have gone into a number of ventures around the island. One of them, a proposed holiday village at Alakadi to the east of Girne, was said to have soaked up over £40 million with hardly anything to show for it. That stretch of the island's coastline is rugged and unpopulated. The small winding roads around it are scarcely wide enough to allow two vehicles to pass.

The events of 1990 left northern Cyprus in an economic limbo. Ten years after Asil Nadir first brought business and hope to the region, it had the same hollow feel as when he first arrived. Shake it and its loose-fitting society would rattle. This feeling increased in winter when the few foreign tourists who do make it to the resort towns of Kyrenia (or, if you prefer, Girne) and Famagusta (or Gazimagusa) are lowest in number. With a war around the Persian Gulf a few hundred miles away, the economic stillness of the island became eerie.

Near Lefke, on the west coast, the skeletal remains of a huge copper mine and its attendant jetties are a reminder of the fact that Cyprus was for centuries a rich source of the metal which took its Greek name (*kupros*) from the name of the island. At Gazimagusa, a mere morning's drive away, yet on the opposite side of the island, the concrete hotel slabs stretching to the south of the town are half-destroyed and wholly empty, out-of-bounds to the public and frequented only by bored Turkish troops.

Even in Kyrenia, the pretty little northern port favoured by English expatriates and immortalised by Lawrence Durrell in his book about the island, *Bitter Lemons*, the young rightly complain that there is nothing to do; neither work nor play. Just outside the town, Jasmine Court can count its guests on the fingers of two hands. Its 150 apartment suites are almost all empty but for their touching faith in Polly Peck accessories: a kettle and a toaster from a UK subsidiary, Russell Hobbs Tower; an Imperial television from the group's Italian electronics firm; Niksar bottled water from its spring deep in Turkish Anatolia; and a copy of *Turquoise*, Mr

Nadir's own glossy English-language magazine about the region.

Despite this depression caused partly by his collapse, Asil Nadir is still a local hero. On his last visit before his arrest, farmers from Güzelyurt showered him with flowers as he told them he would sort everything out for the best. The prime minister, Dervis Eroğlu, and the president, Rauf Denktash, pledged their support. Four thousand Turkish Cypriots marched to the British High Commission in Lefkoşa to deliver a letter to the commissioner and to Oscar Camillion, the UN representative on Cyprus, supporting Mr Nadir and accusing the Greek Cypriots of being behind his downfall. A local civil servant who told the news agency Reuters, 'We must be realistic about Polly Peck. If we explain everything as a Greek plot, who will believe us?', resigned shortly afterwards. 'What has happened to Asil,' said Mr Denktash firmly, 'is related to Cyprus.'

Yet for some twenty years in the middle of his life, Asil Nadir never visited the island of his birth. Soon after the Nadir family arrived in England he was packed off to university in Istanbul to study economics. As a student he was undistinguished. He went around with a foreign crowd – Turks from Greece or Yugoslavia, and even Turkish Cypriots from London. Cyprus was scarcely ever out of the news at the time and Cypriots in Istanbul received much sympathy if not much status. However, Asil was not tempted to revisit the island.

At this time he was very shy and not very sociable, hindered in part by his poor Turkish. He formed a five-man pop group called The Asils in which he played the piano and sang. He also developed some skill on the violin, which is invariably mentioned in profiles of him.

Despite this, music was never a particularly important part of his life. At the pinnacle of his fame he would play raucous Turkish pop cassettes as he cruised in his private jet from one city to another. At his first public appearance after his arrest he sang delightedly at a charity dinner alongside a Turkish pop singer called Semra Turel. But classical music cassettes bought for him in bulk by friends remained unheard.

At university Asil was very generous to his friends – as he continued to be for the next thirty years. He is best remembered by them for the red MG convertible motor-car which he brought over from England at a time when such luxuries were almost unheard of among Turkish students. The red MG was to play a very significant role in his life.

One day a young schoolgirl spotted the car on an Istanbul street. She had just broken off with a boyfriend who was a relative of Ismet Inönü, Atatürk's right-hand man in the founding of the Turkish republic. The boyfriend had also owned an MG convertible, probably the only other one in the city. The girl had loved the smell of the car's interior and, as she hung around Asil's red convertible trying to catch a whiff of the captivating aroma, the owner returned. He introduced himself, and fell in love.

The girl's name was Ayşegül Tecimer, and she was the beautiful, fun-loving daughter of an Istanbul businessman. The middle-class Tecimers were originally Laz, a people from the eastern Black Sea coast who are the frequent butt of Turkish jokes – in much the same way as the Irish are for the English.

Ayşegül swept Asil off his feet, and she found him very handsome, quietly amusing and kind. She loved dancing and going to parties and the two of them became a familiar sight at the 'in' night-spots. Eventually he persuaded her to marry him, and their wedding took place in Istanbul while he was still a student there. But from the beginning the two were very different. She came from a background that was accustomed to having maids and cooks. His mother sewed skirts in a back room and had a mouthful of gold teeth.

When, in the middle of his university course, Asil decided to drop out and return to London to work with his father, Ayşegül found it tough. She was like a fish out of water in the house in Romford, Essex, which they shared with his parents, and she would stay in bed until midday to avoid the oppressive atmosphere.

Things improved when they moved to the first home of their own – a small flat in Bayswater. But Asil was already working long hours. He would come home late to find Ayşegül dressed and ready to go out for what was left of the evening. Her day began just as his ended.

In 1964 Ayşegül gave birth to their first child, Birol. When the child was born Asil was not present, but to compensate for his absence he sent the new mother some red roses. In each was hidden a small diamond. The gesture was probably more extravagant than he could afford, for when Birol was only a few months old the family travelled inexpensively to Istanbul by train rather than by plane. On the trip they lost all their luggage in Bulgaria, but Asil was his usual calm self, assuring everybody that it would turn up. Sure enough, a week later it did.

Despite a couple of divorces and several estrangements the couple were to stick by each other for the next thirty years. Ayşegül vouched for £500,000 of Asil's bail money at Bow Street Magistrates' court, and she appeared at all his court hearings. When he entered the building she was the first person he greeted and kissed, even though they had been living apart for several years.

Increasingly, Asil began to demonstrate the workaholic trait which characterised him throughout his business life. Couples who met the Nadirs in their early years in London often found themselves dining as a threesome: Ayşegül would apologise for Asil's absence: he was either working or travelling abroad. Even on the Saturday in the late 1960s when the couple moved into a vast new house on The Bishops Avenue, a wide street in the most exclusive part of London's Hampstead, popularly known as Millionaires' Row, Asil was absent. Ayşegül had to manage the move with the help of his mother and father.

Thereafter Asil became famous for his fifteen-hour workdays. As a young man in London in the heady 1960s he was unusual. Love and peace, meditation and self-discovery were in the air. The Beatles and the Rolling Stones were beckoning all to twist the night away. But Asil would have none of it. He once said, 'Pain is a tremendous teacher; it gives you a chance to learn much faster.' Did the pain of his shyness teach him early on that his greatest comfort and pleasure lay in solitary work? Whether it did or it didn't, his heavy working days necessarily cut him off from developing other aspects of his life, in particular the social skills that might have enabled him to do for his country what Greek shipowners' *joie de vivre* had done for theirs.

While Asil's father might have been happy to have his only son back home to help him with the business, his mother, with true Cypriot devotion to the value of education, never forgot that he had not finished his degree course. When Polly Peck was growing fast Asil would report to her that the company had ten subsidiaries in five countries and was worth £100 million. She would reply that that was very good, 'But it's a pity that you never graduated, my son.' A year later he would tell her that Polly Peck now had twenty subsidiaries in ten countries and was worth £200 million. Again she would say that that was very good, 'But it's a pity that you never graduated, my son.' Eventually he gave in. In the late 1980s, after his father had died of cancer, he returned to Istanbul University to take his final exams. He passed them with unconventional though adequate answers.

The Nadirs were always a close family. For anybody brought up in the post-familial age of western Europe, where independence is sought and granted early, the strength of the family community in the eastern Mediterranean is alien. It remains in force there partly at least because there is no adequate social security system to provide alternative support, but partly also because families are less afraid to show their emotions to each other and can thus bear to live together longer.

As children in Cyprus, Asil and his two sisters, Bilge and Meral, would help their parents prepare orders after school. In London Asil's mother would come every day to the Wearwell offices in a black Mercedes. Brothers-in-law, aunts and uncles all worked for the company. Close friends would come in and out doing temporary jobs. Even as adults the Nadir children never showed anything but the greatest respect and affection for their parents. They were a typical Mediterranean business family, born of a culture where the idea of a public company owned by thousands of distant, disinterested shareholders was (and still largely is) totally unfamiliar.

In 1965 Asil left his father's firm, which rejoiced in the rather unmodish name of Nadir Modes, to set up his own company, which he called Wearwell. (The Turks have a propensity for choosing discordant names for their English businesses.) Nadir Modes and Wearwell remained close, with Wearwell selling the cheap and cheerful garments that Nadir Modes produced.

Wearwell's office was in Commercial Road in London's East End, the traditional home of the English rag trade. At the time the business was dominated by Jewish immigrants who had stamped their own mark on it. Nowadays the rag trade has been infiltrated by other more recent immigrants – many of them Muslim, from East Africa, Pakistan and Bangladesh.

But in the 1960s the Nadirs were one of the few Muslim families to set up in the Jewish heartland of the rag trade. And from the beginning their style was different. In an area where Jewish manufacturers would usher visitors into unprepossessing offices and showrooms, the smartness of Wearwell's premises stood out.

At that time it might have been more natural for a Turkish Cypriot to have moved to the area that was the nearest London had to a little Lefkoşa. Newington Green is typical of many areas to the north and west of the city where dull state-owned apartment blocks, surrounded by desolate concrete play-areas, sit cheek by jowl with chic owner-occupied houses in tree-lined avenues.

Set in a corner of the north London borough of Islington, Newington Green was the area that most Turkish Cypriots fleeing the communal violence at home in the 1960s headed for. It became full of youngsters who spoke English with a broad Cockney accent, but whose fathers or uncles had been killed in a faraway place that they were nervous of visiting. By 1990 it was centred on a small shabby square where the Hodja Nasreddin restaurant rubbed shoulders with the Turkish Women's Project, and almost every shop sold *döner kebab*, the minced lamb cooked on a slow-turning spit that is (wrongly) most Englishmen's idea of the beginning and end of Turkish cuisine.

Around Newington Green there are still a number of textile and garment firms run by Turkish Cypriots. Had Asil Nadir not aimed so high he might be running one of them today.

Just to the south of the Green, once-faded Victorian squares have been gentrified by professional folk – in particular by those who work in the City of London, conveniently close, and by those from the left wing of the political spectrum, attracted by the borough's traditionally radical politics. The families in these houses became a sort of British prototype in the 1960s and 1970s – the mother in loose Laura Ashley dresses ferrying children around; the father, with hair slightly too long and a job in media or advertising.

The close proximity of this English style to the Turkish street culture of Newington Green might have been expected to appeal to Mr Nadir who, years later, could happily sit all day in the Georgian splendour of his office in Berkeley Square and then while away sleepless nights watching Turkish pulp movies. The fact that he did not limit his horizons by staying within his traditional community, but instead set up in the heart of the established textile businesses of the day, says something about his *modus operandi*. When he started his businesses on mainland Turkey in the 1980s (fruit, water-bottling, electronics and, eventually, newspapers), he again confronted the established firms head-on, as he had done in the East End. It was a strategy that did not win him many friends.

In 1968 Wearwell was still a very small business. On a turnover of some £370,000 it made a mere £10,000 profit. But over the next six years the Nadirs stumbled upon a successful formula which took the company's annual turnover to over £4 million and its annual profits to £672,000 by its accounting year to April 1973. With that track record Wearwell decided to become a public company, quoted on the London Stock Exchange.

The Wearwell formula was simple but revolutionary. Unlike most garment manufacturers who design 'samples' which they then hawk around to retailers in the hope of getting orders to be delivered in several months' time, Wearwell opened a number of cash-and-carry outlets. Cash-and-carry was a hot new retailing concept in the late 1960s, a sort of wholesaling from a shop. Wearwell's customers (shop-owners from up and down the country) would come to its outlets and buy garments immediately off the peg, but strictly for cash.

This had several advantages over the traditional method of selling, but most importantly it did wonders for the company's cash flow. Finished garments were bought and paid for long before Wearwell had to pay suppliers for its own raw materials – fabric, buttons, labels, etc. On the other hand it did depend on having flexible and fast production which could not be too far away from the point of sale. It was no good having stuff sitting on racks for months in an industry and an age when last season's styles were about as desirable as a rancid yoghurt. So only a few days' sales were kept in stock, freeing seamstresses to switch to any new-fangled fashion that suddenly appeared (like hot pants), and as often just as suddenly disappeared.

Under this system the man who controlled the business and ensured its success was the one who kept his eye on the stock. Asil Nadir – owner, managing director and chairman of the company

– seems to have been expert at this. It mirrored a time later on when computers had taken over from accounting books and Mr Nadir, by then the hugely successful chairman of Polly Peck, could scarcely take his eyes off the flickering screen in his office which provided him with up-to-the-minute information on financial and other markets. Fast information meant control, and control by Mr Nadir, who never doubted his own ability, meant success.

Wearwell expanded its cash-and-carry operations, opening branches in Birmingham, Glasgow and Leeds. At the same time it expanded from its basic womenswear into suede and leather goods, and then into menswear. It remained very British, with scarcely any foreign input or output.

Despite the company's success, some commentators were sceptical when it offered 3.2 million shares (40 per cent of its equity) to the public in the summer of 1973. 'It is difficult to draw convincing conclusions from the achievements of a company which scarcely existed five years ago,' said the left-wing *Guardian* newspaper. More representative of the establishment, *The Economist* said that 'The company is really too young to go public.'

Certainly, the nature of the company's business and the state of its cash flow meant that it did not need the money. What was left of the £1.47 million proceeds of the share sale after the bankers, brokers, lawyers and accountants had had their cut went into Mr Nadir's pocket.

But the sale was a success. Other retailers seen as revolutionary at the time – like the frozen-food group Bejam and the Sainsbury's supermarket chain – were currently in favour with the stock-market. Promoted aggressively by L. Messel (the firm that was to remain stockbroker to Mr Nadir's companies all the way until 1990), the Wearwell issue was over-subscribed and the share price started to rise from the day (24 July 1973) that dealing in the shares began.

By September there were the first signs that the Nadir magic was beginning to grip the stock-market. Wearwell's shares had risen to 78 pence from the 46 pence at which they had been issued, a 70 per cent profit in two months. On top of the more than £1 million he had pocketed from the issue in July, Mr Nadir had made a £1.5 million gain on paper from the 60 per cent of the company that he still owned – in just sixty days. He was already a seriously wealthy man, and impressed with the mathematics of the market.

The problem with any successful business formula is what to do for an encore. Wearwell's formula continued successfully for a couple of years until in its accounting year to April 1975 the company touched the magic figure of £1 million pre-tax profits. Then it hit a rock.

Competition in the cash-and-carry business was reducing the advantage that Wearwell had from being first with the idea, and Mr Nadir was not a man to sit around doing the same thing year in and year out. For a while he took his eye off the importance of Wearwell's cash flow and branched out into mail order – selling garments by catalogue.

Mail order is a business that depends on giving customers credit and having enough stock to meet unpredictable demand. It is a business that has brought down far bigger firms than Wearwell. For Asil Nadir it was almost disastrous. The UK economy was in the doldrums following the big first oil-price rise, engineered by OPEC the year before, and inflation was running away at over 24 per cent. The rag trade was particularly badly hit as the English made do with hand-me-downs and last year's summer clothes. Wearwell lost over £650,000 in the six months to October 1975.

Mr Nadir came out of this first serious business setback with flying colours. He shut down the mail-order business almost immediately, and he retrenched into the company's core cash-and-carry operation. Profits returned in the following year (1976/77), but Mr Nadir had made an important decision. He had decided that the UK market was not to be relied upon. Wearwell had to go out and find export markets, even though to do so might dangerously stretch the company's finances.

Asil Nadir bought a bunch of plane tickets and set off around Europe and the Middle East. He could not turn just to markets that he knew. Isolated northern Cyprus, three years after the invasion by the Turkish army, was too small and too cut off to be worth much effort. And mainland Turkey was a major cotton-grower with a large textile industry of its own. The industry was well protected behind high tariff barriers whose purpose was to make the price of imported garments uncompetitive.

So Mr Nadir turned his attention to the newly oil-rich countries of the Middle East, countries such as Libya and Iraq. They liked the idea of dealing with a fellow Muslim (albeit never a particularly religious one) who could bring them goods of Western quality. In the first half of 1977 Wearwell exported more than it had done in the whole of the previous year.

But the export drive put great strain on the company's chairman and on its finances. It required Wearwell to extend credit facilities to new customers in order to build up confidence in markets where it was totally unknown. Some idea of the financial strain can be gleaned from transactions at the time. In September 1977 the company sold 10 per cent of its equity to a leather supplier, Strong & Fisher, in return for credit facilities and the cancellation of a trade debt of only £144,000.

At the same time Mr Nadir sold a large chunk of his own shares, reducing the family's stake to less than a majority. With the proceeds he repaid a loan that he had taken from the company. This loan had caused the company's auditors to qualify the previous year's accounts when they had felt obliged to bring to the attention of the company's shareholders the fact that the loan, which at one time was as much as £86,000, was to a director and, as such, was in contravention of the 1948 Companies Act.

These auditors were a smallish firm of accountants called Stoy Hayward. Like the broking firm L. Messel they stayed with Asil Nadir throughout the 1980s, auditing Polly Peck's accounts for all of those years. They too grew rapidly during the period, gaining a reputation as the auditor of ambitious entrepreneurial firms. Inevitably, Stoy Hayward was to find itself at the centre of the storm that broke out in the autumn of 1990 when Polly Peck was taken over by administrators. Shareholders who wanted to know why their shares were so suddenly worthless looked to the company's accounts (and to its accountants) for an explanation.

Despite the financial constraints, Wearwell's export drive paid off. In 1979 the company started to pay dividends again – the first since 1976 – and the magical £1 million profit figure was exceeded in the financial year 1979/80, for the first time since 1975.

At the time Wearwell was not exporting anything to Cyprus. But the company's change of tack, away from total dependence on the UK market and a business perspective that did not extend much beyond the end of Commercial Road, had brought the Nadir family back in touch with its roots.

The export business was a financial burden because it was conducted in the traditional rag-trade way, based on giving credit: orders were taken and production could proceed over a number of months. There was not the same need for speed and flexibility as in the cash-and-carry business. That was especially true because of the sort of export orders that Wearwell was winning – for example, what was said to be a £3.2 million-a-year order to supply Libyan schoolgirls with uniforms. These were not fashion-sensitive items, and could be processed with long lead-times.

Where speed left off, price took over. Anything that could cut production costs, almost regardless of the time it took, would help win orders. So Wearwell moved some of its labour-intensive machining from Britain, with its high wage costs, to Cyprus where they were much lower. Irfan and Safiye Nadir returned to the now peaceful island to supervise an operation that distributed cut pieces of fabric to village women around the island for sewing. The garments were then returned to Britain to be finished. Despite the additional transport cost, the savings were considerable – according to one estimate the unit cost of machining in the UK was £3 while in Cyprus it was 75 pence (including the shipping).

By the end of the 1970s more than 80 per cent of Wearwell's sales were being exported, and the company was regularly picking up the Queen's Award for exports. When Mrs Thatcher was first elected prime minister in 1979, Asil Nadir was already the sort of entrepreneur that she admired and wanted to encourage – a self-made immigrant who had scoured the world for business in order to bring profits to Britain.

The City of London was more impressed with the fact that Mr Nadir had proved that he was a businessman who could come up with good ideas (the cash-and-carry operation) and put them into effect. And he was a man who had seen his business almost in tatters, yet had pulled it up again by dint of hard work and another successful strategy (export and overseas production). This was the sort of person with whom a bullish, Thatcher-influenced City could fall deeply in love. There were too few of his sort to be found in a Britain deadened by the weight of politicised state industries and the power of the labour unions.

Asil Nadir could probably have raised millions from the City over the next few years to do almost anything he liked. Since he was by now already gripped as much by the idea of doing deals as by doing business, the City was not going to have to wait long for a chance to back him.

And sure enough, with his links with northern Cyprus firmly re-established, a deal was being cooked. It was cooking right by the sea in old Famagusta, just beyond Othello's Tower, the grandest corner of the city's Venetian ramparts. For this new venture Mr Nadir searched around for another quoted company to buy. He argued that the new project would sit uncomfortably within Wearwell since it had absolutely nothing to do with the rag trade.

A suitable company was soon found. It was Polly Peck, and it became the vehicle for the Famagusta venture: a plan to convert two bullet-riddled sheds into a cardboard packaging factory, the bullet holes a relic of the intense fighting that had taken place there in the 1960s and early 1970s.

CHAPTER THREE

POLLY PUTS A KETTLE ON

BY the time Asil Nadir first took an interest in Polly Peck, the company had been quoted on the London Stock Exchange for many years. It was one of a number of look-alike Jewish rag-trade firms, manufacturing and distributing women's clothing. Although its head office was in Great Portland Street, in the area behind Oxford Circus that sports most of the showrooms of the UK's fashion industry, much of its manufacturing was done in the East End, a stone's-throw away from Wearwell's offices on the Commercial Road. Polly Peck's chairman, Raymond Zelker, and his family owned most of Polly Peck's shares, as the Nadir family did with Wearwell.

In the early 1970s Mr Zelker had been faced with a similar business problem to Wearwell. The rag trade was very competitive. There were plenty of newcomers and fly-by-nights who were able to push the profit margins on traditional business down very low. Polly Peck made reasonable profits for a few years in the late 1960s and early 1970s, but they were flat and never likely to set the industry or the stock-market on fire.

In order to improve profits, or to stand out from the competition (which, after all, is the normal ambition of most firms), the Wearwells and Polly Pecks of the early 1970s had two choices: either they could introduce some revolutionary new idea into a staid, established business (which is what Wearwell did with its cash-and-carry idea) or they could go into something completely different. Both choices involved a considerable degree of risk. Polly Peck chose the latter.

The property business has always been volatile and has always attracted more than its fair share of spivs. In good years it can reap tremendous profits, but in bad years it throws up a disproportionately high number of bankruptcies. In 1972 Polly Peck's profits fell by some 40 per cent, and in order to change tack the company decided to plunge into the property business, then in one of its irregular good moods.

Towards the end of that year Michael Clore joined Polly Peck's board. He was the nephew of Sir Charles Clore, a legendary property developer of the 1960s, and he set about turning the company into a property and fashion business. By the end of 1973 Mr Zelker was able to say, 'We are basically a property firm. Our plans are long-term but very lucrative.'

Long-term they may have been; lucrative they were not. After one year (1973/74) when the profits from property almost matched those from fashion, the property market took a steep dive as interest rates soared and the cost of loans (the basic raw material of almost all property deals) rose in line. In the following year Polly Peck's losses on property more than wiped out its profits from the rag trade. It was not the only company to suffer from property losses at the time. In 1974 the Bank of England launched its famous 'lifeboat' to rescue stranded banks that had put too much short-term money into long-term property development. Slater Walker, the darling of the early 1970s, got stranded too and ended up being owned by the Bank of England.

Through all this, however, Polly Peck's fashion business was doing well. At one time the company ran some fifty boutiques which were pioneering what was to become the popular idea of 'shops within stores' – renting floor space in big department stores (including the gem of all England, Harrods) to sell their wares. For many Londoners their first awareness of the name Polly Peck came from seeing these shops in the mid-1970s.

However, the fashion business could not be insulated from the fatal foray into property. For a number of years Polly Peck struggled to sort out its property debts and to return to what it knew. In 1976 its shares were suspended for three months while 'the company clarifies its financial position'.

After a brief return to profit, Polly Peck was making losses again by the end of the decade. Unlike the Nadirs, the Zelkers had been unable to pull themselves cleanly from a bad patch. As the 1980s beckoned, Polly Peck's share price was a mere 6 pence, putting it among the band of so-called 'penny stocks', shares whose price could scarcely fall any lower without the company disappearing altogether.

These penny stocks were closely watched by the stock-market 'tip-sheets', cheaply produced newsletters which recommended shares for the amateur investor to buy. These newsletters flourished in the early 1980s on the back of Thatcherite enthusiasm for the stock-market, and they could often perceptibly move the price of individual shares. They specialised in spotting penny stocks because a small turnaround in their fortunes (or in a rumour of their fortunes) could lead to a massive increase in their share price in percentage terms; investors could literally double their money overnight. That is what most of them were after.

On 14 February 1980 it was announced that a company called Restro Investments had made a cash offer for the penny stock Polly Peck. The offer was worth 9 pence per share, 50 per cent more than the price at which the shares had been languishing in the preceding months. Restro Investments was a private company based in Jersey, a favourite tax haven for Englishmen and their companies.

Restro, in turn, was owned through another insular tax haven, the Isle of Man. An Isle of Man company called Wearwell Isle of Man Holdings, indirectly controlled and owned by Asil Nadir and his family, owned Restro. Clearly, Mr Nadir was already being well advised as to fiscally advantageous 'offshore' ways in which to hold his expanding industrial empire. These offshore tax havens had the advantage not only of charging low tax rates but also of disguising the ultimate owner of assets held through them.

Raymond Zelker, his wife Sybil and another director accepted the offer, and that was enough to give Restro 58 per cent of Polly Peck for a price of £270,000. (Exactly ten years later 58 per cent of Polly Peck was to be worth just over £1 billion, a 4000-fold increase.) At the time Mr Zelker described the offer as 'financially prudent given that the current economic downturn may last for a while'.

The economic downturn did last for a while, but Mr and Mrs Zelker, who remained on the board of Polly Peck, were soon to regret that they had accepted the Restro offer. For they had failed to take into account the Nadir factor. As soon as Mr Nadir's interest in Polly Peck became known, the company's share price began to rise, so much so that it rose way above the offer that the Zelkers had accepted. Only a month after he had said yes, Mr Zelker advised other shareholders to say no. They took his advice. Restro picked up scarcely any Polly Peck shares other than the Zelkers'.

In the months following the takeover Polly Peck's share price rose as high as 85 pence, the biggest price rise of any share that year. During those few months the Polly Peck phenomenon was born. On his £270,000 investment in March, Asil Nadir had reaped a paper profit of £2.25 million by June. Yet the company had done nothing to merit the rise other than to hold out a vague promise of exciting things to come.

On 8 July 1980 Asil Nadir revealed what all the excitement was about. Polly Peck was raising £1.5 million through a rights issue, an issue of new shares on which existing shareholders have first option. It was an extraordinary thing to do since at the same time the company announced a loss of £89,000 for its most recent financial year. Most of the money was to be used to buy a company called Uni-Pac Packaging Industries which was already owned by Mr Nadir personally.

Uni-Pac had a lease on the concrete sheds by the waterfront in the port of Famagusta. The plan was to turn these old buildings into a sophisticated cardboard box factory, using the most up-to-date European machinery. The scheme had been put to the Nadir family by the Turkish Cypriot government. Since the Turkish invasion six years earlier the region's economy had gone limp. Tourism, once the major source of foreign currency, had dried up. In 1978 a mere 8000 non-Turkish tourists made it on to the thousands of beds available in the northern part of the island.

The area's other main industry was agriculture, and citrus fruit in particular. But much of the citrus crop was being left to rot under the trees, partly because much of it was technically still owned by absent Greek Cypriots who watched zealously any attempt to export it, and partly because northern Cyprus lacked the business skills to farm and market it profitably.

The Turkish Cypriot government had identified Mr Nadir as someone who might be able to help them. His father and mother were already back on the island and in touch with local officials and local issues. One of the problems facing the citrus farmers was that there was no suitable local packaging to transport the fruit abroad and keep it in good condition.

A potentially serious stumbling-block to the scheme had been overcome in the courts of London in 1978. The House of Lords decreed that year that English courts could not rule on questions of trespass in Cyprus. As far as Britain was concerned, the Turkish Cypriots were free to export the fruit from the orchards once owned by Greek Cypriots. At the time the British were keen not to depress the Turkish Cypriot economy so far that it became totally dependent on mainland Turkey for survival. The High Court ruling effectively allowed Turkish Cypriot produce to arrive in London's fruit and vegetable market at Covent Garden. It opened the doors to everything that followed from Polly Peck.

When it was first proposed to him by the Turkish Cypriots, Mr Nadir was sceptical about the Uni-Pac project. Not only was it something entirely new for him, but it was also in an industry (food) which suffered from some of the same problems as the rag trade. It had low profit margins, and it was susceptible to outside factors beyond its control: the weather in this case; fickle fashion in the case of the rag trade. However, a feasibility report commissioned from a British firm of consultants suggested that the project was a goer. Uni-Pac would be the first packaging plant in Cyprus, and the saving to be made from manufacturing boxes there rather than importing them could be dramatic. One estimate was that an imported box would cost fourteen times as much as a locally-made one.

The Uni-Pac project encapsulated what was to become the essence of Polly Peck's strategy in the coming years, and a very alluring strategy it was too – the combination of Western capital and technology with developing-country natural resources and cheap labour. 'Building bridges' was how Mr Nadir liked to describe it.

The 1970s had seen hundreds of billions of Western dollars poured into developing countries in the form of loans from American, European and Japanese banks. Much of this money was channelled through banks in the City of London, and much of it was lost in the grandiose schemes and corruption of local governments. The whole process ground to a halt after 1982 when Mexico, one of the most indebted countries, effectively admitted that it could no longer keep up-to-date on repayment of its loans.

One flaw in this process was that the lending banks retained little control over the money once it was lent. Much of it went directly to governments, who could not be told what to do. The banks comforted themselves with the thought that countries never went bust – a thought from which the holders of old and worthless Russian and Chinese bonds could quickly have disillusioned them.

Bankers could only bring usury, however. What the developing countries were lacking was foreign direct investment – investment by Western companies which could bring the whole panoply of skills necessary to turn a forest clearing into a profitable industrial enterprise. Polly Peck was one of the few British companies that set out to do just this on a large scale. In all its investments it injected not only money but high-quality Western plant and machinery, and Western (usually British) experts. The process started on northern Cyprus but was soon to spread to the mainland of Turkey where there was a vast market of over 50 million people hungry for the quality of Western products.

Also in the formula was an assumption that the goods produced would be of such a standard that they could be exported back to Western markets. Again, Cyprus was the model. There was no way the northern part of the island could consume all the fruit it produced, or indeed all the planned output of the Uni-Pac factory. From the beginning Mr Nadir made it clear that only one-third of the Uni-Pac factory's output of cardboard boxes would be for the local market. He hoped to develop new markets abroad to take up the slack, in particular in Turkey.

Turkey is an extraordinarily rich agricultural country. Early civilisations arose in places where people didn't have to worry too much about finding their daily bread, and Turkey had an abundance of early civilisations whose sustenance literally fell off trees.

In the late 1970s no traveller to the country could have failed to notice the countless number of lorries labouring across mountainous terrain loaded down with fruit and vegetables: melons, oranges, tomatoes, aubergines – almost anything you like to name (apart from bananas and pineapples) was available in quantity. But by the time these laden vehicles reached their destinations half their load had rotted, suffocated and pressed down by the weight of other fruit on top of it. Until it could be sorted, graded, packaged properly in boxes and then protected from damage by paper wrapping and polystyrene trays, all this abundance was a wasted export and a loss of valuable dollars. Whoever could harness that export potential could expect to make a lot of money.

In London the rights issue to pay for the Uni-Pac project was a success. Investors were increasingly keen to get a slice of Polly Peck for two reasons: the forecast that Uni-Pac would make a profit of not less than £2.1 million in the year to the end of August 1981, and, more importantly, Mr Nadir himself. He had proved attractive to investors not only for his track record at Wearwell but also for what he was and what he represented.

He was very different from the stereotype image that northern Europeans have of people from the eastern Mediterranean. He did not have a dark moustache; he spoke English very well; he dressed as the City of London expected its visitors to dress; he was slim (then) and good-looking, with a boyish charm and mesmerisingly beautiful eyes. And he was always, but always, polite and soft-spoken in public – although he could swear like a trooper when among friends or colleagues. In England, politeness and appearances could still then go a long way.

Asil Nadir had a unique combination of characteristics born of his background. From Istanbul he had some of the dour sophistication of the Ottoman Turk; while from Cyprus he had the warmth of the Mediterranean and an understanding of the British. On top of that he had an inner self-confidence and a stubborn persistence that came, perhaps (as it has for others), from being a very able member of a persecuted minority.

He had great confidence in his own ability to solve problems when all about him were in despair. 'Don't worry' was a sentiment he expressed often, in English and in Turkish. This calm confidence, of course, appealed greatly to the English who panic at nothing so much as the sight of panic itself. He was also an optimist and an enthusiast who gave an impression of great depth. 'A man with Messianic vision'; 'a volcano about to erupt'; 'one of the most generous men I ever met', are some of the descriptions of him by people who knew him well.

These qualities enabled Mr Nadir to inspire small meetings of two or three people in a remarkable way. His enthusiasm and optimism would get the adrenalin going. People would talk of him as a 'charismatic charmer', a man who saw the grand picture, not a man for detail. Unfortunately he could never weave the same spell on larger groups. When speaking to the company's dealers, or at the openings of various new projects, he was visibly ill at ease, often with his upper lip twitching uncontrollably in the tic that became a hallmark of his nervousness.

Before the Uni-Pac sheds in Famagusta had produced their first cardboard box, Polly Peck was off to pastures new. The company bought a controlling interest in another 'penny stock', rather as Asil Nadir had bought the original stake in Polly Peck itself. The stock was called Cornell Dresses, and it was another dowdy loss-making rag-trade business that happened to be quoted on the stock-market. Like Raymond Zelker before him, Cornell's Jewish owner Samuel Cohen sold his shares and then, when he saw the subsequent share price rise, advised other shareholders, in his capacity as a director, not to follow suit. Polly Peck ended up with a 57 per cent stake in Cornell.

As soon as the Nadir connection was known, Cornell's share price rocketed from 26 pence to well over 100 pence – and this despite Mr Nadir's statement at the time that the board of Polly Peck had no intention of expanding Cornell's business 'by either diversification into new areas of activity or by the injection of existing trading assets'. Rightly, as it turned out, nobody believed him.

Press comment was a mixture of incredulity and scepticism. 'The stock-market's most highly rated man' was both an enigma and a joy in the dreary autumn of 1980 when recession was biting hard in Britain. The Young Turk (in England he was more usually seen as a Turk than as a Cypriot) got a boost on 12 September that year when the military under General Kenan Evren took over in Turkey. Violent civil strife and the breakdown of parliamentary rule in the late 1970s had threatened for a long while to degenerate into civil war. Now that possibility was remote.

The Nadir gaggle of companies (Polly Peck, Cornell and Wearwell) was already linked to Turkey in the average Englishman's mind, even though they had no business at all there except for the promise of exporting cardboard boxes from Uni-Pac. With a strong military ruler in place, the chances were that business would pick up in Turkey – more especially since in January 1980 the prime minister's young assistant in charge of economic affairs had introduced a package that opened up Turkey's hitherto closed economy to the outside world in an almost revolutionary way. The assistant's name was Turgut Ozal.

Britain may be in decline, the argument went, but Turkey was a place whose star was in the ascendant. Brazil and Mexico had been a false start for the developing countries. There were places like Taiwan and South Korea with development programmes that were really working. They could become the new Japans, and the new Turkey might join them.

For a while the Nadir companies' share prices continued to levitate on little more than promise and a good set of results from Wearwell, the only company in the group doing real business at the time. Then, suddenly, the levitation was threatened. In May 1981 the first seriously critical article on Polly Peck appeared, in the *Daily Mail*. The paper had had the sense to send out a correspondent (Michael Walters) to see the source of the Polly Peck phenomenon. He went to Famagusta and 'was underwhelmed' by what he saw: 'a bullet-scarred shed on the waterfront, with the roof next door still open to the sky and twisted from rocket attacks'. This was a factory that was supposed to be producing over £2 million profit in the eighteen-month accounting period to August 1981. Delays meant that it had not started production until February that year, and in May it was still only working at half-capacity.

Asil Nadir always showed great determination to fight against setbacks. A few weeks after this article appeared he accompanied a group of bankers, brokers and investors out to northern Cyprus in his first visit to the island for over twenty years. What these moneymen saw obviously reassured them. When Geoff Bowman and Peter Jones of L. Messel, the company's brokers, returned home, they produced the first full brokers' report on the company. In it they described Polly Peck as a 'unique and exciting situation'. They stuck with their forecast of a profit of over £2 million, and foresaw profits of £10 million and £20 million in the next two years. That was a staggering increase, but only expectations of that order could justify the Polly Peck share price.

The £2 million was based on an expected production of 8 million cardboard boxes from a plant which was scheduled to have a maximum capacity of 35 million boxes in future years. It was said at the time that Mr Nadir could land a case of lemons at London docks for a total cost of £1.90, and then sell it wholesale for between £3.50 and £4. The icing on the cake was the expectation that the government of northern Cyprus would shortly ban the import of corrugated cardboard boxes, giving Polly Peck a monopoly in the local market, which used some 12–15 million boxes a year. In addition, Mr Nadir was getting more involved in the local fruit business that had been the *raison d'être* for the cardboard boxes in the first place.

At the time, the City of London was giving one of its not infrequent shows of xenophobia. An attempt by a colonial upstart, the Hongkong and Shanghai Bank, to take over the ancient Royal Bank of Scotland was dismissed as 'unwelcome' by the governor of the Bank of England. After much fuss, the bid was eventually blocked by the government, and the Royal Bank preserved for Scotland.

Any incipient xenophobia towards Polly Peck was brushed aside by its results. Its annual report, when it appeared in January 1982, duly showed the forecast profit of £2.1 million, giving an astronomic return of almost 50 per cent on the capital invested. In a note to the accounts, the auditors Stoy Hayward pointed out that £2.16 million of the company's total turnover in packaging of £3.82 million was from sales to Nadir Holdings, a company owned by Asil Nadir and his father Irfan Nadir. When the accounts were closed at the end of August 1981, £2 million of that £2.16 million was still owed to Uni-Pac by Nadir Holdings.

Asil Nadir's explanation for this was that his private company had guaranteed to fulfil orders for boxes from farmers who were nervous about the delays in getting the Uni-Pac plant into production. So the farmers had signed contracts with Nadir Holdings which supplied them with Uni-Pac boxes. If Uni-Pac had not come up with the goods, Nadir Holdings would have had to buy boxes from abroad at a high price to supply them to the farmers at a guaranteed low price. It was a risky deal that could have lost the Nadirs a lot of money had the Uni-Pac plant been subject to further delays.

At the same time Mr Nadir reduced his stake in Polly Peck from 58 per cent to just over 40 per cent by selling 1.3 million shares for £4.5 million. He was prepared to give up his controlling stake because, he claimed, financial institutions were ravenously hungry for the stock and there just weren't enough Polly Peck shares to go round.

By now Asil Nadir was looking for his next leap, and it was big in principle if small in practice. It involved his first investment on the Turkish mainland.

Doing business in Turkey is very different from doing business in northern Cyprus. Turkey is a large country with a number of developing industries. Monopoly profits do not come so easily there. Since Mr Ozal's free-market package in January 1980 had opened their markets to newcomers, Turkish industrialists had been doggedly trying to conserve the monopolies that they had grown up with. Any industrial interloper was viewed with great suspicion and a knee-jerk hostility.

The first Nadir venture into Turkey was, again, into something new. But it was small, far away from Istanbul and relatively inconspicuous, ideally screened from the jealous glare of the old-time industrialists. More than half-way across Turkey's great breadth, east of Ankara, is a small town called Niksar. Three hours' drive from the nearest airport at Sivas, it happens to have a fresh-water source which has been in use for fifteen centuries.

Turkey has plenty of delightful-tasting natural waters. But at the time bottled water was being shipped from Europe to the newly-rich Middle East at enormous prices. It did not take a genius to think of setting up a sophisticated bottling plant at one of Turkey's sources, to under-cut European competition in the nearby Middle Eastern markets.

Polly Peck tried a large number of different waters and sent a short-list to Europe for chemical testing. Niksar was chosen, despite its geographical inconvenience, because it was judged to resemble most closely France's famous Evian water. But geography was not its only disadvantage: there was not enough water flowing from the source ever to produce many more than 60 million bottles a year. That amounted to only just over one bottle a year for every Turk – never mind the demand from abroad.

A feasibility study had suggested that Polly Peck could sell up to 100 million bottles of mineral water in the Middle East at around 17.7 pence a bottle. On sales of 43 million bottles a year (which is what Polly Peck expected from Niksar in its first year), the accountants' calculators said the profits should be £3.6 million.

Mr Nadir decided to use Cornell Dresses as the vehicle for his proposed water-bottling plant at Niksar. In April 1982 a company called Su ve Şişeleme Sanayi (Water and Bottling Industry) was registered in Turkey. Mehmet Sakir Yener, the man who set up many of Mr Nadir's early operations in Turkey before the two men fell out, was chairman and a founding shareholder.

Niksar was the first of many businesses that Mr Nadir was to set up in Turkey. Ten months later Mr Yener became chairman and founder of another Polly Peck company, Meyna Tarim Urunleri Sanayi ve Ihracat (Meyna Agricultural Products Manufacturing and Exports). Later on Meyna was to grow into one of the largest branches of Polly Peck, containing all its fruit, packing and processing businesses on the mainland of Turkey. The company was formed on an inauspicious day: 23 February 1983, the day that the Greek Cypriots, smarting over their stolen property, almost managed to bring Polly Peck to its knees.

Back in September 1982 Cornell announced that it had made losses in its most recent financial year, but at the same time asked shareholders to subscribe to a £2.76 million rights issue to help finance the bottling plant at Niksar. The rest of the £6 million cost of the plant was to come from Polly Peck.

It was almost a carbon copy of the Polly Peck rights issue in 1980. Shareholders had then been presented with losses and asked to come up with money in order to finance a project that could be the only justification for the price at which their shares were standing in the market. If the project didn't go ahead (or a similar one that Mr Nadir could pull out of his hat), their shares were worth little. It was Hobson's choice.

Another pattern to Polly Peck's progress was beginning to emerge. No sooner was one project on the drawing-board than Mr Nadir's mind was on another. As the years passed, this tendency became more pronounced. By the late 1980s Mr Nadir would talk about deals that he would like to do as if they had already been done. That applied to Del Monte and to Sansui, deals that did eventually happen; it also applied to deals that Polly Peck did not consummate, such as Mr Nadir's intention to take over the Sheraton hotel group.

The deal that was brewing in Mr Nadir's mind at the end of 1982, however, turned out to be one of his most stunningly successful. The taps had not even been turned on at Niksar before the gossip was about that Polly Peck's next deal was going to be in electronics, manufacturing colour televisions in Turkey. It was going to mark the company's first joint venture, and the likely partner was the British firm Thorn–EMI, virtually the only manufacturer of colour television sets left in Britain.

Thorn–EMI was an old-fashioned firm trying to be modern. Long before Japan's Sony bought America's CBS it had had the bright idea of bringing electronics hardware (Thorn) together with electronics software (EMI, a music-maker which recorded artists ranging from Itzhak Perlman to David Bowie). But the firm's old-style managers were not making much of their new-style company. Its profits were lower in 1986 than they had been in 1982.

With such a project Mr Nadir knew that he had to face something that the Niksar venture had avoided: full-frontal competition with Turkey's industrial establishment. Two manufacturers in particular, Arçelik, which belonged to the vast Koç conglomerate, and Profilo, which was run by an Istanbul entrepreneur, Jak Kamhi, dominated the electronics industry. Neither was going to take kindly to a new boy, particularly one with the backing of powerful Western capital and technology.

For the project Mr Nadir also had to expand his small circle of acquaintances. He called on a number of Turkish Cypriots who knew the business community on the mainland to help introduce him to the sort of commercial and political contacts he was going to need to make an ambitious electronics business work. Marketing people, public relations people, lawyers and political fixers flew back and forth between Istanbul and London. People who worked on the project at the time said that Asil Nadir inspired a great feeling of camaraderie. This was to be a breath of fresh air for Turkey, a new team taking on the established powers. There was a feeling in the air around Mr Nadir that nothing was impossible.

There were to be two prongs to the project, which was initially called Star Elektronik: first, the manufacture of colour televisions in a country that was about to get its first colour transmissions (in 1983); and second, the manufacture of video-cassette recorders, which were already having a field-day with the Turkish public, starved as they were of decent broadcast television. Broadcast programmes were only available from the state-owned channel, and the military was still keeping a close eye on what was broadcast. Their censorship of foreign films in particular would have been amusing had it not been so crude.

Nowadays Istanbul is spattered with satellite dishes which bring foreign television into many homes and keep the state-owned channels on their toes. CNN, the Atlanta-based American news channel, became a household name during the Gulf War. BBC's satellite transmission is also available. But in 1983 the best form of home entertainment was on video and at the time the two Japanese electronics giants, Sony and Matsushita, were engaged in a dog-fight over their incompatible technologies. In most of the world Sony's Betamax system was losing out to Matsushita's VHS system, sold by its JVC subsidiary. Turkey, however, was 'Beta country', with as much as 85 per cent of the video market accounted for by Sony's Betamax system.

Asil Nadir made the brave decision to go into Turkey with JVC's VHS system. Maybe he foresaw that it was going to wipe Sony off the video map within a couple of years (which it did in the rest of the world), but he had to go with VHS because it was the technology used by Thorn–EMI, his new partner.

Star Elektronik, which was the name of half the corner-shop electricians in Turkey, soon changed its name to Vestel. This was short for Western Electric in a country whose alphabet does not possess the letter W. But a change of name could not protect Vestel from what was becoming a regular Polly Peck problem. Asil Nadir was announcing new projects that the London Stock Exchange was greedily feeding off so far ahead of their practical realisation that their completion was inevitably ending up as a mad rush.

Vestel's television and VCR plants were originally due to come on stream in 1983. By the beginning of that year little was ready. Not even a suitable factory had been found. At the last minute a disused plant in a place called Manisa was seized upon. It had belonged to a company called Borusan which made pipes (the underground variety, not the Meerschaum ones for which Turkey is famous). Manisa is a small provincial town and not an obvious site for a grandiose industrial project.

With the benefit of hindsight, though, Manisa made a lot of sense. It was not far from one of Turkey's main ports and its third-largest city, Izmir, through which the high-tech parts that Vestel was going to process could pass. It had been described in the Turkish press as the country's future Silicon Valley. And the local authorities were keen to encourage 'clean' industries into their special industrial development area, an area that had already attracted names like Pierre Cardin textiles and Raks video-tapes. But the reality was that the Borusan plant was available at short notice when everything was having to be done in a rush.

Vestel was to become the jewel in Polly Peck's Turkish crown, an operation that fought against many odds and came out a winner, with a network of licensing agreements and joint ventures with some of the greatest names in the world of electronics. Its factories impressed everybody who saw them and eventually stretched far beyond the original Borusan building which remained as the administrative headquarters. At the end of 1990 Vestel had 19 per cent of the Turkish television market, 36 per cent of the market for video-cassette recorders, and 46 per cent of the market for music-centres.

The official opening of the factory was attended by Turgut Ozal, by then prime minister, and it was accompanied by the sort of razzamatazz that was becoming another Polly Peck hallmark. Shareholders and bankers were flown over from London; low-flying planes dropped leaflets on the assembled dignitaries; the municipal band played and thousands of coloured balloons floated up in the air mingling with simultaneously released pigeons. For Manisa the good times had come, and so they had for Turgut Ozal, fed up with seeing his country filled with Europe's technological cast-offs. Vestel looked like a classy operation. Asil Nadir, he believed, could be an example to the rest of the world of what could be achieved in Turkey with first-class foreign investment.

From London Mr Nadir kept his hand very firmly on the Vestel tiller, assuring his team in Turkey that it was better for him to watch from a distance. A crucial factor in building up the company was finding dealers who would sell its products. Luckily there were a number of independents who were not tied in with rivals Koç or Profilo. They were attracted by the Nadir name, and they were not put off by the great man's unimpressive appearances at their annual get-togethers, meetings of rough, simple men. Their main complaint was that Polly Peck made only 'brown goods' (televisions and other electronic gadgetry housed in dark containers), and not 'white goods' (fridges, washing-machines and the like). Koç and Profilo made the lot, so working with them provided a dealer with a wider range of products to sell. One of the last things that Vestel did before Asil Nadir's downfall in 1990 was to start manufacturing white goods in order to honour a promise he had made to his dealers.

Despite its substantial and real achievement, profits did not flow to Vestel in the same easy way that they had to Uni-Pac. The company did not make real inroads into the local television market until the end of 1987, and Turkey did not turn away from the well-entrenched Betamax VCR system overnight. Even in 1990, by which time Vestel was a quoted company on the Istanbul Stock Exchange in its own right, the group's latest reported profit was a mere TL22 billion – just over £6 million. Turkey was not the same pot of gold that Cyprus had been; and electronics was not going to give the group the same sort of sustenance as had agriculture and packaging.

Yet back in early 1983 the City of London was blindly assuming that Turkey would lay golden eggs like Cyprus – only bigger ones, much bigger ones. And it was not distracted by Britain's own electronics promise, evidenced by the growth of the M4 corridor and the rise of Swindon Man. With Polly Peck's shares standing at £35 at the end of January 1983, the *Sunday Telegraph* explained their Himalayan stature thus:

> The reason is the extraordinary profit projections being made by some analysts. A recent visit by accountants Coopers and Lybrand to Turkey has raised expectations that the Polly Peck and Thorn–EMI video deal starting in September [sic] could itself produce profits of as much as £55 million alone in the 1983/84 financial year. When added to non-video profit forecasts of some £43 million for that year, the bulls' projections of almost £100 million pre-tax compare with an estimated £25 million in the current financial year and £9 million last year.

But how many of these bulls had ever been to Turkey, let alone to Manisa or Gazimagusa? The Thorn–EMI project did not produce a single product until almost the end of the 1983/84 financial year. By February 1983 the stock-market was already sniffing for the next Polly Peck deal, perhaps carrying Asil Nadir along with it in its belief that the electronics business was complete, established, yesterday's story. Maybe pharmaceuticals would be next, indicated Mr Nadir. But actually what was next was a nasty shock.

The Greek Cypriots had been licking their wounds since the case in the House of Lords in 1978 which had allowed Turkish Cypriot produce into London's Covent Garden. As Polly Peck's shares were soaring at unbelievable heights, the Greek Cypriot High Commission in London announced that it was considering taking action against both Polly Peck and Wearwell for 'exploiting property owned by Greek Cypriots', which was 'prejudicing a settlement of the Cyprus problem'.

This was the Greek Cypriots' main concern. But at the time they also claimed that 'There are a number of questions relevant to the accounts of Polly Peck plc and Wearwell plc which merit investigation.'

Another allegation made by the Greek Cypriots was that much of the group's profits arose from currency movements – shifts in the exchange rate between the Turkish lira (in which it did its business) and sterling (in which it denominated its accounts). This point went almost unnoticed at the time, but it was to come very much to the fore in later years. The Greek Cypriots also claimed that Polly Peck should have told its shareholders at the annual general meeting held earlier in 1983 that the Turkish Cypriot Ministry of Finance was trying to retrieve £620,000 of unpaid tax from the company.

The Greek Cypriots sent a lengthy report on the issues to the British Foreign Office, to the Department of Trade and Industry, and to the Stock Exchange, then under the chairmanship of Nicholas Goodison. Although the Greek Cypriots never got a reply from the Stock Exchange, after their announcement that they were considering taking action against the company Polly Peck's share price shrank like a dehydrated grapefruit.

When the price had been almost halved, the Stock Exchange suspended trading in the shares pending an announcement from the company about its tax status in Cyprus. After much discussion, including a telephone conversation between Mr Nadir and the Turkish prime minister Bülent Ulusu, a decree was rushed through the Turkish Cypriot parliament. It confirmed that there would be a tax holiday for Uni-Pac's operations in the free port of Famagusta, and wiped out the £620,000 potential liability. The share suspension lasted for only twenty-four hours.

The British government decided not to investigate Polly Peck further for failing to divulge the tax position. 'Although the company's liability for overseas tax is at present uncertain,' said Gerard Vaughan, the minister of consumer affairs at the time, in a written answer to a parliamentary question, 'the indications are that when the company's annual report was sent to shareholders recently, the directors had reasonable grounds for believing that no such liability existed.'

The challenge from the Greek Cypriots had not only wiped out half the wealth of Polly Peck's shareholders, it had also played on the paranoia of Mr Nadir and other Turkish Cypriots that the Greek Cypriots were bent on destroying them. And it had put at risk two important developments going on within the company at the time. Investors had been complaining for a while that the interweavings of Wearwell, Polly Peck and Cornell were getting too tangled, and that Mr Nadir should bring together the three companies in which he was the driving force. N. M. Rothschild, the impeccable merchant bank, had been called in to advise on consolidating the three companies, but after the Greek affair (which adversely affected the share price of all three) their merger was postponed.

The second crucial development at the time was not put off as a result of the hysteria on the stock-market. On 14 March 1983 Polly Peck had signed the exclusive agreement with Thorn–EMI to assemble and market colour television sets in Turkey.

For a short while Polly Peck tried to return to normal. But it was frustrated by what was subsequently described as 'an Exocet missile' from Michael Gillard, an investigative journalist on the *Observer* newspaper who had been following the Polly Peck story closely for some time. Mr Gillard was to continue to be a thorn in the flesh of the company for years to come, through the things he wrote both for the *Observer* and the satirical magazine *Private Eye*. *Private Eye* never had a kind word to say for Polly Peck, but then it never had a kind word to say for anybody.

Like Michael Walters of the *Daily Mail* two years before him, Mr Gillard actually went to Cyprus and Turkey to see what Polly Peck was up to. His unflattering report, published on 24 April 1983, pushed the Polly Peck share price down by less than had the threats of the Greek Cypriots, but the impact of his report, and of others that followed, probably hurt more deeply.

Peter Jones, for long the analyst at the stockbrokers L. Messel who had sung Polly Peck's praises loudest, believes that the Gillard articles constrained Polly Peck's ability to raise proper finance for the electronics project. From then on, he maintains, the company was over-stretched financially and under-capitalised for what it was doing.

Like so many things surrounding the history of Polly Peck, the articles suffered from exaggeration. They hurt Mr Nadir particularly because they had nothing good at all to say about the company. Throughout his business success (and he undoubtedly had a lot) Mr Nadir could become incensed by the most insignificant critical comment in a publication with a circulation of a few thousand. He always longed to be appreciated for what he felt he had achieved – *inter alia*, an almost single-handed revival of the Turkish Cypriot economy, and a demonstration to Turkey of what that country could do if it kept a closer eye on the quality of its industrial production.

But the *Observer* articles raised some valid questions, in particular about the slow progress of the Niksar plant and about the profit projections for the Thorn–EMI electronics venture. The article also asked questions that Polly Peck's shareholders themselves should have asked about the company's accounts. Were the company's auditors, Stoy Hayward, doing proper checks on the all-important Cypriot accounts which were audited on their behalf by a local firm? And why was there no geographical breakdown of profit and turnover in the accounts? The London Stock Exchange's rules demanded that quoted companies give such a breakdown, but Polly Peck had obtained a special exemption from the Stock Exchange on the grounds that giving such information would be 'commercially damaging'. This vacuum, said the *Observer*, 'only serves to encourage speculation, if not suspicion'. Mr Nadir did not help his case by refusing to meet Mr Gillard and put across his point of view.

The press criticism reached a peak a month later when Polly Peck came out with its half-year results. The *Financial Times*, the doyen of British financial journalism and a newspaper not given to hysterical exaggeration, commented on the results in its Lex column. Lex is an anonymously written section on the back page of the distinctively pink newspaper that analyses corporate and financial news. It is written by some of the paper's brightest journalists and was then essential everyday reading in the City of London, rather as the *Wall Street Journal*'s Heard on the Street column was in New York.

Lex said:

> The skeletal profit statement for the half-year to March produced by Polly Peck yesterday would have been inadequate in any circumstances. In the light of the rapid expansion in profits and turnover, the speculation surrounding the shares, not to speak of the litigation in which the company is involved, it is disgraceful. . . . While Polly Peck provides details of future projects, present operations rate a few bland lines.

The word that stuck in people's minds was 'disgraceful'. But it did not stick firmly enough to detract for long from the future projects that Polly Peck was signposting: the electronics deal; the construction of a second box factory and a third packing plant in Cyprus; and plans for a box factory and two packing plants on the mainland of Turkey (through Meyna). The City was in no mood for bad moods. The main stock-market index had risen by almost 30 per cent over the previous year, and the UK economy was growing at the almost unheard-of rate of 4 per cent a year. Polly Peck's shares soon began to rise again.

The Turkish halo was also shining brightly at the time. Free elections were due in November 1983 that would return democracy to a country that had been under military rule for three years. Despite the military rule, the Turkish economy had been growing strongly and opening up to outside trade and investment. Democracy promised a continuation and acceleration of that process.

Indeed, so brightly was the halo shining that the City of London started to play a new game. It was called 'Spot the Turk'. Any deadbeat company that could boast a Turkish connection was suddenly full of Eastern promise. If the Turkish connection was in any remote way linked to Asil Nadir, so much the better. In 1982 a young man called Touker Suleyman bought a stake in a hitherto moribund south London clothing firm called Mellins. Mr Suleyman was said to have been at school in Famagusta with Mr Nadir, and on the strength of their common education Mellins's share price rose from 6 pence to £2.52 over the next twelve months. That made a large fortune for Mr Suleyman despite Mr Nadir's statement that 'If Mr Suleyman and I went to school together, either I was very thick or he was very bright. He is thirty. I am ten years older. We are not great buddies.'

Mehmet Tecimer, the brother of Mr Nadir's wife Ayşegül, performed a similar magic. He bought 76 per cent of a Cheshire-based company called Bellair Cosmetics at 8 pence a share. Almost before the slightest scent of profit could be sniffed the share-price was on a high of £7. Mr Tecimer performed the trick again with Harold Ingram, a knitwear company. When Wasskon Establishment, a Liechtenstein company controlled by Mr Tecimer, took control of Harold Ingram, the knitwear company's share price shot from 64 pence to £3.23 on the strength of the Nadir connection. The Stock Exchange, increasingly worried about the City's Turcophiles, briefly suspended Harold Ingram's shares.

To their credit, these Turkish entrepreneurs tried to calm down the excitement, saying that there were no fundamental trading reasons for share prices at these levels. But the stock-market seemed as deaf to their warnings as it had been in the long run to those of the Greek Cypriots or of Michael Gillard. Was it crazy, or did it just know better than anybody else? There were plenty who believed that it did. After all, Thatcherite economics was about restoring faith in markets and in 'market economics' where the laws of supply and demand were freed from interference by the state or by the labour unions. And was the stock-market not the closest thing that Britain had to a 'perfect market'?

CHAPTER FOUR

THE CITY STOKES THE FIRE

ONE fact which proud financial institutions in the City of London find it hard to come to terms with is that they owe their wealth and success to trade. The Square Mile around St Paul's Cathedral which they inhabit provides them with plenty of reminders of this. There are the ancient livery companies with their splendid halls – the Fishmongers, the Goldsmiths and the Merchant Taylors. Until recently the fish market, Billingsgate, used to be within smelling distance; Smithfield, the wholesale meat market, still is. And as a backdrop there is the River Thames, the stretch of water which placed London where it is and whose heavily-laden ships provided the city with some 25 per cent of its jobs in the eighteenth century. All this trade required plenty of financial services, like banking and insurance. Without trade there would be no City.

For much of the time the City sniffily ignores this, behaving as if trade should be left to stevedores. In practice, however, it has usually realised where its own best interests lie. A staunch supporter of free trade, it has also appreciated that where the Port of London left off, the airport of London (Heathrow) took over. If there is one thing that has turned the City into the world's busiest international financial centre (apart from its great good fortune that the English speak English), it is the proximity of Heathrow, the world's busiest international airport. Whereas clippers and square-riggers used to carry exotic seamen, merchants and slaves into the City's gloomy, poky streets, now jumbo jets ferry bankers and brokers of every nationality to and from those same gloomy, poky streets. Foreign faces have never been unfamiliar to the denizens of Lombard Street, the heart of the banking district, as sombre as when the fourteenth-century financiers from Lombardy first set up shop there.

The City of London has always been a mish-mash of financial and commodity markets, only a few of which had a role in Polly Peck's story. But these few provided the financial fuel for the whole phenomenon. They were Britain's unique contribution to the extraordinary story, and they included the merchant banks and clearing banks, the stockbrokers and the so-called 'long-term financial institutions', like insurance companies and pension funds.

In the 1970s the relationship between the City and Britain's trade and industry was uncomfortable. Industrialists from the hinterland would enjoy coming up to London to have lunch with their bankers or brokers, especially since the City firms provided some of the best cuisine in the country in the days before Continental chefs discovered that the English could be persuaded to spend money on dishes other than roast beef and custard. But the industrialists' visits were short and unproductive. The hospitality was rarely returned.

Much time was spent discussing whether British industry was well served by the City. The City claimed that anything that British industry asked for it could have. But industrialists who did ask were put off by 'them-and-us' attitudes. A Lloyds bank manager once began a discussion with two businessmen by regally advising them, 'We are not a charitable institution.'

In the City there are two sorts of banking: boring banking and interesting banking. As somebody once put it, bankers live on either their deposits or their wits. Boring banking is the almost exclusive monopoly of the clearing banks which 'clear' people's cheques and listen to the imprecations of small businessmen from Bolton who have run out of cash.

Interesting banking used to be the almost exclusive monopoly of a small number of merchant banks which had formed themselves into a club called the Accepting Houses Committee (AHC). These banks did not like to sully their hands with money. They existed to give advice – to companies and to governments – on how they could raise money from others.

The AHC stood at the pinnacle of the City pecking order. In return for being seen to behave like gentlemen, its members received special privileges from the Bank of England, the central bank which ruled the City, not with an iron rod and a rigid rule-book but with a nod and a wink. There was an assumption that people behaved honourably unless proved otherwise.

The AHC included all the most august banking names: Rothschild, Hambro, Morgan Grenfell and Schroder – none of them, incidentally, founded by Englishmen. Polly Peck's bank (and Wearwell's before it) was Singer and Friedlander, one of the smaller members of the Committee and the most recent newcomer. (It joined the club in 1973.) As a small newcomer Singer and Friedlander had to find a niche that others had ignored if it was going to grow and join the big league. The niche it chose was Britain's medium-sized companies, like Polly Peck, and to reach them it did an almost unheard-of thing. It opened branches in the provinces outside London. It was the natural merchant bank for Polly Peck in its younger days.

Polly Peck began to move into the big league at the end of 1982 when it employed N. M. Rothschild to mastermind a merger of the three inter-related companies: Polly Peck, Wearwell and Cornell. Singer and Friedlander was given the job of advising Wearwell, and Arbuthnot Latham, a member of the AHC until it did the unseemly thing of being bought by a foreigner, advised Cornell.

Until 1981 the most important privilege of the accepting houses was their right to discount bills. A bill is a sort of post-dated cheque given by a buyer of goods to a seller. The seller, usually an industrial company, can take the bill immediately to an accepting house and have it guaranteed, at a price (the 'discount'). Then it is as good as cash: if the buyer of the goods goes bankrupt, the bank will pay. The exclusive privilege of the accepting houses was that they, and only they, could have bills that they had 'accepted' rediscounted by the Bank of England. So if the bank went bust the Bank of England would pay, and that guarantee was literally as good as gold.

This exclusive privilege was worth a lot of money to the sixteen or seventeen merchant banks that had it in the late 1970s. It enabled them to be relaxed about their other business, such as advising British industry on how to raise capital for new investment. Even at times in their 150-year histories when their acceptance business was not particularly thrilling, the merchant banks had been fairly relaxed about British industry. Sorting out the financial affairs of foreigners or of governments was usually a grander and more profitable way of exercising their skills.

The security of their acceptance business freed the directors of the merchant banks to indulge in some of the time-consuming rural pursuits, such as hunting, shooting and fishing, that their upbringing had taught them to enjoy. Banking attracted new recruits from the same background – partly because it was a career that allowed them to follow their hobbies; partly because in a world of gentlemen's agreements the bankers believed that people who went to their schools and rode with their hounds were the most likely to be gentlemen. Since their schools admitted no women, neither did their banks. In 1981 seven of the chairmen of the sixteen accepting houses came from Eton, and all but two had been educated at one of the top English public schools. Those two had been educated abroad.

However, 1981 was the last year of an era for these merchant banks. For in that year the members of the AHC lost their exclusive access to the Bank of England, and with it the monopoly profits from their acceptance business. They were suddenly faced with the need to find new businesses that might support them in the style to which they had become accustomed.

The City's stockbrokers generally came from the same social class as the merchant bankers, but from a lower classroom. They too had their own clubby ways, ruled by the Stock Exchange itself. The Exchange's ruling council was made up of 'members' who themselves approved and vetted other members. Only members could be partners or directors of stockbroking firms and until 1971 they had had to be British.

In 1971 one member of the Stock Exchange council, Graham Greenwell, had written a letter to *The Times* in which he maintained that the Exchange was a private gentlemen's club and not 'an institution which exists to perform a public service'. This attitude still pervaded the stockbroking and merchant banking community in the early 1980s. Their business was nobody's business but their own. The merchant banks were allowed to keep 'hidden reserves', which meant that nobody outside the bank (not even their own shareholders) knew what their true profits were. Secrecy was the order of the day.

The best-known stockbroking firms (though none of them exactly courted publicity) were James Capel, which was probably the biggest (though nobody could tell since it never published any figures), and Cazenove, which revelled in a haughty disdain for all but those fortunate enough to be chosen as its clients.

Polly Peck's broker (and Wearwell's before it), L. Messel, was an old-fashioned firm whose speciality was gilts (government securities), but which had a good list of solid industrial clients, companies like Glaxo, Grand Metropolitan and Mothercare. For many years Messel's relationship with Polly Peck was almost exclusive, with the firm acting as a sort of Delphic oracle for Polly Peck's increasingly exciting profit projections. Not until the company had been battered by the Greek Cypriots' allegations and adverse press reports in 1983 did other brokers (like James Capel and Laing & Cruickshank) join Messel in seriously analysing the company.

Once they did, however, they battled to outdo each other in the size of their profit projections for Polly Peck – Messel and Laing & Cruickshank in particular. One year Messel forecast profits of £50 million; Laing & Cruickshank upped it to £68 million. The next year Messel tried £80 million, but Laing & Cruickshank came out with a forecast of over £100 million. These were very big figures indeed and were sure to bring Polly Peck to the attention of a wide audience beyond the City's walls.

The place where the City met the general public was in the branches of the clearing banks. They were a stodgy oligopoly which included Lloyds, Barclays, Midland and National Westminster. These four collected huge deposits from savers and in the 1970s had eagerly shovelled them out to Brazil, Mexico and other poor countries. By the early 1980s they were beginning to realise that this might not have been such a good idea. Their developing-country clients were having a hard time repaying their loans.

But the banks had to lend their huge deposits to somebody or else they could not pay the interest due to their depositors. Like the merchant banks, they too had to look around for new areas of business.

They plumped on two groups – private individuals and companies. To individuals they began to offer mortgages, loans to buy houses. Until the end of the 1970s these had been the almost exclusive prerogative of the building societies, solid local organisations with names like Northern Rock and Cheltenham & Gloucester. But with Mrs Thatcher exhorting all and sundry to buy their own home (i.e. to have a mortgage) there was plenty of business to go round.

The clearing banks also began to encourage the growth of consumer credit – loans to individuals to buy consumer goods like dishwashers, video-cassette recorders or a new dress. Much of this consumer credit was channelled through increasingly popular credit cards, like Barclaycard and Access. Access had been launched with the unforgettable advertising boast that it could 'take the waiting out of wanting'. That was the Holy Grail for the 1980s.

Credit cards gave their owners a credit limit which, in theory, card-holders were not supposed to exceed. In practice, many were astonished to find that as soon as they exceeded their limit it was raised, so as not to interrupt their spending spree. The banks were encouraged to push these loans because of the very high interest rates they were able to charge on them. Individuals, unable to find such convenient loans elsewhere, used them freely.

The clearing banks' eagerness to lend to companies was not so easily satisfied. Several things were conspiring to take their corporate business away from them. For a start, the opening up of the stock-market made it easier for companies to raise equity and thereby reduced their demand for long-term loans from banks. Second, blue-chip companies like ICI and Shell realised that it was more beneficial for them to lend their surplus short-term cash directly to each other (through various short-term financial markets) than it was for them to deposit the surplus in a bank in order that others might borrow it from the bank. This process was called 'disintermediation' and threatened to cut the banks out of the business of lending to top companies altogether.

Finally, there was the competition from all the foreign banks in London. They were finding that with a minimal amount of extra effort they could undercut the sleepy clearing banks and do business with a number of big British companies. In the early 1980s the finance director of a reasonable-sized British company could expect several calls a day from different banks offering him money in one form or another.

This *embarras de richesses* had some unfortunate side-effects. It altered the traditionally uncomfortable relationship that had existed between banker and industrialist. Companies used to stick with one bank (even if reluctantly) for most of their financial needs. But now they were being encouraged to shop around, taking the best deal on offer wherever it came from.

This was called 'transaction banking', by contrast with the old method of 'relationship banking'. It was a system that Polly Peck exploited to the full. Asil Nadir himself once said that Polly Peck did not 'practise the attitude that you appoint a merchant bank and at every instance you call that bank . . . the company itself at different times has used different lawyers, different bankers and different advisors. Your saying in this country, horses for courses, is appropriate.'

Finding horses for courses was further encouraged because bankers themselves were moving around like never before. The large number of new banks arriving in London were ruthlessly pinching the limited amount of banking talent on offer. Good bankers ratcheted up their salaries by moving quickly from one bank to another. Even if a company had stuck with only one bank 'relationship' it was unlikely to have been served by the same person or team of people for any length of time.

The only way that companies could be sure of retaining the same banker was to employ him themselves. And that is what Polly Peck did in 1983 when it persuaded a twenty-nine-year-old lawyer called Mark Ellis to leave Arbuthnot Latham (the bank that was advising Cornell on its merger with Polly Peck) and to join Polly Peck as joint managing director.

The infidelity between bank and company, and between banker and bank, put a horse and cart through the proper controls that steady relationships should impose. Companies began to play one bank off against another and, given certain basic requirements (such as a sparkling set of accounts), found that they could have what the City had always told them they could have: whatever they wanted.

At its extreme, this put billions of pounds in the hands of over-reaching executives who wanted to buy companies many times the size of their own. In April 1983 a couple of unknown Americans, Marshall Cogan and Stephan Swid, who ran a company called GFI/Knoll (the GF stood for General Felt), attempted to take over Sotheby's, the grand auction house which Thackeray had described 134 years earlier as being 'full of snobs and odious bombazine women'.

Sotheby's was shaken to its well-bred core. In the event it managed to find a more acceptable American – Mr Alfred Taubman, who was married to a former Miss Israel – to rescue the company from the fate of General Felt. But the message was clear: armed with a friendly banker anybody could take over anything.

In such an environment Polly Peck had no trouble raising whatever bank facilities it needed for its various projects. The fulsome attitude of banks throughout the 1980s lends credibility to Mr Nadir's statement that eleven 'world-famous' banks were prepared to lend him the £1.5 billion that he would have needed for his ill-fated attempt in August 1990 to buy the company back.

In fact it was so easy for Polly Peck to raise money that in the end this worked against the company. For example, among the many banks that came offering it loans in its early days were a number of Turkish banks, several of which had offices in London. Mr Nadir was able to brush them aside – so casually that when he came to them in late 1990 asking for help to bail out Polly Peck, there were no favours to be returned.

Mr Nadir has admitted that one of his biggest mistakes was to have been too casual about Polly Peck's bank loans. Too much was left callable on demand – i.e. the banks could ask for their loans back whenever they liked. Just before its collapse Polly Peck was negotiating a deal with a group of banks that would have put its loans on a more fixed, long-term basis and that might have prevented its collapse.

The last feature in the financial background to Polly Peck was the 'long-term financial institutions' – a general term for insurance companies and pension funds. The insurance companies grew up as self-help organisations among the working men of Victorian England. The biggest of them, the Prudential, has a huge Gothic brick headquarters just outside the City, a building that reflects its age and glories in much the same way as St Pancras station does those of the railways.

With the growth of industrial wealth these companies attracted more and more savings, which they invested largely in government securities and industrial shares. By the 1960s they were the largest single shareholders in most big British companies.

While they too had a smattering of public schoolboys on their boards, unlike the merchant banks they were actually run by their managers. These bright men were expert at the grim task of calculating the probability of death, but they were not so good at owning companies. Their emphasis was on their role as guardians of the savings of millions of working people.

The same was true of the pension funds, which were even more nebulous than the insurance companies, and growing even faster. Whereas their total assets had been worth less than £5 billion in 1963 they were worth over £125 billion by 1984. Anthony Sampson described their managers in his book *The Changing Anatomy of Britain*, published in 1982:

> Few of them came from the public school or Oxford and Cambridge background of bankers and stockbrokers, and there are some faint rumblings of class warfare. The old guard treat them with wary politeness, as they might treat upstart millionaires who have suddenly become lords of the manor.

As owners of shares these institutions were passive at best, and failed to play their full role in the Anglo-Saxon capitalist system of which they were an increasingly important part. As family firms became public companies quoted on the Stock Exchange they were thrown into an ownership limbo. Big firms like Sainsbury, Marks and Spencer and Pilkington were still largely run by their founding families. But their largest shareholders were likely to be the Legal and General insurance company or the British Railways pension fund.

The same happened to smaller family companies that became quoted on the Stock Exchange. By the time of Polly Peck's annual general meeting in February 1983, when Mr Nadir told assembled shareholders, 'Your company has unlimited expansion potential,' almost 4 per cent of Polly Peck was owned jointly by just three institutions: Friends Provident, Phoenix Assurance and the Iron Trades Employers Insurance Association. Later that year, Legal and General and Friends Provident each owned more than 5 per cent of Polly Peck.

This separation between ownership and management left a company's managers too firmly in charge of its affairs. In particular, it left quoted family firms free to be run as if they were still private family firms. The institutions were rarely represented on the boards of the companies they owned, and they had little influence over the company's non-executive directors who were, at least in theory, the guardians of their interests against the vested interests of the managers and executive directors. It meant that rotten management continued to rot unchallenged until a company's share price was so weak (because its results were so bad) that it became vulnerable to a takeover.

That sequence of events was, perhaps, not surprising. The British, ever weak in industrial management but strong in finance, had worked out a financial solution to a management problem. But it was like cutting off a company's head to cure it of a headache.

Britain's financial system was (and still is) peculiar, and Polly Peck would never have been financially nourished in the same way elsewhere. At the root of the peculiarity is a sharp divide between the way that industry is financed in Britain and the United States, and the way that it is financed in Germany and Japan. In the first two countries industry is more dependent on financial markets, like the stock-market; in the latter two, it is more dependent on banks. In 1984 almost 80 per cent of Japanese companies' external cash came in the form of bank borrowing. The percentage was similar in West Germany. But in the same year the roughly comparable figure for the United States was 40 per cent and for Britain 55 per cent.

This greater dependence on banks in West Germany and Japan leads to a much closer relationship between industrialists and bankers: 'transaction banking' is rare and frowned-upon. In West Germany banks also hold large equity stakes in the companies they lend to, and they also provide directors for those companies' boards. For example, Deutsche Bank (the biggest bank in Germany) owns 28 per cent of Daimler–Benz (the biggest industrial company in Germany). When Alfred Herrhausen, the chairman of Deutsche Bank, was murdered at the end of 1989, he was also chairman of Daimler–Benz, and of many other German companies besides. His successor at Deutsche Bank almost automatically became chairman of Daimler–Benz too. In Britain it is unthinkable that the chairman of Barclays Bank should also be chairman of British Aerospace, or of GEC, or even of Polly Peck.

The question of 'leverage' (the ratio of a company's debt to its equity) was at the heart of one of the biggest financial debates of the

1980s. On the one hand, the great post-war industrial success stories (Japan and West Germany) rejoiced in highly leveraged companies. On the other hand, Anglo-Saxon attitudes instinctively thought that debt was bad, equity good.

Henry Kaufman, a popular American financial guru of the time, put equity on a par with apple pie and motherhood. In the mid-1980s he wrote:

> The roles of debt and equity in corporate finance – and for that matter in our society – should be clearly defined, understood and publicly reinforced. Debt can never be a substitute for equity . . . the abuse of the debt-creation process debauches the essence of an economic democracy. Equity, in contrast, allows freedom of decision-making and often reflects confidence in society and its political and economic institutions. If we diminish the role of equity, we also invite social and political change.

Either that makes Germany and Japan politically unstable, or else the nature of equity is somewhat more prosaic.

One lesson of the 1980s is that the nature of a company's sources of finance (and the balance between them) matters less than the degree of control that is imposed by the suppliers of that finance on its users. In Britain (and in the United States) neither the suppliers of equity capital (the long-term financial institutions) nor the suppliers of loans (banks) are sufficiently involved with what the users of their money actually do with it. Otherwise how could Polly Peck's bankers and shareholders have been so shocked by the company's downfall that they switched overnight from offering it almost limitless billions to withdrawing absolutely everything?

MUCH of the wind of change in the London financial scene in the 1980s blew in with the radical politics of Mrs Thatcher. Normally the City votes Conservative to a man, but in 1979 there was some trepidation that Mrs Thatcher's policies might be less palatable than the moderate socialism it had become familiar with over the previous five years. Its fears were calmed by the promises from the Thatcher camp of privatisations to come.

These sales of rheumatic state-owned industries would bring the City's banks and brokers big fees from underwriting the attendant issues of shares, and they would give the long-term institutions something new to buy with their policy-holders' savings.

But the City was never going to have an easy time with Mrs Thatcher. She disliked the clubby ethics which had been a bulwark of her Conservative predecessors and which permeated the City. And she deeply mistrusted all institutions, with the possible exception of the British parliament. Its rules and management she defended against any whiff of foreign influence quite as fiercely as the executives of Sotheby's did theirs when first they spied Messrs Cogan and Swid.

Initially, Mrs Thatcher's influence on the City of London came from two directions – privatisation and deregulation. The former was designed to de-institutionalise the nationalised industries, the latter to sweep restrictive practices and club membership out of British commercial life.

Ultimately, Mrs Thatcher realised that there was no point in releasing state industries from the dead hands of state ownership if they simply moved straight into the dead hands of the long-term financial institutions. So privatisation was tailored to sell shares to individuals, and to shift the balance of share ownership away from Mrs Thatcher's dreaded institutions. In her firm belief in the ability of the individual to overcome institutional evil Mrs Thatcher may have thought that would be enough to cure the problems of British industry.

If so, she misread the motives of the new individual shareholders she created. Perhaps she thought that they would care for their companies in the same way that they cared for the houses they owned. But these people were not out to buy a share in a company. What they were after was a casino chip with which they might hit the jackpot. As Polly Peck turned to the stock-market for more and more money throughout the 1980s it was turning to a pack of hungry-to-get-rich-quick gamblers. It was not turning to people who were concerned to build up a business.

If privatisation turned the City into a casino, deregulation turned it into an uncontrolled one. Tight, gentlemanly self-regulation (which, though exclusive, had nourished the City for centuries) had to struggle for survival in the teeth of the Conservatives' zeal for deregulation – a philosophy that hastily hoovered its way into every nook and cranny of the British economy.

The first significant piece of City deregulation came in August 1981 when the Bank of England increased the number of banks whose bills it would accept from the sixteen members of the AHC to a motley selection of ninety-six foreign and British banks. That kept the merchant bankers of the AHC at their desks long after they might at one time have been galloping across the English shires. They were busily looking for new business, and what they found first was new equity issues for companies. Later they were to become eager pedlars of mergers and corporate takeovers.

As the Conservatives had been bringing the principles of good housekeeping to the management of government finances, there was more money available at the time for industrial equities since so much less was required by the state. With its experience of raising capital for smaller quoted companies, Singer and Friedlander had had little trouble raising £1.5 million in 1980 for Polly Peck to set out on its Cypriot adventure. Likewise Arbuthnot Latham easily raised £2.76 million for the loss-making Cornell to buy the water-bottling business at Niksar. And N. M. Rothschild subsequently raised £42.6 million for Polly Peck's electronics venture at Manisa.

Only later did Polly Peck partake of the merchant banks' other big service: advising on mergers and acquisitions. In 1988 it set off on an extraordinary corporate buying spree, helped by a number of enthusiastic merchant banks. Like many men before him, Asil Nadir had by then discovered that buying a going concern brought quicker returns than starting a new business.

To cope with all the new business that poured in during the early 1980s, and with the fierce competition for it, the City had to recruit large numbers of new workers. Of necessity many of them came from outside the City's traditional recruiting grounds, and most were young, loud and self-confident. They had in common an ignorance of their own ignorance, and a sense of history that stretched no further back than yesterday's closing stock-market prices. They had never known hard times.

A new word was created to describe these people: yuppies, young upwardly mobile professional people. They worked hard and frantically, and they earned more in one year than their fathers had done in a lifetime. Money gave them Porsche cars, property in London's trendy Docklands, and short sharp holidays in the Seychelles or Phuket.

There was to be even more of this life later in the decade, although as early as 1983 *The Economist* said that the partners of some City broking firms were expecting to take home seven-figure pay packets that year. This bounty arose largely because the brokers' fees from buying and selling shares for clients had more than doubled since 1980. That they had done so was largely a result of the government's privatisation programme.

The Conservative Party's privatisation crusade had begun well before Mrs Thatcher's first election victory in 1979. Nicholas Ridley, the old Etonian younger son of a baronet with vast estates in Northumberland (and an unlikely close ally of the meritocratic Mrs Thatcher), had devised a plan in 1978 to reduce the nationalised industries' dependence on state subsidy. This plan did not embrace the then revolutionary idea of selling the state industries to the private sector. But it was not long before Mrs Thatcher was talking to Sir Frank McFadzean, the chairman of British Airways, about selling off some of the national flag-carrier. The model then was of minority private and majority public ownership along the lines of BP, 17 per cent of which had been successfully sold to the private sector in 1977.

The privatisation snowball rapidly gathered pace, and by the time of the general election in May 1979 even British Gas was being talked about as a possible candidate for sale to the public. The original idea of reducing government expenditure on subsidies to state industries had developed into a plan for actually raising revenue for the government. As such it was a considerable success: some £27 billion was raised from selling state-owned companies to the public during the 1980s. The plan rather blindly assumed that the new owners of these ex-state companies would automatically change the companies' management attitudes, the root cause of many of their problems. But in Britain shareholders did not buy shares in order to behave like owners.

It took longer to sort out the practicalities of privatisation than the theory. The sell-off began modestly, with some of the easiest candidates going first: the National Freight Corporation, British Aerospace and the British National Oil Corporation, all the sort of straight-down-the-line industrial companies that sat most uncomfortably in the state sector.

The first real sign that the privatisation programme might become something more than a way for the government to raise money came in early 1982, when an obscure company called Amersham International, which manufactured medical equipment and had a futuristic research centre, was sold. The sale of the company was twenty-two times over-subscribed – which meant that for every share on sale there were a phenomenal twenty-three offers. Some of the frustrated twenty-two bidders set about buying the shares as soon as they became available on the stock-market, and Amersham's share price rocketed.

Until that time shares had been something owned by financial institutions, the very wealthy who had 'portfolios', and the great-aunts of the middle classes. Almost overnight, the man in the Clapham omnibus realised that here was an almost foolproof way for him to make good money quickly. For the first time everybody, from taxi-drivers to shop assistants, started to talk about buying shares. The popular tabloid papers increased their coverage of the stock-market, and stockbroking firms like Quilter Goodison made it easier for the general public to buy shares by opening booths in places like Debenhams department stores.

Stock-markets know that they need both serious investors and speculators to keep their markets healthy. If they only had serious investors then everybody would be buying the same shares on the basis of the same information. Speculators come in with a contrary view of things, buying when the serious investors are selling, and vice versa.

Stock-markets also know that newcomers to stocks and shares almost invariably start out as speculators. Privatisation brought a lot of newcomers to the stock-market, so the balance between serious investors and speculators shifted dramatically. The speculators were much more prepared to buy the shares of unproven companies that seemed to have great promise and fast returns. And the growing number of tip-sheets were advising them on shares to back. One share that was constantly brought to their attention was Polly Peck.

Some of the practices of the stock-market enabled these speculators to go further than they should have. The best-known of these practices is called 'dealing in the account'. Stockbrokers divide the calendar into 'accounts' – periods of up to two or three weeks in which an investor can buy shares without paying for them. Deals done during the account are all settled at the end of the period. The brave speculator could thus buy shares at the beginning of an account in the hope that the share price would rise before the end of the account and enable him to sell his shares at a profit before he had been asked to put up any money for them.

In 1983 the *Financial Times* interviewed a café owner in Commercial Road, Mr Lou Sidoli, who was doing just this. 'Loads of people in the East End were punting in Polly Peck shares,' said Mr Sidoli. 'My broker has a large client who was going in and out each account and making thousands of pounds every time. I thought I'd follow him.'

There was an extra twist to dealing in the account, and it was called 'cash and new'. For a commission, some stockbrokers would allow their clients effectively to carry forward their position at the end of one account into the next. This rolling-over allowed a speculator whose unpaid-for shares had fallen in price to hang on longer in the hope that they would rise eventually. In Mr Sidoli's day it was estimated that £6 million-worth of Polly Peck shares were riding from one particular account to another on a 'cash and new' basis.

All this speculative froth helped make Polly Peck's share price extremely volatile. In the smart restaurants that were springing up in smart parts of London to feed the new breed of yuppies, on more than one occasion stockbrokers were heard inviting the whole restaurant to toast Polly Peck, whose hyperactive shares had contributed so much to their incomes.

By the beginning of Mrs Thatcher's second term in office, the stock-market punters were less enchanted with Polly Peck, whose share price had been halved by the Greek Cypriots' (unfulfilled) threat to take legal action against the company. But the Iron Lady soon gave them something to re-ignite their enthusiasm for the once arcane practices of the stock-market. In November 1984 51 per cent of British Telecom, a cumbersome utility with a monopoly on Britain's telephone calls, was to be sold to the public.

The sale of BT was designed to fetch £3.5 billion, by far the largest issue the London Stock Exchange had ever seen. But it was not just big; it also marked a second new step in the progress of privatisation. From being a means to raise money for the government, privatisation became elevated into a full-blown philosophy. 'Our aim now,' said John Moore, a junior Treasury minister at the time, 'is to build upon our property-owning democracy and to establish a people's capital market.' Popular capitalism was born.

The BT sale could not be allowed to fail, so every effort was made to persuade as many people as possible to buy the shares. All BT employees (almost 250,000 of them) were to be given £70-worth of free shares, and more of these were to fall from heaven if employees actually paid money for some shares as well. Telephone subscribers (i.e. most of the adult population of the country) were enticed by an £18 cut in their quarterly telephone bills for every £250-worth of shares they bought. Since everybody knew that the government would price the issue so that there was an immediate premium when trading in the shares started on the Stock Exchange, this was money for old rope. Santa Claus had come to town, and it was not yet November.

In case there were some who had not got the message, the government spent £8 million on an advertising campaign which, for the first time ever, used television to tout a share issue. Over 800,000 people rang or wrote to a special information centre in Bristol in order to ask for the mini-prospectus. This was yet another first for the issue – a simplified form of the full prospectus document that precedes all share issues. It was simplified, presumably, so that ordinary folk would not be confused by information that is normally regarded as essential for investors to make a proper judgement as to whether to buy a share or not.

Needless to say, the sale was a success. It was almost four times oversubscribed – i.e. £16.5 billion pounds ended up chasing the shares of a fossilised utility. In Glasgow a local refuse cart was spotted screeching to a halt at a branch of the Royal Bank of Scotland. The driver rushed into the bank at the last minute with his share application forms.

Over 2 million people ended up applying for BT shares, and the government's distribution policy for the shares ensured that most of these popular capitalists got something. What BT got was the most unwieldy share register ever seen.

As predicted, all these investors made a quick buck. When dealing in the shares started in early December it was as if the Rio carnival had come to the Stock Exchange floor. Silly hats were the order of the day and trading was frantic. The visitors' gallery at the Exchange was packed with new BT shareholders wondering what they had let themselves in for as they watched the pandemonium on the floor of the Exchange below. They were soon comforted by the sight of their shares selling at a considerable premium (of up to 90 per cent) on the price that they had only just paid for them.

As the *Daily Mail* wisely said at the time: 'The sight of investors everywhere scrambling for BT shares does not seem to square with the reality of a telephone company whose service is still terrible.' But their company's business prospects were not foremost in the minds of BT's new shareholders. Popular capitalism *à la* BT was not about creating a share-owning democracy, it was about gambling. Even the language of the market changed to reflect this: 'investors' became 'punters', and 'blue-chips' became just 'chips'.

In a 1990 survey on capitalism in *The Economist*, entitled 'Punters or Proprietors', the author wrote that in the Anglo-Saxon world 'a share is little more than a betting slip . . . What is wrong with the British and American system is that far too many shareholders, both institutional and individual, do not behave like owners . . . that abdication is not inevitable: other countries do things differently.'

Mrs Thatcher, however, succeeded in persuading a number of other countries (including Turkey) that they should do things her way. By the end of her reign she was better known outside Britain for her privatisation programme than for almost anything else. Britain came to be seen as the laboratory in which an experiment that everybody must do had first been performed.

When the countries of eastern Europe shed their communist shackles in the late 1980s they joined the ranks of curious observers of the British privatisation laboratory. At the last Conservative Party conference that Mrs Thatcher attended as prime minister, held in Bournemouth in October 1990, delegates were slightly bemused by a parade of eastern European political leaders, come to bear witness at the shrine of privatisation and to praise its high priestess.

In the end, privatisation did not stop the remorseless concentration of British company shares in the hands of financial institutions.

By 1990 institutions owned some 60 per cent of all UK quoted company shares. Pension funds, which owned 7 per cent of all shares in 1965, owned 32 per cent. Admittedly, more Britons owned shares than before the privatisation programme began, but they owned a smaller percentage of all the shares available.

What had held back Britain's nationalised industries was not government ownership *per se*. Rather, it was government management. One chief executive of a privatised company has talked about a 'middle-management damp course' of civil service types defending the status quo. Another told of receiving Treasury approval for a bid on a contract made six years earlier. Privatisation was little more than another British attempt to find a financial solution to a management problem. Polly Peck too was to suffer from Britain's narrow focus on finance as the be-all and end-all of corporate life.

CHAPTER FIVE

WARM TURKEY

AFTER the enforced sale of Polly Peck's fine collection of English Georgian furniture in 1991, Mrs Nadir was indignant at the auctioneer's suggestion that her husband had been trying to be an English gentleman. 'He is not trying to be an English gentleman,' she insisted. 'He doesn't need to become something else. He is a Turkish gentleman.'

Many Turks did not see him that way, however. An Istanbul press baron, incited by Mr Nadir's talk of the need for the press to support its country, once told him that he was nothing more than an Englishman born in Cyprus. The hostility may have been mutual. A friend once said that 'Asil never really liked the Turks. No Turkish Cypriot does.'

To the Turks, Cypriots are too Mediterranean ever to be truly Turkish. In Turkey, as in England, accent is important in social status. Somebody from Cyprus can never speak with the sing-song Ottoman intonation that is an essential accoutrement of a Turkish gentleman in the sense implied by Mrs Nadir.

Asil Nadir was a cultural chameleon: a Cypriot patriot when it suited him; a Turkish industrialist when it suited him; and even an English businessman on the few occasions when that suited him. He was also a gentleman, but a stateless one, usually perceived as being from somewhere other than where he was doing business.

For most people in Britain he was a Turk, and Polly Peck became almost synonymous with investment in Turkey. That carried its own baggage of uncomfortable associations. Turkey is not a country the West finds it easy to like. While Greece is typified by films like *Shirley Valentine*, a mix of middle-aged sex, funny accents and shining white villages, Turkey has had to put up with *Midnight Express*, a fictionalised account of a drug trafficker's torture in a Turkish prison. Even the Greeks would admit that it is not that black and white. But nationalities get forced into stereotypes, and the Turks are seen as gloomy Muslim torturers, while the Greeks are smiling Christian bottom-pinchers.

A British Labour member of parliament once said that going into the Labour Party and saying that you were pro-Turkish was rather like going into a bar in Los Angeles and saying that you had AIDS. It is little different in the Conservative Party.

Religion is at the root of much British hostility to Turkey, though few care to admit it. In the sixteenth century Martin Luther taught as part of his Protestant reforms that there were three manifestations of the Devil – the Pope, the Jew and the Turk. For one of the three, such teaching led to the Holocaust; *vis-à-vis* the Turk it led to a belief that humanity ends just east of Athens. In modern times the question has become: How can such a country, 99 per cent of it Muslim, ever be part of a European Community?

In 1986 Lord Hailsham, then Lord Chancellor of England, gave a speech in Athens in which he praised the Greeks, but for whom a mosque might have stood today on the site of St Paul's Cathedral in London. For this, said Lord Hailsham, the Greeks deserved the gratitude of every civilised European and every 'percipient Christian'. After his speech he received a warm hug and a kiss from Melina Mercouri, the actress best known for her role as a prostitute in the film *Never on Sunday*, who was then Greece's minister of culture.

A true portrait of the Turk lies in none of this, but rather in the strange collection of fables about a legendary figure called Nasreddin Hodja. He is said to have been a thirteenth-century villager and wise man. In reality, he was a rolling stone that gathered apocryphal Turkish wisdom over many centuries.

Nasreddin Hodja's homely moral stories are deeply embedded in the Turks' collective psyche. They illustrate many Turkish characteristics: their fatalistic acceptance of anything that life can throw at them; the strength of the family unit; the changing fortunes that can so swiftly affect rich and poor alike; their inordinately well-developed *amour propre* which makes them easy to offend; their strong sentimental streak; a touch of cruelty; and a dry sense of humour.

Nasreddin Hodja is a wise comedian who, when asked why he always answers a question with a question, replies, 'Do I?' His props are a nagging wife and a stubborn donkey, and every Turk knows at least a few of his stories. They will quote just the punch-line at appropriate moments in life.

Typical is one story known as 'The Cat Ate It'. This recounts how Nasreddin Hodja had returned one day from the market with a choice piece of meat. He was dreaming of how delicious it would taste and he could hardly wait for dinner-time. He gave it to his wife to prepare and then went to a local tea-shop to smoke a water-pipe, have a tea, and relax before the meal.

In the meantime his wife had chopped up the meat, stuck the pieces on skewers and invited all her best friends to come and eat her *shish-kebab.* Just after the guests had left, the Hodja returned. He couldn't believe his eyes when he saw only a bowl of soup placed before him for dinner.

'Where is the meat?' he demanded.

'Oh, the cat ate it,' his wife replied.

'But I bought a kilo of meat.'

The Hodja went and fetched the cat, which was actually a very thin cat, and then took a pair of weighing scales. He put the bemused cat on the scales, and it weighed exactly one kilo.

'So if this is the meat,' he exclaimed, 'where is the cat?'

It is difficult to categorise Turkey because it is easier to say what the country isn't than to say what it is: it is neither East nor West, neither Arab nor Christian, neither developed nor under-developed. Istanbul's streets are full of a crazy assortment of physiognomies which reflect the city's role as a honey-pot (and a melting-pot) for people from thousands of miles around for many centuries. Slant-eyed Mongols rub shoulders with blond Caucasians and tall dark Kurds. Peasant women swathed in headscarves walk beside elegant ladies in *haute couture*. Swish apartments by the Bosphorus change hands for hundreds of thousands of dollars while new immigrants build slums called *gecekondu* (literally 'put down overnight') for next to nothing. Look down from the smart restaurant on top of the multi-storey Sheraton hotel and the lights below twinkle like the gas lamps of Dickens's London.

Although nowhere else are such contrasts as pronounced as in Istanbul, they are to be found throughout the country. In Ankara politicians and diplomats meet in elegant open-air cafés while porters (known as *hamals*, not to be confused with *hamams*, the Turkish baths that are one of the country's greatest gifts to humanity) heave unbelievable burdens along the streets outside. On the southern Riviera, topless sunbathers are overlooked by goat-herds and their bell-ringing charges.

All this undefinable hotchpotch is held together by one man, and he has been dead for over fifty years. Kemal Atatürk was a remarkable despot who died in 1938 with, if not of, cirrhosis of the liver. He was born Mustafa Kemal of solid peasant stock in what is now Salonica (and part of Greece). He rose high up in the army (a very egalitarian organisation in Turkey), and was a brilliant military tactician who took most of the credit for expelling the nations that occupied the country after the First World War. His spirit still influences most of the important decisions that Turkey takes today.

Having become the first president of the new Turkish republic in 1923, Mustafa Kemal called himself 'Atatürk' ('Father of the Turks'). This was more than a demonstration of conceit. Turkey was then – and still is – a young country. It was formed this century from the hard core of what had been the Ottoman empire – an empire whose borders had waxed and waned from Vienna across Cyprus and around the coast of North Africa. For the imperial Ottomans of Istanbul, the Turk was from Anatolia, merely one among many uncouth provincials under their suzerainty.

The new Turkish republic needed to make all its people proud to be called Turks. Mustafa Kemal's honorary title of Atatürk was part of that process. In the end the process went too far, denying almost any ethnic identity inside the country other than what was considered to be truly Turkish.

If a young country, Turkey is an even younger democracy. Only in 1946 did voters get their first choice at the ballot-box. Before that there was only Atatürk's Republican Party to vote for; and before that there was nothing to vote for. Countries with the confidence of hundreds of years of democratic tradition seem to think that democracy is like pregnancy: you can't be half-democratic. Yet in less than seventy years Turkey has succeeded in becoming half-democratic, or maybe even three-quarters so.

Atatürk's inheritance did not stop at the creation of a republic. He also created it in a very particular image, that of a Western-oriented modern industrial society. The fez, the traditional rimless hat of the Ottomans, was banned in 1925 as being a ridiculous hangover of a backward people. Typically, Atatürk was tyrannical in putting his reforms into effect. On one occasion his insistence that the Egyptian ambassador remove his fez at an Ankara reception almost led to a break in diplomatic relations between the two countries.

Women were forbidden to wear headscarves and encouraged to go to school and to work. As early as 1934 they were given the right to vote and to be elected to parliament, long before they had those rights in 'democracies' like Switzerland. Again Atatürk's enthusiasm for enforcing reform went to extremes. His adopted daughter Sabiha was set up as an example of what modern woman should be. Not only did she qualify as Turkey's first woman pilot, but in the 1930s she flew a brand-new American bomber on a semi-official tour of the Balkans.

Perhaps the most overt symbol of Atatürk's wish to westernise was his change of the Turkish alphabet from Arabic script to Roman. While this allows Europeans to mouth Turkish words, it has left much pre-1928 Turkish literature and history inaccessible to those who cannot read Arabic.

The course set by Atatürk turned the face of Turkey firmly towards Europe, and he diligently set about courting those European countries with whom Turkey had had chequered relations in the past. Among them was Britain, which had been considered an enemy since the First World War. That changed, however, on the day in September 1936 when King Edward VIII steamed into Istanbul on a yacht called *Nahlin.* Among the King's party for the Mediterranean cruise was an American divorcee called Mrs Simpson.

Although the visit was officially an informal one, Atatürk came down to Istanbul to meet the King. There were parties galore. Bunting and the two countries' national flags were waved in abundance as the King drove in an open car with the Father of the Turks through the bedecked streets of Istanbul. Lord Kinross records in his authoritative biography of Atatürk that at one of several dinners held in the King's honour a waiter dropped a large dish of food on the floor. This prompted Atatürk to turn to his royal guest and remark, 'I could teach everything to this nation, but I couldn't teach them to be good lackeys.'

For years afterwards coffee-houses remained adorned with photographs of Atatürk and King Edward sitting under their respective flags, a visible emblem of the new-found Anglo-Turkish friendship.

When Mrs Thatcher visited Turkey in 1988 there was no such *entente cordiale*. She spent her time browbeating the Turkish government for not giving one of her favoured companies, Trafalgar House, the contract to build the second Bosphorus Bridge. No Turkish coffee-shop was ever adorned with Mrs Thatcher's photograph.

Yet Turkey's relations with Britain remain special, and for more reasons than their shared experience in Cyprus and the long-ago visit of the *Nahlin*. The Turks like the undemonstrative British character, which is so much closer to their own than that of their Mediterranean neighbours. And sometimes they feel an affinity and respect for a nation that coped rather better than they did with an empire and with the loss of it. The fact that Polly Peck was British and Asil Nadir respected in the City of London was an added bonus when he first brought business to Turkey.

Recently, however, Britain has been seen increasingly as just another member of the European Community. And Turkey has felt accepted by Europe only under sufferance. For sure, it is a member of some of Europe's most exclusive clubs – for example, NATO, the Council of Europe, the OECD, and the Eurovision song contest – but the less than warm postponement of its application to join the European Community in 1989 aroused all the Turks' feelings of insecurity. What they saw as rejection led them to look to the countries around the Black Sea (Romania, Bulgaria and the Soviet Union) as potential partners in a new regional club. Some thought that Israel, Egypt and Turkey would make an even better regional alliance. Turkey's deep longing to belong knows few bounds.

The main guardian of Atatürk's inheritance nowadays is not his own Republican People's Party but the Turkish army. And it intervenes periodically to protect that inheritance from political abuse. To most Turks there is little wrong with an army that they are proud of sorting out a bunch of politicians who can still behave like kindergarten kids. Most of the top military brass have spent long spells in the West through Turkey's membership of NATO. Many of them speak foreign languages and understand foreign ways. They do, however, find the West's manic abhorrence of 'military intervention' both peculiar and inappropriate.

Asil Nadir employed a number of retired military personnel to help run his businesses in Turkey. These included Erkan Gürvit, the son-in-law of General Kenan Evren, leader of the military coup of 1980. Mr Gürvit was the general manager of one of Mr Nadir's Turkish businesses. Mr Görgülü, the head of all his Turkish newspaper operations, was a former governor and chief of security. To those who found something sinister in this Mr Nadir would point out that only between five and ten of his 25,000 employees in Turkey had a military or secret service background – not an unusually high proportion. Turkey has the second-largest army in NATO (after the United States) and many of its officers retire early to take up business careers.

Over the past thirty years the Turkish military has intervened three times in politics, and each intervention has been more sophisticated than the last. The first (in 1960) was an oriental affair. Adnan Menderes, whose Democrat Party had defeated the Atatürkist Republican People's Party in every election since 1950, was prime minister at the time. He was a man who was suffering from delusions of grandeur, heightened by his escape from a plane crash at London's Gatwick airport in which many of his entourage were killed.

His economic policy had proved a disaster, based as it was on financing huge budget deficits by foreign borrowing in the belief that there was no limit to the depth of the West's purse for Turkey because Turkey was where it was (i.e. next door to Krushchev's communist machine at the height of the Cold War). For many years in the 1960s and 1970s Turkey over-estimated its capacity to borrow from the West. This led to resentment that the West was not doing its economic bit to keep NATO member Turkey within the Western fold.

Adnan Menderes and his foreign and finance ministers were vengefully sent to the gallows about the same time as Asil Nadir arrived in Istanbul to study at the university. From the island of Büyükada, where Asil and Ayşegül danced some of their student nights away, could be seen Yassiada, the bleak rock across the Sea of Marmara on which Menderes awaited his execution.

The next military intervention was a gentler affair. By 1971 there was widespread terrorism centred on the universities. Students had heard of what their counterparts had achieved in Paris, and set out to do the same. The military told the government to restore order, or else. The government resigned, a new coalition was formed, and martial law was imposed in the most troublesome regions.

But the wound was not healed. Throughout the 1970s the violence escalated, and it was no respecter of persons. Ex-prime ministers were assassinated and so were poor kids in the *gecekondu* slums. For some time it was enough to be carrying a newspaper of the wrong political persuasion to become the target of a bullet.

The government was tossed between the two equally helpless main parties. The right-wing Justice Party was headed by Suleyman Demirel, a bald, overweight populist who rejoiced in his peasant origins. The Republican People's Party was headed by Bülent Ecevit, a bespectacled intellectual who left political analysts in the West swooning with his broad knowledge and perfect English.

If the unpolitical Mr Nadir had a political hero, it was Mr Ecevit. For in 1974 it was Mr Ecevit, then prime minister, who ordered the Turkish armed forces into Cyprus and, in Mr Nadir's eyes, gave him a homeland and the pride to walk with his head held high. When Polly Peck collapsed and Mr Nadir turned to Turkey for help, it was Mr Ecevit who came out with the strongest declarations of support.

However, Bülent Ecevit's intellectual approach and his élite pedigree left him too diffident and out of touch to be the successful leader of a large under-educated population. When over 100 people were killed in communal violence at the end of 1978 in the eastern town of Kahramanmaras, martial law had to be imposed. From then on it was only a matter of months before the military would intervene for a third time.

They waited until 12 September 1980. (By then Mrs Thatcher had been prime minister of Britain for sixteen months.) For Asil Nadir, the military intervention came at a perfect time. In the previous month Polly Peck had successfully completed the rights issue to fund the cardboard box plant in Famagusta. Achieving the profits projected for the plant depended on exporting large quantities of the product to Turkey. That would be so much easier in a country not riven by civil strife. The share price took note, and climbed steeply.

The relief on the city streets of Turkey that day in September 1980 was palpable. The military was rounding up suspected terrorists by the hundreds. There was soon a sense of optimism in the air, a feeling that this was going to be a case of 'third time lucky'. The eminently respectable head of the armed forces, Kenan Evren, looked like a man who would clean up the political and constitutional mess once and for all.

OUT of the chaos of the late 1970s emerged a fat, friendly little man with a Chaplin-esque moustache who was to have a great influence over the future course of Turkey and of Polly Peck. His name was Turgut Ozal, and he was to reign over the longest period of uninterrupted stability and economic growth in the short history of the Turkish republic. A bright boy from a modest Anatolian background, he worked his way through scholarships that eventually took him to university abroad.

After a spell as an economist at the World Bank in Washington, Mr Ozal returned home in the 1970s to head up the State Planning Organisation (SPO). The SPO was an étatist institution formed in the 1960s to counter the free-market fantasies of Adnan Menderes. The SPO endlessly wrote and rewrote five-year plans that allocated funds to the country's mammoth state industries.

These were among the less welcome parts of the Atatürk inheritance, created by him in the 1930s as the engine of industrialisation for a country that had neither the capital nor the skill to build an industrial society out of the private sector. By the 1970s the state industries' inefficiency had become legendary, partly because their generous employment policy had turned them into a surrogate social service. While the unemployed did not get hand-outs from the government, they could always hope for a pointless job in a state organisation.

While at the étatist SPO Mr Ozal seems to have travelled the metaphorical road to Damascus and converted into a rabid non-interventionist free-marketeer. By 1980 he was economic advisor to Suleyman Demirel's right-wing government, and in January that year he introduced an economic package full of the free-market principles that were to become the dominant ideology of the 1980s.

The package freed interest rates, cut subsidies, promised tax reforms, and released the Turkish lira into a contrived float against the dollar. It was an entirely new direction for the hitherto inward-looking Turkish economy and it took it out of the protectionist cocoon which had sheltered it for decades from the rising standards of Western manufacturing. It was far more revolutionary than the military intervention that followed nine months later.

Mr Ozal was undoubtedly influenced by the World Bank (where he had worked) and the International Monetary Fund, the two mighty Washington organisations that were urging heavily-indebted countries everywhere to adopt free-market policies as a precondition for any more foreign financial favours. But the main model for Turkey's free-market experiment was in many respects Thatcherite Britain. Mr Ozal knew the country well, and so did his younger brother Yussuf who had studied at Liverpool university where he had shared a student flat with a close friend of the family, Yildirim Aktürk. (Both Yussuf Ozal and Yildirim Aktürk were to head the SPO in later years. Yussuf was also to become a minister in his brother's government.)

The influence of Britain's free-market economics on the Ozal years in Turkey was strong, and the country even looked to British-style privatisation as a solution for its own fossilised state industries. But this it found even harder to put into practice than did the British, and by the end of the 1980s only minimal gestures to privatisation had been made. Several cement factories were sold off and 22 per cent of Teletas, a telecommunications manufacturer.

Whatever influenced the pragmatic Mr Ozal also seized the Turkish military. For they approved of his policies enough to make him deputy prime minister with special responsibility for economic affairs in the puppet government set up after 12 September 1980. But the portly technocrat only just made it. In 1977 he had narrowly failed to be elected as a member of parliament for the National Salvation Party, a right-wing religious party that was opposed to much of the secularism enshrined in Mustafa Kemal's republic, and in which Turgut's other brother Korkut was a leading light. After the military takeover all parliamentarians were banned from politics for seven years. Had he won the 1977 election, Turgut Ozal would have been banned too.

Mr Ozal's policies in Turkey were as fortunate for Polly Peck as were the changes taking place in the City of London at the same time. If the City gave Polly Peck fertiliser, Turkey gave it seedlings. The prize that Mr Ozal sought most in return for opening Turkey's markets to the outside world was foreign investment. Turkey had neither the skills nor the capital to produce goods that could compete with the imports which were now much more free to come into the country. The success of Mr Ozal's free-market experiment depended crucially on the arrival of foreign capital and skills.

And they were very slow a-coming. The Turks watched the foreign investment figures like hawks, and tried to give the impression that they were greater than they were by focusing on the amounts that were authorised. But much of this was never converted into actual investment. In 1981 $338 million of foreign investment was authorised, but the actual net inflow that year was a mere $95 million. As late as 1987 the net inflow was only $106 million.

When Cornell invested in Niksar and, more importantly, when Polly Peck started its electronics business with Thorn–EMI, it was like an answer to Mr Ozal's prayers. At the opening of the electronics plant at Manisa in May 1985 he was a very happy man. This should demonstrate to the world what could be done in Turkey. All it had to do now was to show a profit.

Mr Ozal's joy was apparent to others. Polly Peck had flown some sixty bankers and brokers over from London for the occasion. On their return one of them reported that 'The political acceptance of Asil Nadir was manifest.' Another said, 'We are optimistic about the Turkish economy. Its industrialisation offers great potential.'

While Mr Ozal and Mr Nadir never seem to have been particularly close, they talked frequently and met each other on many occasions. Mr Ozal often held Mr Nadir up as an example to visiting foreign businessmen and to domestic industrialists. He was also very supportive during Polly Peck's early years in Turkey. In August 1985, for example, the government gave a 2.75 per cent tax rebate to fresh fruit and vegetable exporters, a gesture that was very helpful to Polly Peck.

In the following years the Ozal influence on Turkey grew and grew. And as it grew, Mr Nadir's path to do other things in the country became smoother and smoother. The red tape and obstructions from petty-minded officials in Ankara became less and less – as, indeed, they did for any foreign investor in Turkey.

As Turkey changed so did Mr Ozal. From being a kindly, clever uncle who would receive foreign journalists in his dressing-gown and slippers, he gradually became the head of a dangerously powerful dynasty. Even in his first civilian government after the military stood down in 1983, he filled his Cabinet with family and friends. By the time he was elected president in 1989, in succession to Kenan Evren, Turkey found that it had more than a president; it had a First Family.

The Ozals became soap-opera material for the gossip columns, much like the Windsors in Britain. Daughter Zeynep married a drummer from a pop group; son Ahmed was a sort of fixer who brought influential people together and into his father's entourage. Ahmed gained a reputation for persuading American-educated Turks to return home to high office in his father's government or in the state industries.

The queen of the Ozal show, however, was the president's wife Semra. Short and portly too, she had met her future husband in the 1950s, when she was a mere typist in a state ministry. But she was no meek stay-in-the-kitchen wife, obediently at her husband's side whenever he appeared in public. As she herself once said, 'I don't sit in the corner and do as protocol dictates.' A favourite (probably fictitious) story is of an official visit to Turkey of a foreign head of state in the mid-1980s when Mr Ozal was prime minister. On leaving the country he was asked what he thought of the prime minister. 'Very astute and very able,' was his reply. 'But her husband's a bit quiet.'

Mrs Ozal became a highly controversial figure, exemplifying the best and the worst of the Ozal years. She once had a military helicopter fly her couturier from Ankara to the family's summer house on the Aegean coast, and she was branded a collector of arms when she bought a couple of gold-plated Colt revolvers in Los Angeles. On the other hand, Semra Ozal's most notable persona was that of the secular woman upholding Atatürk's ambitions for the female half of her country. She set up an organisation called The Foundation for the Strengthening and Recognition of Turkish Women (known locally as The Daisies), and she campaigned boldly for the conversion of religious marriages, where the wife has few rights, into civil marriages, where she has many more.

Through his wife and his brother Korkut, Mr Ozal found

himself at the vortex of the religious/secular debate in Turkey, a debate which erupts periodically and angrily. In the presidential household, though, Semra was well able to hold her own, and was said to have thrown her proselytising brother-in-law out of the house more than once.

THE family atmosphere in political Ankara was mirrored by a family atmosphere in commercial Istanbul. The great Turkish corporations are not known by faceless acronyms or by their leading brand names. They are known by the names of the families which started them and which invariably still control them: the Koçs, the Sabancis and the Eczacibasis.

In Britain family firms rarely get very big before they become public companies run by professional managers for the faceless owners of their shares. In Turkey, as in much of Continental Europe, family firms can become very big indeed, and still be controlled by the family. Giovanni Alberto Agnelli, the nephew of Fiat chairman Gianni Agnelli, is being groomed to take over at the top of his uncle's family firm, the largest private enterprise in Italy. In France François Michelin, grandson of the founder, is chairman of the world's largest tyre company. And even in Germany Siemens still has the flavour of a paternalistic family firm thanks to the large number of third- and fourth-generation Siemens family members who occupy senior management positions. In these companies, ownership and management have not become divorced in the way that has left such a gap in Anglo-Saxon corporate governance.

This might change as the Anglo-Saxon stock-market model is embraced by other countries in a blind assumption that where finance is concerned London and New York know best. The Istanbul Stock Exchange, dormant since the First World War, was revitalised in 1985 on a wave of euphoria for stock-markets as an essential element of a free-market economy. The Exchange was wildly speculative for a number of years, although it gradually began to trade in more and more shares.

However, the big family firms which floated parts of their companies on the Exchange took care to ensure that control remained in the family's hands. The requirement for quotation in Istanbul was only that at least 15 per cent of the shares be owned by more than 100 people. Vestel, Polly Peck's Turkish electronics subsidiary, came to be quoted on the Istanbul Stock Exchange (and remained so while Polly Peck's shares were suspended in London and Zurich after the administrators took over the company). But only 15 per cent of Vestel's shares were freely traded. The rest were owned and controlled by Polly Peck.

Of all the Turkish business families, two stand head and shoulders above the rest. The Koçs and the Sabancis dominate the industrial scene. Their activities cover almost the entire industrial spectrum, ranging from car manufacture to cotton-picking, from trading to banking. Representatives of both families appear in most listings of the richest billionaires outside America.

When Asil Nadir first returned to Turkey he was extremely concerned about how he would be received by these ruling families. He was competing with many of them head-on, not complementing them. His electronics business was in direct competition with Profilo and Arçelik. His luxury hotel in the south was up against the Koç hotels in an over-supplied market, and his proposed car venture with Peugeot struck at the heart of the Koç and Sabanci empires. One-third of all Koç's turnover came from the automobile industry, and Sabanci had a joint venture with Toyota to set up a major manufacturing operation in Turkey.

The industrial families welcomed the newcomer with polite hostility. They were noticeably absent from Polly Peck social occasions, such as the grand reception thrown by Asil Nadir in Istanbul in the summer of 1989 to celebrate the fifth anniversary of Vestel. And they lost few opportunities to spread bad news about his businesses. The Sabancis insisted for many years that Niksar was losing money.

Not that any of this was going to make Mr Nadir pack his Louis Vuitton bags for an early retirement in Cyprus. Quite the opposite. The Koçs and the Sabancis were his goals and his role models, and he inspired his Turkish workers with a sense that he was a new broom come to take on the changeless might of the establishment.

Tahsin Karan, the president of Vestel, Polly Peck's chief Turkish subsidiary, and a main board director of Polly Peck itself, clearly viewed Koç and Sabanci as the yardsticks by which to measure Polly Peck in Turkey. Interviewed in 1989, he described Vestel largely in terms of the ways it was different from Koç and Sabanci. Unlike them, it was 'not looking to sell mainly in the local market' and, also unlike them, it was looking to do business 'beyond Eskişehir'. Eskişehir is an old industrial town less than 200 miles to the east of Istanbul.

As individuals the Koçs were more to Mr Nadir's taste than the Sabancis. The Sabancis' empire was built on cotton fields around Adana, the main town in the agricultural south-east, and the family had not thrown off its Adana accents and a taste for the arabesque. The Koçs, on the other hand, like the Nadirs, had developed a liking for beautiful antiques, large jewels, fast boats and old houses. Cigdem, once married to Rahmi, the only son of Vehbi Koç the grand old man of Turkish industry, became a close friend of Ayşegül Nadir. Like Ayşegül, Cigdem was a beautiful woman with taste and a particular weakness for shopping. Moving between Harrods and Sotheby's, she and Ayşegül consistently helped to support the UK retail sales figures throughout the 1980s.

But the Istanbul business dynasties have a puritanical streak that left them aghast at Mr and Mrs Nadir's free-spending ways. Vehbi Koç's autobiography is a paean in praise of health, hard work and the family. He recounts the story of a man called Nafiz Kotan who was the leading contractor in Ankara when the Koç business was starting there in the 1920s. Nafiz Kotan was enormously wealthy by the standards of the day. He had a car and a house full of servants. When he went to Istanbul he would order shirts by the dozen from Strongilo, a famous Greek shirtmaker of the time. He also had a lot of friends who were bank managers. However, his business collapsed and Nafiz Kotan died in poverty in the east. This salutary tale left a lasting impression on the then young Vehbi Koç. 'Nafiz ultimately failed in business,' he declared in his autobiography, 'because of his irrational work habits and his spendthrift ways.' Turkey has seen a lot of business meteorites fizzle into dust. Many of them have borrowed too much from banks, and spent too much in shops.

The difference between the Turkish continental-style family business and the Anglo-Saxon public company goes beyond the nature of ownership and structure. It applies also to appearances and style. It would not be surprising if Asil Nadir, who moved frequently from one style and country to another, sometimes felt schizophrenic about what sort of businessman he was meant to be: the dominant father figure, dressed to impress, that his Turkish workers wanted, or the sober-suited committee man that some of his English investors expected.

The Turks, along with many other Europeans, find a man like Virgin's Richard Branson, who runs a multi-million dollar empire wearing pullovers and corduroy trousers, and likes to mess about in balloons, slightly odd. Their business élite is only interviewed in its offices, smartly dressed in a suit and perfectly knotted tie.

Offices matter. Like a well-decked wife they are a visible appendage of a successful man. Rahmi Koç's suite in the group's headquarters is a treasure trove of Ottoman antiques which stands comparison with the Georgian furniture which adorned Polly Peck's headquarters in London's Berkeley Square. The Koç headquarters themselves are a group of beautifully restored minor Ottoman palaces, with white wooden walls and the top-heavy roofs typical of much fine Turkish architecture.

Another of the trappings of office in Turkey is the teams of advisors and sycophants which surround the holders of all important posts. In the rambling building in Ankara which served as the finance ministry in the early 1980s, the lonely minister sat at one end of a room that could have hosted two grand balls simultaneously. Beyond his door was an assistant cramped into a few square metres with piles of files and dozens of supplicants seeking the minister's ear.

In Istanbul the aura surrounding the powerful is less exaggerated, but apparent none the less. When a top industrialist rises from his desk others rise too – secretaries, assistants, senior managers, even the *kahveci* (the coffee boy) – swooping around and collecting the paraphernalia that the great man needs. This quite normal support system, which offends nobody, is alien to Britain. Not surprisingly, it was to cause more than a little confusion in Berkeley Square where Mr Nadir could be surrounded at any one time by Cockney secretaries, Cypriot accountants, bankers from the Home Counties, and Turkish cooks.

CHAPTER SIX

THE ROAD TO BERKELEY SQUARE

IT took Polly Peck a long time to impress the City of London with its achievements in Turkey. After the extraordinary gyrations of its share price in 1982 and 1983, when it was every speculator's favourite punt, the company was cold-shouldered by the stock-market for almost the whole of the next four years.

This was demonstrated most clearly by the lowly price–earnings ratio of the shares throughout this period. The price–earnings (P/E) ratio is a key indicator of what the market thinks of a company. It compares the price of a share with the earnings per share (i.e. the company's most recent profits divided by the number of shares in issue). It is also (roughly) a measure of the number of years that it will take a shareholder to earn back the price that he or she paid for his share.

At the height of its popularity in early 1983 Polly Peck's P/E was as high as 37 – i.e. it would have taken thirty-seven years of unchanging profits for a share to earn as much as it cost. A thirty-seven-year 'pay-back' period is more than the vast majority of investors would ever contemplate. But investors in Polly Peck, of course, were betting on a rapid increase in earnings in the near future to reduce that thirty-seven-year period dramatically.

By the end of 1984, Polly Peck's P/E ratio had plummeted to a humble 4. By the end of 1985 it was 3.5; and by late 1986 it was down to 3. This fall was all the more remarkable because at the time the London stock-market was going through one of the most bullish periods it had ever known. The main index doubled between the beginning of 1983 and the beginning of 1987.

Some of the reasons why Polly Peck went out of favour were not hard to find. The Greek Cypriots' attempts to stop the company from 'exploiting property' that they claimed they owned in northern Cyprus had alerted the stock-market to a fundamental fact. The eastern Mediterranean may be exotic and full of promise, but it is also a politically uncertain place. A booming business today could be bogged down in a legal morass tomorrow.

The alert was reinforced in November 1983 when the Turkish Cypriot leader Rauf Denktash unilaterally declared independence (UDI) in an attempt to overcome the debilitating non-recognition of the area. After UDI there were fears of all sorts of reprisals – perhaps a Rhodesian-style embargo on fruit exports from northern Cyprus, or Greek Cypriot retaliation in the form of electricity cuts to the region.

The political uncertainty was heightened by any discussions that threatened to reunify Cyprus. During such discussions in January 1985 the Greek Cypriots made it clear that in any new Federal Republic of Cyprus they would not allow Polly Peck to continue to receive the favours it had been granted by the Turkish authorities in the north. These included special leases on property, tax holidays, and monopoly rights on the supply of cardboard boxes to the north of the island.

Polly Peck would issue reassurances saying that any change in the political arrangements of Cyprus would not affect it materially. But it was hard to believe that there would be no adverse effects at all from reunification. Polly Peck's chances of continuing to produce remarkable profits looked good only for as long as the status quo remained on the island.

The company's other problem with the stock-market was that its credibility had been shot to pieces. It had been a company built on promise since Asil Nadir first took it over in 1980. And from those beginnings the excitement surrounding it had been continually fed by a drip of prospect after prospect. This was a natural way for Mr Nadir to operate since he, as an individual, was always at least one step ahead of reality. He preferred to plan for tomorrow rather than get bogged down with today.

Promises are fine things for as long as they are fulfilled, but a broken promise is the surest way to end a friendship. And with deal after deal Polly Peck was failing to come up with the goods. Either there were delays, or hints of things to come came, too soon, to nought.

Cornell's water-bottling plant at Niksar had been projected to produce profits of £3.6 million in the company's 1983/84 financial year. In practice it did not open officially until the end of August 1984, a few days before the 1984 financial year was closed. In its first eleven months of operation it was reported as having contributed £1.9 million to the 'share of results of related companies'.

Even more strikingly, the electronics plant at Manisa, on which so many hopes were hung, did not open officially until May 1985. In January 1983 some had been led to believe that the Manisa plant alone could produce profits of as much as £55 million in the 1983/84 financial year. By January 1985 that had been scaled back to £15 million for the current year. In the event, the plant was reported to have produced pre-tax profits of £1.9 million for the 1984/85 financial year.

Then there were the hints of new deals to come in the promised land of Turkey: there was to be a packaging and canning operation with the old-established British firm of Metal Box; there was to be a defence-electronics venture with one of the most exciting young British high-tech companies, Racal; and there was to be a car plant with the Japanese company Daihatsu. None of these materialised.

Moreover, pharmaceuticals, which had been signposted as a major new industry for Polly Peck (four full pages were devoted to it in the company's 1983 annual report), failed to appear in the portfolio. The one pharmaceutical venture that did materialise was insignificant and delayed. In September 1983 Polly Peck agreed to buy a company called Inter-Channel Pharmaceuticals (ICP) which had a very small business in Cyprus. By January 1985 Polly Peck was saying that the signing of the contract with ICP had been 'unavoidably delayed'. The deal was not completed until August of that year.

Finally, there was the delay in consolidating the three companies in which Mr Nadir was interested: Polly Peck, Cornell and Wearwell. N. M. Rothschild had first been appointed to work on this at the end of 1982. Eventually, in July 1984, Wearwell was brought into the Polly Peck group, but not until June 1985 did Cornell (i.e. Niksar) become part of Polly Peck.

Despite the market's disappointment over all these things, Polly Peck's pre-tax profits continued to grow in an astounding way – which is one reason why the P/E ratio fell so low. The price could scarcely be expected to keep up with the pace of the company's earnings. From £10.5 million in the year to August 1982 they rose to £30 million in the following year, and to £50.6 million in the year to August 1984. For several years the company's profits were higher than the previous year's turnover.

By early 1985 the remorseless appeal of these figures was beginning to restore Polly Peck's reputation – to such an extent that in February the company was able to raise £42.6 million through a rights issue. This was underwritten by N. M. Rothschild and was Polly Peck's first rights issue since the famous occasion in 1980 which had funded the cardboard box factory in Famagusta. Since then, the company had raised some £10 million by placing new shares privately with investors, but the rights issue (to finance expansion of its electronics and fruit businesses in Turkey) was a visible demonstration of the company's return to favour with the investing public.

Other things helped to put the company further in favour. Mr Nadir spread charm and positive assurance at a number of City lunches, and in the spring of 1985 what was described as 'a tribe' of analysts, bankers and investors was invited on a trip to see the group's operations in Turkey and northern Cyprus. 'I was very impressed with the efficiency of the operations,' said Nigel Utley, an analyst with Laing & Cruickshank and one of the travellers.

In April 1985 Polly Peck appointed two heavyweight non-executive directors to its board – Neil Mills, a former chairman of Sedgwick, a large insurance broker, and Lawrence (Larry) Tindale, deputy chairman of 3i, a venture-capital outfit owned jointly by the clearing banks and the Bank of England.

In the summer Polly Peck was recategorised on the Stock Exchange as an overseas trader, instead of the paper and packaging company that it had hitherto been. This was more important than it might sound, for the stock-market categorises companies by their industrial sector. Different expectations attach to different sectors. In particular, they are expected to have different P/E ratios. So, whereas the paper and packaging sector had an average ratio of over 11, overseas traders were less highly rated at below 10. As an overseas trader Polly Peck's lowly P/E ratio would look less out of synch than it would as a paper and packaging firm. Therefore it would be less likely to rise.

Although confidence in the company was slowly being rebuilt, it was a delicate thing, and it was back in tatters by the end of the year. In November, Polly Peck's faithful stockbroker L. Messel reduced its forecast of the company's profits. It trimmed its original estimate of £82 million to something between £68 million and £75 million.

This was not a huge drop, and would still have left Polly Peck with a 40 per cent or so increase on its profits of the previous year, an increase that would cause most companies' shareholders to break open the champagne bottles. But so intoxicated were Polly Peck's investors with preternatural profits that the reduced forecast from the oracle Messel was enough to send the share price tumbling by almost 25 per cent in a day. That wiped over £55 million off the value of the company, and lost Mr Nadir over £13 million in less than twelve hours.

Messel's change of mind was worrying because it came only a few weeks before Polly Peck was itself due to announce its results, and many weeks after the financial year in question had come to an end. In previous years Messel's forecasts had been disarmingly accurate. For 1980/81 it had forecast profits of £2 million and they had turned out to be £2.1 million; its forecast for 1981/82 had been £10 million and the actual figure was £10.5 million. This time Messel's Polly Peck analyst Peter Jones was giving a range of numbers and saying that his revised profit forecast was 'a stab' because 'there is no way that you can analyse the currency movements'. Currency movements? My goodness, said the speculators, what on earth are they?

They were of course nothing new to Polly Peck – merely the result of borrowing money in a relatively strong currency (sterling) to invest it in a relatively weak one (the Turkish lira, the currency of northern Cyprus as well as of mainland Turkey). But it was the first time that the currency effect on Polly Peck's accounts had been raised seriously in public, although the Greek Cypriots had mentioned them *en passant* in 1983. Currency movements were to become a key issue in subsequent retrospective analyses of Polly Peck's results.

At the beginning of December Polly Peck announced results that were even below the lower end of Peter Jones's final forecast. Pre-tax profits were £61.1 million, trimmed by as much as £15 million, it was said, by currency fluctuations. The Turkish lira, which had been fairly stable against the pound in the first half of the year, had depreciated by some 44 per cent in the second half. And sterling had also been strong against the dollar, the currency in which most of Polly Peck's export sales of fruit and vegetables were denominated.

To understand how this affects profits, consider an example. Suppose Polly Peck received an order in January to supply Libya with $150,000-worth of pink Cypriot grapefruit in March. In January, suppose the exchange rate is $1.5 to the pound, so in sterling (which is what Polly Peck's accounts were denominated in) the order is worth £100,000. But by March the dollar has depreciated so that each pound is now worth $1.8. The Libyan order is then worth only £83,333 as far as the accounts are concerned. The difference is lost profit.

The picture is complicated even further by the fact that the cost of the grapefruit (including both the labour to collect it and the raw material itself) was denominated in Turkish liras. One day there would be 1000 liras to the pound; a few weeks later there would be 1200 to the pound. At what exchange rate should those costs be converted for the purposes of the sterling accounts?

This kind of currency-translation problem existed in almost all Polly Peck's businesses. Since so few of them were in the United Kingdom it seemed rather ridiculous to switch all the company's costs and revenues into sterling just because its registered head office was in England. But the rules of the game said that it should be so, and so it confusingly was.

After its brief return to favour, Polly Peck was cast back into the shadows – again for frustrating so many people's expectations. For Mr Nadir personally it was a depressing experience, topped by the death of his father of cancer in the spring of 1986.

He withdrew more and more from the public eye, leaving his young and industrious joint managing director Mark Ellis to act as company spokesman. 'I'm not going to talk about anything that is going on at the group until it actually happens,' said Mr Nadir. 'It's time we took the hope element out of Polly Peck.' There was also a concerted attempt to distance the company from the forecasts being made by the brokers' analysts. The company talked more about 'consolidating' its existing operations, and less about its future plans.

That did not mean, however, that Mr Nadir did not have any future plans. His withdrawal from the front line in favour of Mr Ellis gave him more time to think about them. In a way his position was similar to the one he had been in almost ten years earlier with Wearwell. Then he had seen a period of remarkable success disappear rapidly, to end (that time) almost in bankruptcy. But he had fought back with a different strategy and had turned Wearwell round. He still saw himself as a fighter contending against eternally hostile elements.

As he gloomily pondered the stock-market's persistent failure, as he saw it, to appreciate the true worth of Polly Peck – and, therefore, of his 27 per cent stake in it – he gradually developed another new strategy. It had two main prongs: one was to reduce Polly Peck's heavy dependence on Turkey and Cyprus, whose unpredictable currency and politics were a nightmare for long-term plans. The other was to eschew new 'green-field' businesses (like Vestel, Niksar and Uni-Pac) in favour of buying up-and-running operations.

By early 1987 the strategy was being revealed. Mr Ellis told the press that 'the idea, over a three- to five-year period, is to have equal-sized businesses in the same range of businesses in the Far East, Europe and America'. (At that time the group had three main businesses: textiles, agriculture and electronics.) And Mr Nadir told shareholders who turned up in freezing cold and snow to attend the annual general meeting at London's Savoy Hotel in January 1987 that the company was on the look-out for acquisitions, which it would buy with cash, not shares.

The proposal to buy with cash was forced on Mr Nadir for as long as Polly Peck's share price languished below what he thought it ought to be. Say he thought the shares should have been selling for twice the £1.50 that was their price on the stock-market. To buy a company for £300 million he would have had to give the purchased company's owners 200 million Polly Peck shares. But if Polly Peck's share price had doubled he would have had to give away only half as many shares. Hence he preferred to buy with cash, if enough could be found.

The groundwork for the strategy had been laid some time before Mr Ellis's and Mr Nadir's public statements. In the summer of 1986 the board was boosted with the appointment of four new executive directors. David Fawcus was recruited as finance director, replacing

Anil Doshi, the Indian accountant who had been by Mr Nadir's side since the early days of Wearwell and who remained as an advisor to the company. Mr Fawcus had a sound industrial pedigree. He came directly from Guinness, the brewer, and before that had been with Unilever for twenty years. Unilever was acknowledged as one of the best management-training schools in England.

Mr Fawcus was joined on the board by Tahsin Karan, the head of the Vestel operation in Turkey, by Joe Harris, the head of a textile subsidiary, and by Evan Potts, an agricultural specialist who joined the company from the Deciduous Fruits Board.

At the same time Polly Peck began to expand geographically – in several directions at once. In February 1986 the American authorities gave the go-ahead for trading to begin in Polly Peck's shares in the United States. This opened up a potentially huge new market of investors and speculators, and Mark Ellis set off on a promotional trip to the States. This was organised by Shearson Lehman, the large American brokerage firm which had bought a 5 per cent stake in L. Messel in 1984, with the intention of increasing it to 100 per cent when restrictions on foreign ownership were lifted by the Stock Exchange.

American interest was soon tickled. Like London, the New York Stock Exchange had been enjoying one of the longest bull markets in its history. But it was getting tired of its own domestic stocks which had been bought and analysed *ad nauseam*. It was hungry for something a little exotic, first from quaint old Europe, then from even quainter developing countries. Polly Peck suited the bill, a UK stock with its business in Turkey. 'We love Turkey,' said the American brokers Arnold & S. Bleichroeder, who became particularly keen on Polly Peck.

Within a year American investors were said to own as much as 20 per cent of the company. Their buying accounted for much of the second huge rise in Polly Peck's share price, a rise that began in early 1987. The Polly Peck phenomenon in the early 1980s was a purely British affair; the company's second coming in the late 1980s was largely fuelled by the interest of American and other non-British speculators.

Polly Peck started to make some smallish acquisitions in its existing businesses, but in new parts of the world. It paid about £5.5 million for a Hong Kong garment company called Impact

Textiles, and then it bought two good old British brand names – Russell Hobbs and Tower Housewares – for £12 million. The British companies made electric kettles, toasters and pots and pans, and employed almost 1000 people in the Midlands. It was Polly Peck's first serious investment in Britain.

There was also the promise of a brand-new line of business: in early 1985 Polly Peck had commissioned a feasibility study on a 300-room luxury hotel in Antalya in southern Turkey. At the time the project was to have been undertaken jointly with another quoted company – Strong & Fisher, the leather-goods manufacturer with whom Mr Nadir had had close ties since Strong & Fisher had helped to rescue Wearwell in 1977. Richard Strong, the chairman of Strong & Fisher, was still on Wearwell's board, and on Polly Peck's too until his resignation in April 1985. Mr Nadir sat on the board of a Strong & Fisher subsidiary in Turkey.

A year later Mr Strong announced that he was pulling out of the deal to concentrate on his company's core activities. It had been proposed that Strong & Fisher should invest £1.5 million for a 25 per cent stake in the Antalya Hotel. Polly Peck went ahead with the project on its own and the hotel eventually became the $60 million Sheraton Voyager.

By the spring of 1987 confidence in Polly Peck had been largely restored. It had been a long hard struggle to return to favour, but Mr Nadir had learned a lot during the process. One lesson in particular stood out: the stock-market could make or break Polly Peck, and the company ignored it at its peril.

In the first five months of 1987 the company's share price doubled, increasing its potential to make acquisitions by issuing paper (its own shares) rather than by handing over cash. The company took on some more experienced managers to help it grow. Among the newcomers was a tall, bespectacled, rather humourless young man who became group treasurer at Polly Peck. His name was Tim Wood and he had been the retail analyst with Capel-Cure Myers, a firm of London stockbrokers. Before that he had worked in the corporate planning division of the BHS department store. Tim Wood was soon joined by another City analyst, David Stoddart, a former colleague at Capel-Cure Myers. He was to be in charge of acquisitions.

Then in September came the biggest new appointment of all:

Anthony Reading, one of the top executives at the hugely successful conglomerate BTR, joined the company as group managing director, a new post with a seat on the board.

The newcomers brought a sense of excitement to the company, a sense that it was the beginning of another great future. But the lodestar was still to be Mr Nadir. There was no question that his position at the pinnacle of Polly Peck International plc was anything other than totally secure. Mr Nadir is 'a broad and strategic thinker' said Anthony Reading respectfully.

The second age of Polly Peck was about to begin. But the vision was of an age of a magnificent global trading company. Such a company could not be run from the depths of London's East End. The style of the new Polly Peck was of the West End, and the company needed a West End headquarters to match.

FOR the great companies of England the City of London had always been the end of a cul-de-sac. The flow of industrialists on their trek to City lunches was from the capital's West End. None of them could believe that anything serious went on east of the Tower of London and down the Commercial Road.

However much they may have paid lip-service to the 1970s' fashion to 'decentralise' their operations out of expensive London property, all these companies retained impressive executive headquarters in the small area bounded by Marylebone Road to the north, Edgware Road to the west, St James's Park to the south, and Regent Street to the east. The most exclusive enclaves for these companies' brass plates were around pretty St James's Square, hard by traditional English clubland, and in the costly lanes of Mayfair huddled behind the Dorchester and Hilton Hotels on wide Park Lane.

In 1983 BTR had taken over a little-known old-fashioned company called Thomas Tilling in what was at the time the biggest takeover deal that Britain had ever seen. Among Thomas Tilling's senior executives was Anthony Reading, and among its other assets was one of the most fabulous pieces of real estate in the whole of London. The company's headquarters was in Crewe House, the most magnificent mansion in the whole of Mayfair. The unassuming BTR promptly sold it and it became, more appropriately, the Saudi

Arabian embassy. BTR kept for its headquarters (in unglamorous Victoria) a building which has been likened to a public library fallen on hard times.

Crewe House alerted British shareholders briefly to the opulence that some of their companies' managers indulged in. BTR's corporate modesty was an exception for the flamboyant 1980s. By the end of the decade corporate offices in Mayfair and around St James's Square were in such demand that rents in the area touched those for the City's golden square feet, which had for long been the most expensive in Europe.

Polly Peck joined the crowd moving to Mayfair and settled on a handsome Georgian town house at 42 Berkeley Square. Half-way up the west side of the square, this became the new head office of Polly Peck International. (The company had significantly added 'International' to its name in February 1985.) When questioned about the unassuming nature of his offices in the Commercial Road Mr Nadir had once said, 'One does not better oneself by moving to another area.' Moving to Berkeley Square may not have bettered Polly Peck, but it brought the company into daily contact with a very different style and different influences. In the 1980s Berkeley Square became home to a number of high-flyers whose ambitions were fuelled by borrowed money. Whether this bettered Polly Peck or not, it was sure to change it.

Berkeley Square was best known for the 1930s song about a nightingale that once sang there, but by 1980 it had become a busy thoroughfare for traffic going from Oxford Circus across to Hyde Park Corner. Long gone were the bright young things who once sought support against its railings on their way home from some debutante's ball. The closest Turkish connection it had was a blue plaque on number 50 informing the passer-by that George Canning, statesman and prime minister, had lived in the Square in better times. George Canning's cousin Stratford de Redcliffe had been British minister in Constantinople for over twenty years in the first half of the nineteenth century.

The Square's rough grass and elderly trees were home, first and foremost, to the American advertising agency J. Walter Thompson. Located at number 40, this most gentlemanly of agencies considered the Square almost its own. Its biggest non-American office stood aloof from shabby Soho where a bunch of younger agencies was busily creating a worldwide reputation for British advertising, and a taste among British consumers for goods like cars and clothes that they could no longer produce. The thoughts of the founder, Commodore Thompson, were a reminder that this was an agency with tradition. Taken from the commodore's 1899 *Red Book on Advertising*, they included gems such as 'The foundation of most fortunes may be directly traced to advertising'.

Between J. Walter Thompson and the new tenant at number 42 stood an anonymous building with its front door in a side street facing Polly Peck's. The restraint of number 41 was understandable because this was the London office of Citibank Private Bank. This offshoot of America's most powerful financial institution described itself as 'the largest non-Swiss private bank in the world'.

Secrecy and discretion were essential for an organisation which boasted that, above all, it was 'a relationship business with long horizons'. This was not a branch that people popped in and out of for the odd transaction. Citibank Private Bank handled 'in a highly confidential personal manner' some $67 billion of the money of individual 'wealth-creators'. Before long it was handling the affairs of the individual wealth-creator next door. One of the people who looked after Mr Nadir's affairs at the bank was a middle-aged Englishwoman called Elizabeth Mitchell Forsyth.

Around Berkeley Square were some of the accoutrements to go with discreet private banks and corporate headquarters. Its only shop sold Rolls-Royces and Bentleys, at the heart of the square mile that can probably boast the world's greatest density of Rolls-Royces. In 1990 this emporium was joined by a second shop – one which sells only Blüthner grand pianos.

Once the shops and offices closed the clubs opened: Mortons at number 28 and Annabel's at number 44. By 1980 Annabel's had become one of London's most famous and exclusive night-spots. Named after the wife of the founder, Mark Birley, it was a Mecca not only for the rich and aristocratic English but also for wealthy foreigners.

Among these foreigners was a sprinkling of sophisticated Turks who found it (and Les Ambassadeurs club off Park Lane) closest to the night-life they enjoyed in other places they frequented: St Moritz, Nice or New York. Asil Nadir was a guest at Annabel's many times before he moved his office to the house next door but one.

Annabel's came to set the tone for Berkeley Square. It was expressed in the rows of double-parked Rolls-Royces and Jaguars to be found outside its door on most nights after midnight, protected from police interference by a bevy of chattering chauffeurs. The idea of having his headquarters only two doors away from this landmark for the international jet set may well have appealed to Mr Nadir.

This rich mix in Berkeley Square eventually attracted one of the emblems of the Thatcher years. In 1988 the Saatchi brothers took over and redeveloped the ugly building known as Lansdowne House which occupied the whole of the south side of the square.

Maurice and Charles Saatchi, two Baghdad-born Jews whose family name is a Turkish word meaning 'watch-maker', ran the most successful advertising agency in the pantheon of British agencies which during the 1970s and 1980s came to dominate the industry throughout the world. Their fame was established in cramped offices on Charlotte Street, surrounded by cheap Greek restaurants and cut-price electronics shops. Like Asil Nadir, they felt that their beginnings did not match their achievement or their ambition.

The Saatchis had first become widely noticed through the campaigns they had run for the Conservative Party (one of which had the classic slogan 'Labour isn't working'). This had brought them to the attention of Mrs Thatcher, and one of the agency's chief executives, Tim Bell, became one of her closest advisors.

The Saatchis followed the pattern of admired Thatcherite entrepreneurs. Immigrant outsiders, they had built up a successful business from scratch and then taken their company public in the late 1970s with a quotation on the London Stock Exchange. That had been a pioneering move because the stock-market had traditionally been suspicious of service industries whose assets went in and out of lifts every day. It had preferred to back assets that stayed still, like factories and machines. But Maurice Saatchi, the businessman of the two brothers, succeeded in allaying the market's suspicions about 'people' businesses so convincingly that the agency became one of the most glamorous stocks on the market.

Being a favoured public company had enabled Saatchi & Saatchi to raise huge sums of money with which it bought a string of agencies and related businesses on New York's Madison Avenue, then the capital of the world advertising industry. By 1986, after it had paid $450 million for the Ted Bates agency, Saatchi & Saatchi was the biggest advertising group in the world – a mere sixteen years after it had been founded.

This was a performance worthy of Berkeley Square, home of Saatchi's venerable rival J. Walter Thompson. The Saatchis set about transforming Lansdowne House into a showcase of their achievement. Its dull flat brick was replaced by a sparkling grey marble which Londoners could not ignore. Inside was a high American-style atrium, an essential import if the atrophied little offices clustered around it were to be among the most expensive in the world.

Most magnificently, above the building's high arched glass entrance were placed, in big black letters, the words Saatchi & Saatchi. If J. Walter Thompson, the symbol of another age of advertising, had thought that Berkeley Square was theirs, they had to think again.

But this new order was not to reign for long. In 1986 the Saatchi brothers had said farewell to their finance director, Martin Sorrell. Mr Sorrell, a 'bespectacled number-cruncher', had been Saatchi's finance director since 1977, during the critical period when the brothers had been building up their empire through acquisition.

Mr Sorrell left the agency to branch out on his own. This he did in much the same way as Mr Nadir had done with Polly Peck. He bought an insignificant quoted company called Wire and Plastic Products, but he had no intention of using his talents to develop the company's basic business – the manufacture of supermarket baskets and hamster cages. Instead, Mr Sorrell changed the company's name to WPP, and started buying small advertising-related businesses. Then, in 1987, just as Mr Nadir was settling the handsome antiques that he had been collecting into 42 Berkeley Square, all hell broke loose at number 40.

It started in New York where the gentlemanly J. Walter Thompson had gained the attention of Wall Street's insatiable takeover merchants. They were toying with the finance and ownership of corporate America like jungle cats let loose on a herd of deer, and they had discovered a simple formula for making huge fees for themselves. It involved finding a bunch of bankers who wanted to lend a lot of money, and some managers who wanted to own some of what they were managing. Neither was hard to find.

The next ingredient was scarcely more difficult to find: a company whose share price was so dull that its faithless shareholders were happy to sell out to the bankers and the managers. J. Walter Thompson, whose profits had been lack-lustre for some time, was an ideal candidate.

The American boss of J. Walter Thompson at the time was a charming, lean East Coaster called Don Johnston. He had hand-picked as his successor one Joe O'Donnell, a man who, in the mood of the times, hatched up a plan for a group of Wall Street bankers and investors to back him in a sort of management buy-out of the company. Ten years earlier such a plot would have been too ridiculous for words. Now it put the agency, reeling at the time from the possibility of losing one of its biggest clients, the Burger King chain of restaurants, 'in play' with the jungle cats.

Michael Lewis, the author of *Liar's Poker*, an hilarious best-selling account of his career as a Wall Street novice (or 'geek' in his jargon), was working in London for Salomon Brothers, one of the fattest jungle cats, when J. Walter Thompson was 'in play'. (So was Don Johnston's son.)

Mr Lewis's description of how the Wall Street influence was spread to London is amusing – and true:

> There was no obvious barrier to entry in Europe. There was little financial regulation. And the Atlantic cultural divide seemed less daunting than the Pacific to native New Yorkers. When a kid from Brooklyn disembarked at Heathrow airport he was greeted in English. When he sat down to dinner in his expensive hotel (Claridge's and the Berkeley were favourites) he wasn't served raw fish, but stuff that looked pretty much like American food. It was easy for this man to fool himself that Europe was a lot like New York, because on $2000 a day it was. So London became the key link in this drive for world domination; its time zone; its history; its language; its relative political stability; its large pools of dollar-hungry capital and Harrods (don't underestimate the importance of shopping opportunities in all this) made London central to the plans of all American investment bankers.

Against this background it is not surprising that interest in the fate of J. Walter Thompson should have been just as keen in the City of London as it was on Wall Street. Re-enter Mr Sorrell, with a reputation from the hottest advertising agency in the hottest advertising town. Such was the internal consternation at the attempted management buy-out that J. Walter Thompson would have found almost anyone who came along with a better offer more acceptable. So when Mr Sorrell appeared with £350 million for the agency, the American J. Walter Thompson breathed a sigh of relief and became a subsidiary of the British WPP.

That did not mark the end of WPP's ambitions. In 1989 the company bought yet another large advertising agency, Ogilvy & Mather, this time for the even more princely sum of £550 million. With this purchase, WPP vaulted above Saatchi & Saatchi to become the biggest advertising group in the world. That was quite a snook to cock at the big black letters hanging over Lansdowne House.

It was a heady time in Berkeley Square. The nightingales were not alone at night. All around them were young Thatcherite entrepreneurs – the Saatchi brothers, Martin Sorrell and Asil Nadir – burning midnight oil as they cooked up deals that made the 'old country' feel young again. None of their companies had existed twenty years earlier.

Each of them had stumbled on a common path. With the help of small quoted companies they had titillated the stock-market to back them as individual entrepreneurs. They had then 'leveraged' their capital with bank loans that had enabled them to buy bigger and bigger companies.

In the end this gave them something else in common. They all over-reached themselves. Even as the Saatchis developed Lansdowne House their fortunes were turning down. In 1987 they made an absurd approach to buy Midland Bank, the least successful of the four large English clearing banks. Sir Kit McMahon, the South African-born chairman of the bank and a previous deputy governor of the Bank of England, was reportedly astonished at the brothers' ignorance of banking. But ignorance was more than matched by arrogance. The Saatchis believed that if they could run one service industry (advertising), they could just as easily run another (like banking). The City took fright at the impudence of it, and the approach was abandoned.

By the end of the decade Saatchi's heavy debts, used to buy its rag-bag of service companies, were pulling it down. It was narrowly rescued from bankruptcy by a fire sale of its assets and by a recapitalisation that left its shareholders with a fraction of their original stakes. The brothers handed over the management of the company to a new chief executive who declared that, above all, he wanted 'the stock-market to think Saatchi boring'. The company was even forced to evacuate the one floor of Lansdowne House that it had been able to retain for itself. It retrenched back to Charlotte Street, the chrysalis it had sprung from a few short years before.

At about the same time WPP found that it too had reached too far with the debt it had incurred to buy Ogilvy & Mather. In 1991 it was forced to reschedule its debts and to refrain from paying a dividend to its shareholders for a couple of years. The fate of Polly Peck was to be even more dramatic.

CHAPTER SEVEN

WAVING CHEQUES OR DROWNING IN DEBTS?

ON 16 October 1987, southern England was swept by the fiercest hurricane in centuries. One-hundred-mph winds uprooted thousands of trees and almost forced the Stock Exchange to close since no one from the wooded stockbroker belt could get into town. After a weekend of tidying up, the stock-market then collapsed on what became known as Black Monday (19 October). The euphoria that had pushed the main London index up by over 40 per cent since the beginning of the year was blown away as panic selling of shares knocked the index down by all of that and more in just ten days.

No financial market was an island. As soon as the panic hit one stock-market it was instantly transmitted down telephone lines to infect the next. From Tokyo it passed to Hong Kong, and from there to London and New York. This concentration of catastrophe seemed like divine retribution for the excesses of the planet's financial Sodoms and Gomorrahs.

Some thought that at least it must mark the end of an era – of the buying and of the conspicuous consumption of the 1980s. Memories were revived of the 1930s, and of the last major stock-market crash which had plunged the world into a long, deep and utterly miserable economic depression. The British chancellor of the exchequer, Nigel Lawson, relaxed his control of the money supply to reduce the risk of future recession. By so doing he increased the risk of future inflation.

For sure, the crash hurt the City of London. But pride compelled it, and its resources enabled it, to disguise the pain in a remarkable way. Before long the crash appeared to have been almost forgotten. It had slashed Polly Peck's share price by a third, but it had little effect on the company's headlong rush to go global. That had been premised on bank finance, not on money from the stock-market.

Even as the world's stock-markets were collapsing about them, Polly Peck's top executives were in Hong Kong. There the crash caused such a panic that the market simply closed its doors on 19 October. But three days earlier Polly Peck had announced that it was paying £20.7 million for a Hong Kong-based consumer-electronics company called Capetronic.

This was the company's biggest purchase so far. Bold and intriguing, it instantly trebled Polly Peck's turnover in electronics. Capetronic made computer terminals and audio and television equipment for companies in Europe, Japan and the United States who then put their own brand name on them. 'Original Equipment Manufacture (OEM)' was what this sort of business was called, and it was much the same as Vestel was aiming to do: to make reasonable-quality goods with low-cost labour for sophisticated Western companies to stick their names on and to sell as their own.

One of the main reasons for buying Capetronic was that there was going to be terrific 'synergy' between it and Vestel. In the 1980s businessmen discovered that synergy could be used as a justification for almost any deal that they wanted to do. It was a sort of New Math: a way of adding one and one and making three. A company bought another company because together they were more than the sum of their parts. Synergy was the philosopher's stone to making profits out of nothing.

The real magic of synergy was that it could apply in all situations. If a company bought another company that was in the same line of business, then there was synergy from combining production or research, or whatever. If the companies were in different businesses there was still synergy. If an iron and steel works fancied buying some citrus plantations, then there was synergy in supplying the steelworkers' canteen with orange juice from the plantations. There could be synergy between Capetronic and Uni-Pac, for instance. Capetronic's Taiwanese consumer electronics goods could be packed in Uni-Pac's Cypriot boxes. It was all too obviously brilliant.

'Synergy sparks excellent performance,' declared Polly Peck's 1988 report on the electronics division. In the event, the synergy between Far Eastern Capetronic and Turkish Vestel did not amount to much. Most of Capetronic's production facilities were in low-cost, fast-developing Taiwan, one of the 'little dragons' that had taken over the lower rungs of the industrial ladder from Japan. Factory workers were brought from Taipei to Manisa where they worked alongside Turks – supposedly to learn from each other in the minimal English that passed as a common language. Likewise, Turks from Manisa found themselves transplanted to Taipei.

Making one and one equal three required more magic than this. And Polly Peck's directors saw it in Capetronic's high technical reputation. 'Capetronic has a superb research and development team where about 200 people are working,' gushed Anthony Reading from Hong Kong. Vestel was expanding rapidly and was in need of more technical back-up. It had just entered into a joint venture to manufacture microwave ovens with Lucky Goldstar, one of the rising corporate stars of South Korea, another of Asia's little dragons.

The price paid for Capetronic was a not extravagant ten times its most recent year's profit. But it was also five times the value of Capetronic's assets as declared in its books. That meant that Polly Peck was paying a hefty sum for what is called 'good will', the difference between the price paid and the book value of the assets bought. Good will was the value of things like the inventions that the white-coated scientists in Capetronic's laboratories had yet to create.

To finance the deal Polly Peck sold a number of its shares to investors in Tokyo, which was a good entrée into the Asian financial capital in readiness for things yet to come. 'This is a Far Eastern investment,' said Mark Ellis, 'and it's being financed with Far Eastern money.'

At the same time Polly Peck was opening up other sources of finance. In a three-month period at the end of 1987 it borrowed from the Swiss bond market three times, the three issues raising a total of SwFr185 million. The merchant bank to the deals was Soditic, the Swiss subsidiary of the London firm of S. G. Warburg, one of the youngest and most successful British merchant banks. So popular did the issues become with investors in Switzerland that the third one was increased from an original target of SwFr45 million to SwFr50 million. But there were a few who shook their heads at the idea of a company borrowing money in the world's strongest currency when much of it would have to be repaid from earnings in Turkish lira, a currency which was devaluing so fast that it had to run like Ben Johnson in order to stand still.

But Polly Peck needed all the money it could lay its hands on. It had been so short of cash earlier in 1987, coming up to a dividend payment in April, that some staff had gone without pay for a while. The company was also about to go on an extraordinary shopping spree. And for that it would have been very expensive to raise money on the shattered stock-markets.

In January 1988, the company signed an exclusive ten-year deal with Pepsico, the American manufacturer of 'the other cola', to open Pizza Hut restaurants in Turkey. Pizza Huts are run by Pepsico as a franchise operation. Franchisees who are approved by the American giant buy the right to open the restaurants in specified areas. Pepsico was known to be very choosy about who it gave its franchises to.

Despite the fact that Turkey had invented what was almost the first 'fast food' in the world (the *döner kebab*), fast food American-style had not penetrated much further than Taksim Square, a large, messy open space in the heart of Istanbul which was favoured by demonstrators and which had seen the death of more than a few. There, a single McDonalds was doing brisk business, proving that quality fast food and clean surroundings (rather than burnt fat and a fly-ridden 40-watt bulb), could make a lot of money in Turkey. The Pepsico deal added considerably to Polly Peck's international stature.

The company's first Pizza Hut was opened less than a year later in a new shopping mall in Ataköy, a suburb of Istanbul. On the edge of the Sea of Marmara, the mall was an oasis of modern consumerism in the desert of traditional Turkish shopping, more at home in Fort Lauderdale or Milton Keynes than in Istanbul. It stood as a token of the Ozalite years. Packed with imported goods, and boasting a bowling alley and a skating rink, it became a Mecca for wide-eyed Turks who cast off all thoughts of headscarves and Islam as, armed with their credit cards, they tasted the fruits that Mr Ozal and the likes of Mr Nadir had brought them.

Polly Peck's next deal was down in Spain. In February the company paid a humble £750,000 in cash for a citrus fruit-packing plant in Valencia. Then in early March it moved to the United States, paying £4.3 million in cash for a 21.6 per cent stake in

Corporate Data Sciences, a company with interests in paper and telecommunications.

By May it was back in the Far East, paying £36 million to the New Zealand entrepreneur Sir Ron Brierley for a controlling stake in a Brierley company called Rainbow Orient Corporation. Rainbow Orient was nothing more than a pile of cash (£35.5 million-worth of it) and a quotation on the Hong Kong Stock Exchange. Polly Peck renamed it Polly Peck Far East and used it as a vehicle to obtain a local stock-market quotation for some of its motley assortment of oriental textile companies. The quoted vehicle, said the company, would assist further expansion in the Far East.

In June Polly Peck was off to Holland, paying £9.4 million for Jas van den Brink, a fruit and vegetable distributor based in Rotterdam which also had a chain of 106 grocery shops in Holland and Germany. More money (up to £8 million) was to be paid for the Dutch company if its future profits met certain targets. This deal was financed through the issue of shares.

At the same time Polly Peck bought a New York fruit and vegetable importer, Prevor Marketing, for £6.7 million in cash. 'Prevor will give us our first major foothold in the United States,' said Mr Nadir. That it would not be Polly Peck's last had been assured by the announcement earlier in the month that Mark Ellis would be moving to Manhattan in the summer to 'develop the group's interests in North America'. 'The potential in America is so great,' said the thirty-four-year-old Mr Ellis from his swish Manhattan apartment, 'that we thought we should have a main board director there.'

Polly Peck was also busy in Britain that June. At the end of the month it was revealed that it had been quietly building up a stake of almost 5 per cent in Borthwicks, a food-processing company. Borthwicks had recently been turned round into a reasonably profitable business, and the Polly Peck interest pushed up its share price as the market anticipated that Mr Nadir would make a bid for the whole of the company.

In July Polly Peck paid out more cash – £2.5 million for Frio Mediterraneo, a packing and cold-storage facility in Spain. To the untrained eye Frio Mediterraneo's Valencia plant looked to be several times the size of Polly Peck's packing facilities in northern Cyprus. Polly Peck said that 'When fully operational, the capacity of the Spanish facilities will equal those in northern Cyprus.'

Again in July, Polly Peck paid £3.3 million (through an issue of shares) for Joseph Le Shark, a London designer and distributor of leisure-wear. This then looked like a business with great potential as the health-conscious Western world tried to appear more and more as if it were permanently heading for the gym – in loose track-suits and Reebok or Nike shoes.

Although none of these deals individually hit the headlines, their cumulative effect was breathtaking. Polly Peck's turnover almost doubled between 1987 and 1988. The company had quietly bought another company almost the same size as itself. But it had bought it in lots of itty-bitty pieces, and the integration of so many disparate parts would have stretched companies with management resources many times those of Polly Peck.

Part of the process of integration involved more expenditure. In 1985 Polly Peck had bought its first ship – a 1600-ton vessel named *Polly Premier*. This was to ply between Famagusta and various parts of the European continent carrying Polly Peck's Cyprus produce. The secret of the company's melon-sized margins on its fruit business was said to be its control of the whole chain of production – from owning the trees that grew the fruit to owning the shops in western Europe that sold it. Shipping was an important part of this chain. The 'synergy' between orange trees and ships became swiftly obvious to anyone who had it pointed out to them.

From the *Polly Premier* grew a shipping line. By the end of 1988 PPI Lines owned ten vessels with both refrigerated and ordinary cargo facilities. They all had names like *Polly Prudent* and *Polly Progress*, and were chartered out to others when not needed for shipping Polly Peck's wares.

This helter-skelter expansion put an enormous strain on Asil Nadir and his chief lieutenants. They were carried forward by the sense that Polly Peck was like a Saturn rocket about to streak into an unknown yonder that was bright and blue. They were also carried along by the inexhaustible enthusiasm and optimism of Mr Nadir himself.

But Mr Nadir was becoming increasingly inaccessible, and when anybody did get to see him he was inevitably interrupted within a couple of minutes by the privileged few (many of them Cypriots) who seemed to have the right to march into his office without even knocking on the door. He did not, then, give all his visitors the impression of a man in control of a rapidly-expanding empire.

When Polly Peck turned to the stock-market for a £133 million rights issue in October 1988 (its first since February 1985), N. M. Rothschild, who had advised the company on the merger of Cornell and Wearwell, refused to be involved. It would not say why. John Antcliffe, who had joined Polly Peck from Rothschild's to run the company's corporate finance department, left after only a few months to return to the bank. His reason, he said later, was that he disliked 'the extremely commercial nature' of Asil Nadir's business style.

To the outside world, however, everything looked smooth and logical. Tony Reading had brought in an experienced public-relations chief, Tony Bennett (who had spent many years at Barclays Bank), to explain away the doubts of the few remaining sceptics. Polly Peck's shares were recovering much of their loss from Black Monday of the previous October, and sellers of the shares were hard to find.

Asil Nadir took time off to sit next to Princess Anne at a lunch sponsored by Polly Peck at the Goodwood horse trials in Sussex that summer. Horses were becoming part of the Polly Peck motif. David Fawcus was very keen, and Mr Nadir thought it would help foster a reassuringly British image for the company. In the autumn of 1988 Polly Peck agreed to sponsor the three-day horse show at Windsor. The first event under its sponsorship was scheduled for May 1989.

The expansion of Polly Peck at this time was all the more demanding for Mr Nadir because, unable to persuade his board to go along with all his buying ambitions, he was satisfying his hunger outside the company. In the summer of 1988 he bought for himself some of the biggest newspapers in Turkey. These were an expensive, loss-making headache of enormous proportions, as later became apparent.

That summer other members of the Nadir family were buying up businesses. Mr Nadir's son Birol emerged in September as a substantial shareholder in a British company called Harland Simon which made computer systems for the newspaper industry. Through a Cayman Island company called Mountain Dew, of which he was a beneficiary, Birol had taken a 17.3 per cent stake in Harland Simon at a cost of over £5.5 million. The Caribbean Cayman Islands are an even more secretive tax haven than Jersey and the Isle of Man, the more traditional offshore homes of Nadir family businesses.

Then Mr Nadir's sister, Bilge Nevzat, took a controlling stake in a Cardiff-based quoted company called Gnome Photographic. This she bought with her husband, Fehim, through their Cayman Island company, Fairweather Investments. The Nevzats' 65 per cent stake cost £4.5 million. There were bankers in the City who found Mrs Nevzat to have a sharper business mind than her brother, and who were prepared to back her but not him. Mr Nadir had no stake in Gnome, but Mrs Nevzat said at the time, 'He is my brother, and we are very close.'

Gnome made overhead film projectors, but Mrs Nevzat soon set it on an entirely different strategic course. It quickly branched out into travel and tourism, and packaged 7500 British tourists to Turkey and northern Cyprus in its first year of operation. The company changed its name – to Noble Raredon, Noble being the English translation of Asil, Rare being a translation of Nadir. Using Mr Nadir's new airline, Noble Air, it ferried its tourists to the eastern Mediterranean, many of them eventually to stay in Polly Peck hotels. It sounded like a rare lot of synergy.

Mr Nadir was also spending large sums of his own money that year in order to maintain the size of his stake in Polly Peck. Every time that Polly Peck issued new shares (as it did to finance the purchase of Capetronic, Jas van den Brink and Joseph Le Shark) his personal stake was diluted. At the end of 1987 it had stood at 19 per cent of the company. In 1988 Mr Nadir spent some £9 million buying the company's shares in order to bring his own stake back up to 26 per cent. Then, when the rights issue came in October, he pledged to take up half of his rights. That cost him over £15 million and (because of the rights that he did not take up) reduced his stake in Polly Peck to 22 per cent.

BUYING, of course, was in the air at the time, and it was both personal and corporate. The yuppies were at the peak of their American-influenced life-style. Nicholas Coleridge, a writer about fashion and fashions, wrote in the *Spectator* in March 1986 that membership qualifications for the new yuppie club were 'a large salary, minimum £75,000'. Club benefits included 'lively complacent conversation about tax avoidance, accountancy fees, and how to spend what's left.'

Although some of the yuppies would, in another age, have been selling bric-à-brac off a barrow (a group that became known in the City as 'the boys from the Essex marshes'), many of them came from the middle classes and would have entered the 'professions' whatever the decade. They already owned their own flats, and their cars and restaurant bills were on the company. That left masses of disposable income to be disposed of.

Attitudes to this money were no longer discreet; investments, the value of houses, business propositions and expensive tackle became the standard subjects of dinner-party conversations. Brand names thrived – it was not just wine that was drunk, but *premier cru* clarets like Château Latour; clothes were by Hugo Boss or Giorgio Armani; homes were not just decorated, they were designed by decorators. These were not the days of wine and roses; they were the days of champagne and orchids.

The spending was backed not just by high incomes but also by rapidly increasing capital values. People with homes in central London could watch the value of their houses increase each month by more than the salary they would have been earning a few years before. They cashed in on that increase in value by taking out new loans backed by the new value of their homes. With it they bought more homes, or maybe cars from the Continent whose main attraction was that they could travel at speeds far in excess of the legal limit on almost every British road.

Money could no longer be enjoyed at leisure. Those who made it were far too busy. Porsches headed for the City at dawn from their owners' one-and-a-half acres in the Home Counties – acres which for much of the year they never saw in daylight. The car's mobile phone brought news of the Tokyo market before coffee and hot croissant were consumed in front of an ever-present VDU. Everything took place in a rush: fast deals, fast food, fast cars, fast luxury. Foreigners noticed the deterioration in Londoners' driving habits and the lack of courtesy from impatient diners at expensive restaurants.

While the Conservative government made no indication of

any misgivings about the yuppies, there was always an element of Toryism that found them distasteful, and their Party's silent approval of them even more so. Their most eloquent spokesman was Peregrine Worsthorne who, as editor of the *Sunday Telegraph*, had written an influential article in June 1987 that described how 'The yuppies feel confident enough to shed all inhibitions about enjoying the spoils of the class war which they think Mrs Thatcher has fought on their behalf.'

The yuppie ethos began to permeate the headquarters of Polly Peck, not only through its frequent contacts with the City but also through the number of its employees who had worked for banks and brokers. Birol Nadir was working for a City broker where he befriended another young dealer called Jason Caradoc Davies. Mr Davies subsequently moved over to work for Mr Nadir, where his boss was Elizabeth Forsyth. She had moved over from 41 Berkeley Square where she had been Mr Nadir's personal banker at Citibank Private Bank.

On a corporate level the buying mania had to a large extent spread out from the City itself. For the City had been involved in its own takeover spree, a spree of unprecedented foolishness. This had been spurred by something called 'Big Bang', which was what had happened on 27 October 1986 when the stock-market had abandoned some of its long-standing uncompetitive practices.

Big Bang had been announced more than three years in advance, and was part of a deal between the Stock Exchange and the government's Office of Fair Trading. The government had been worried not only about the cliquishness of the Stock Exchange but also about its failure to match up to international competition. The capitalisation of all the stockbroking members of the London Stock Exchange was probably less than that of one of the giant American or Japanese brokerage houses that were beginning to muscle into London, the third corner in the Golden Triangle of money. Unless the London market changed, the argument went, it would become little more than a convenient offshore time zone for New York and Tokyo. Like Polly Peck before it, the London Stock Exchange added 'International' to its name lest anyone accuse of it being parochial.

The deal between the International Stock Exchange and the Office of Fair Trading involved the government in dropping legal action to outlaw the Exchange's uncompetitive practices in return for the Exchange voluntarily giving up some of those practices. In particular, from October 1986 it was to abolish the fixed minimum commissions that its members decided (among themselves) to charge for deals in stocks and shares. Big Bang would also signal the end of rules that restricted who could own a Stock Exchange member firm.

The City had three years to think about the implications of the change in the rules, and one of the first conclusions it came to was that the abolition of fixed commissions meant the abolition of another old (and by then unique) City practice: the division of labour between jobbers and brokers. Jobbers were the dealers in shares who spent most of their time on the floor of the Exchange buying and selling shares for clients. They were seen as the barrow boys of the industry.

The jobbers' clients were not the ultimate buyers of the shares, but the brokers who took orders from clients and passed them on to the jobbers. There was no direct contact between the buyer and the jobber/dealer. This so-called 'single-capacity' system, where men were either brokers or jobbers, was doomed, the City believed, because as soon as brokers could not rely on a minimum commission they would be tempted to cut costs by cutting out the jobber. So London was to go over to the dual-capacity system, found in the United States, where the function of jobber and broker is combined. One consequence of this was to put customers into direct contact with dealers. It made the stock-market much more like a casino or an auction house, where it is all too easy to get carried away by the thrill of the moment. The barrier of agents (stockbrokers), that had effectively kept the gamblers (speculators) away from the croupiers (on the floor of the exchange), was being removed.

A conclusion that the big City financial corporations soon came to was that they needed to buy up these brokers and jobbers as soon as they were free to do so. They had at least two reasons for going shopping in this particular market. One was that old familiar synergy that could be counted on to rear its head as an excuse for any corporate shopping expedition. Another was a favourite of all service industries on the make at the time – whether accountants, lawyers, advertising agents or banks – and that was that their clients demanded it.

Like many reasons for action this was more of a *post hoc* justification than a real influence. Stockbrokers' clients had been demanding negotiated commissions for years, but nobody paid a blind bit of notice to them. As soon as one bank customer said he would like a financial services supermarket, then off the banks all went on a mad stampede to be all things to all customers. They chose to ignore the fact that there were plenty of large insurance companies and corporate customers (including the likes of ICI) which had made it clear that they had no intention of buying all their financial services from under one roof. They had long-established links with particular firms which they did not want to break. In any case, in the new competitive world that was being created in the City it was easier than it had ever been to shop around for services.

The banks themselves should have known better. They had been on expensive stampedes before. In the 1970s they had all been over-eager to lend to South America. Many of those loans have still not been repaid. Then in the early 1980s they rushed off to North America, because their internationalising clients had 'demanded' it. In 1986 Midland Bank had to dispose of its large American acquisition (the Californian Crocker National Bank) at a considerable loss. It was many years before any British bank made worthwhile profits in America.

So the stampede into the London securities business was not abnormal behaviour. But what a stampede it was! At first, outsiders were only allowed to buy up to 30 per cent of a broking or jobbing firm, and the starting pistol sounded when Security Pacific bought 29.9 per cent of Hoare Govett, one of the City's biggest brokers, in June 1982.

Security Pacific is a Californian bank headquartered in Los Angeles, the home of Hollywood. Like all American banks it is forbidden by legislation dating back to the stock-market crash of the 1930s from doing business in securities in the United States. The relaxing of the rules in London presented American banks with a back-door way into a business which their own country considered it unwise for them to be in. Significantly, Security Pacific was followed by Citibank, America's biggest, which in November 1983 bought 29.9 per cent of Vickers da Costa, a broker strong in the securities markets of the Far East.

Goaded by fear that the Americans were going to take over the

London market (despite the fact that Big Bang had been designed to make British firms more competitive with American and Japanese rivals), the British banks moved in in 1984. The pace became so hectic that scarcely a week went by in the early months of that year without a bank buying a broker or a jobber, or two. Among the big spenders were Barclays, which bought 29.9 per cent of Wedd Durlacher Mordaunt, a jobber, for £29.9 million, and a smaller stake in the brokers de Zoete & Bevan; National Westminster, which bought a jobber and a broker; and the Union Bank of Switzerland, which bought the big broker Phillips & Drew.

It was not long before these financial giants began to wonder what they had paid all this money for. Firms of brokers and jobbers were little more than a few skilled people with a good list of clients. Moreover, they were in a business whose future was at best uncertain. The bull market and privatisation could, perhaps, be counted on to increase their turnover, but would this ever compensate them for the loss of a monopoly market, where new entrants had been effectively excluded and where they had fixed their own prices?

The first shock to the buyers came when they realised that their expensive brokers and jobbers could walk out of the door. The partners in the firms they bought had received millions and were tied with 'golden handcuffs', but the so-called 'marzipan layer' of employees just below had got nothing out of the deals. They cashed in on the bonanza by moving to another firm, in many cases for double their previous salary. Shortly afterwards they could move again, and maybe double their salary again.

This switched the City's spotlight on to individuals and away from firms. Stars were born, and they changed hands for sums that would not have shamed top footballers. For clients were no longer buying the services of a firm, but the services of an individual man or woman. When these same clients went to the hairdresser they went to have their hair cut by Tony or Guy or Vidal; when they went to a restaurant they went to taste Anton's or Nico's *ballotine* of *foie gras.* If Guy or Nico moved, their clients moved with them. Likewise when clients rang their brokers they wanted tips from Sebastian or Jason, or Charlie or Dave. The City had joined in the individualistic age.

When the stock-market crash of October 1987 almost halved

the turnover in equities within a year, all the half-baked assumptions on which the banks' purchases of broking firms had been made went out of the window. There was intense pressure on the new broker/dealers to find clients in order to create the commissions that were the source of most of their income. Asil Nadir, with his huge purchases of Polly Peck shares in 1988, was a godsend.

The losses of the securities firms in the last (post-crash) quarter of 1987 almost certainly wiped out their profits from the rest of that year. 1988 was even more disastrous, with the Stock Exchange itself saying that its members lost £265 million in the year. The Americans soon gave up. Security Pacific reduced its stake in Hoare Govett to a small minority, and Citibank closed its securities operation in early 1990, abandoning a plan to take over the converted Billingsgate fish market and turn it into the largest trading floor in Europe. One story had it that the last straw for Citibank was its failure to take into account the destabilising effect on the building of melting the permafrost in the basement. It had been there for 200 years, keeping fish fresh.

But the Europeans carried on, even though the losses mounted. In 1990, Phillips & Drew (owned by the Union Bank of Switzerland) lost £14 million on just one deal in Polly Peck shares at the time of the company's collapse. The City's new workers were not laid off in large numbers. Whereas more than 50,000 new jobs had been created in the Square Mile between 1984 and 1987, less than 10 per cent of those jobs disappeared over the next three years.

Many salaries, however, fell back to earth. In 1986 Nicholas Coleridge had forecast that 'The only good news for those of us outside the winner's enclosure is that the huge salaries will not last.' In late 1990 one broker was told that he could take a cut in salary from £90,000 a year to £18,000, or he could leave. He had twenty-four hours to make his decision. He looked around for other jobs and decided to stay. These were not long the days of champagne and orchids.

If the City had made such a mess of its own acquisitions, what hope was there that the industrial companies it was advising on mergers and acquisitions would make any less of a mess of theirs? Everything was telling them to buy too: there was the great god growth itself; there was '1992' and the need to be everywhere in

Europe's new single-market; there was the polarisation of industry and industrialists into winners (who bought) and losers (who were bought); and there was the fact that it was easier to buy an old business than it was to start a new one. More importantly, though, there was the means to buy – billions in the commercial banks looking for a home – and there was advice galore on how to do it from the merchant banks, the middlemen between the billions and the buyers.

But here another profession has to be put into the pot – the accountants who were inevitably behind every takeover deal. In Britain accountants used to be people who worked in companies and looked after their books, or people who worked for a firm of accountants and audited (i.e. checked) other companies' books once a year. There were many firms of accountants all over the country, but they were dominated by the so-called 'Big Eight' which besieged the City from strategic locations around its perimeter. Price Waterhouse was in Southwark House just across the river from the City, Coopers & Lybrand was in Plumtree Court, just to the west beyond Smithfield market, and Arthur Andersen was in Surrey Street just down from the Aldwych.

The Big Eight (Anglo-American to a man) not only dominated auditing in Britain; they also came to dominate it around the world. By the end of the 1980s, between them they audited more than 70 per cent of the world's major corporations. Interestingly, Polly Peck was not one of them. Its auditor (and Wearwell's before it) was still the relatively small firm of Stoy Hayward, which had its headquarters on London's Baker Street not far from the Sherlock Holmes Hotel. Stoy Hayward specialised in auditing the accounts of some of the more prominent go-go companies of the 1980s. A number of these came to grief – firms like Sophie Mirman's Sock Shop, Roger Levitt's Levitt Group, and Polly Peck itself.

In the 1960s and 1970s accountants had grown to have a special role in the British economy. Training with one of the big firms became a substitute for management education – what Americans would have obtained through a post-graduate MBA. It was entirely in character for a finance-dominated economy to believe that agility with a balance sheet was what mattered most in running a company.

Trainee accountants gradually became better paid, and the

profession attracted some of the brightest graduates in the country. In the 1980s one in every ten British graduates was choosing accountancy as a career. These people were obviously not going to do boring old audits for the rest of their lives. So either they left for top jobs in industry and the City, or they were kept by the accountancy firms with promises of more glamorous work. They would become 'consultants' or specialists in mergers and acquisitions (M & A).

Expanding into these new areas suited the accounting firms: it enabled them to keep hold of their bright young graduates, and it produced higher profits than traditional auditing or tax work. By the end of the 1980s five of the world's top six management consultants were arms of accounting firms. (The odd man out was McKinsey.) Non-audit work accounted for well over half of the big firms' fees. Price Waterhouse could boast that it was among the top thirty European M & A advisors. The other twenty-nine were all banks.

The influence of these highly educated qualified accountants spread throughout British industry. Martin Sorrell was one, so was Sophie Mirman's husband (and Sock Shop's joint founder), Richard Ross. Polly Peck had a number of nimble accountants inside the company – in 1982 its four-man board consisted of two accountants, a Cypriot and a Turk – and plenty with advice to offer from outside. On several occasions it used Coopers & Lybrand for consultancy jobs. It also called on McKinsey's to create a new regional management structure in the summer of 1989.

Unlike the general public, accountants know that accounting is not a science. It is rather like getting dressed – put on something good and well cared-for, and it will look smart. But you can also wear something shabby, spend some time on it, and still look smart.

Accountants are also a bit like economists; wherever two or three of them are gathered you can be sure to find four or five opinions – on almost every aspect of a company's accounts. Auditors have to declare that the figures in a company's accounts present a 'true and fair' view of the company's financial position – the balance sheet as a snapshot of the position at the end of the year; the profit and loss account as a trace of the path followed during the year.

Now, true and fair does not mean 'uniquely true and fair'. There is A's true and fair and there is B's true and fair, and they could truly and fairly be completely different. If somebody other than Stoy Hayward had audited Polly Peck's accounts no doubt they would have come up with different figures. Investors should not be surprised (but they often are) to learn that companies spend a lot of time putting on their best face in their accounts. Just as most people, dressing to go out 'in public', will try to look their best.

The accountants themselves attempt to impose uniform rules on how to treat various items in a company's accounts. These they call 'accounting standards'. But they often allow for exceptions, and sometimes they get abandoned in frustration. Typical of the latter was the accountants' attempt to decide on how to account for inflation.

In the 1970s, when inflation in Britain was repeatedly in double figures, inflation accounting was a hot issue. How a company accounts for inflation dramatically affects its profits. Take one simple example: suppose inflation in one year is 50 per cent. A company that buys a product for £100 in early January and sells it for £160 in late December that year can say it has made a profit of £60. But what cost £100 in January costs £150 in December. So the company's profit is only £10. Or is it?

Many worthy committees were set up to decide on the best way of accounting for inflation. They invariably agreed to disagree, but by the end of the 1970s the accountants had decided that companies should add something called an inflation-adjusted statement to their annual accounts. This was to last for an experimental period of three years.

There were huge sighs of relief when, at the end of three years, inflation had dropped so far and so fast in both the United Kingdom and the United States – which between them effectively set the accounting standards for the whole world – that the problem (and the extra inflation-adjusted statements) could be forgotten. That was fine, except for the fact that in many parts of the world inflation was still raging like a forest fire.

Those parts of the world included Turkey and northern Cyprus where Polly Peck had so much of its business. Inflation in both places was the same since northern Cyprus used Turkey's currency, and from 1984 to 1989 it averaged over 50 per cent a year. In 1988 it was 75 per cent. Since Britain and the United States had abrogated their responsibility to set accounting standards on inflation, these high-inflation countries were left to their own devices.

One perverse thing about inflation is that when accountants follow their guiding principles of objectivity and conservatism – without making special adjustments for inflation – they almost invariably come up with an overstatement of a company's profits. Polly Peck's Turkish and Cypriot accounts were not fully adjusted for inflation. The adjustment came later – when the Turkish lira results were translated into sterling for the group's accounts.

Now, the takeover game depends crucially on a company's reported profits. First, because the stock-market values a company on preconceived ideas of what its P/E ratio should be. So the E (earnings, i.e., profit), determine the P (price). The higher the earnings (or promised earnings), the higher the price. And the higher the price, the fewer the shares that a company has to issue in order to buy another company.

Second, earnings are important because that element of them that is not distributed in dividends becomes part of the company's equity. And that is part of the key 'gearing' ratio (the ratio of debt to equity) that bankers watch when deciding how much to lend to one company to buy another. The higher the equity, the higher the debt that a company can get its hands on.

There are many ways of 'dressing up' earnings. Some of these do not mislead anybody half-witted at reading a set of accounts. But they can make an indelible impression on speculators and financial journalists who choose to go no further than a quick examination of the pre-tax profit figure.

Mergers and acquisitions themselves can do funny things to accounts. When Coloroll, a home decoration firm, bought a company called Crowther in 1988 it set up a provision of £52 million to cover the costs of the acquisition. This cost, however, did not have to go through the profit and loss account. So Coloroll's reported profit of £55.6 million for 1988/89 could have been stated in another way as a mere £3.6 million. Coloroll was forced to call in administrators in June 1990.

Acquisitions also have the effect of making one year's accounts look marvellous compared with the previous year's. The 1987 accounts of WPP, for example, audited by Arthur Andersen, compare WPP at the end of 1986 (without J. Walter Thompson) with WPP at the end of 1987 (with J. Walter Thompson). The company's turnover goes up from £24 million to £284 million, and its pre-tax profit from £1.8 million to £14.1 million. This looks impressive, but says nothing about the underlying health of any of the company's businesses.

This good impression can be reinforced by colourful graphics and by association with the unimpeachable. WPP used its in-house firm of Sampson/Tyrrell for its graphics, and added a statement from its chairman that was rich in quotes from American management gurus of the 1980s, such as Tom Peters and Peter Drucker.

WPP's 1988 accounts were even more lavish, lending strong support to the theory that the glossier a company's present accounts, the duller its future performance. Polly Peck's accounts also got glossier and glossier as the years went by, with liberally scattered pictures of clean fresh fruit and vegetables. In its case, comparisons were clouded not only by acquisitions but by another accounting technique that achieves a similar result. This is to change the accounting period from one year to the next.

Polly Peck did this in the early 1980s. Its 1980 accounting year went to the end of March; in 1981 this was switched to 31 August, for the perfectly sensible reason that the citrus season runs from October to May. Then in 1982 the accounting year ended on 28 August. (The 1982 accounting year of Wearwell, Mr Nadir's other company, ended on the peculiar date of 3 September.) In 1987 Polly Peck's accounting year ended on 29 August. Then in 1988 it chose to stretch its accounting period over sixteen months: from 29 August 1987 to 31 December 1988. This made the reading of successive annual accounts somewhat akin to comparing the bananas and avocados that appeared on other pages of the company's reports.

Polly Peck was always dependent on what was described in its accounts as the 'Near and Middle East' for the vast majority of its pre-tax profits. In the early 1980s it did not give a geographical breakdown of its profits (claiming that the information was commercially sensitive). But even in 1989, by which time it had diversified considerably, 67 per cent of its profits still came from the Near and Middle East (essentially Cyprus and Turkey). However, only 35 per cent of its sales were in the region. In 1986, 57 per cent of its profits had come from just the 'Near East'.

Polly Peck was even more heavily dependent on agriculture than it was on the Near and Middle East. In 1989 agriculture accounted for 79 per cent of its pre-tax profits, but for only 49 per cent of its turnover. In 1986, 92 per cent of its profit had come from agricultural products. That meant that a very large percentage of its profits always came from fruit and veg (not electronics or textiles) in Cyprus and Turkey.

That, in turn, put a heavy burden on the auditor of Polly Peck's accounts in Cyprus. This was a company called Erdal & Co, which was sub-contracted by Stoy Hayward to do the local work. The accountants' rules in Britain state that it is the responsibility of the UK auditor who signs a company's accounts (Stoy Hayward in Polly Peck's case) to ensure that any sub-contracted work complies with UK standards. If for some reason it does not, then the accounting policy used should be indicated in the accounts. The question for Polly Peck in Cyprus was, what were the standards on inflation accounting that Erdal & Co was expected to comply with?

The profits that Polly Peck earned on its agriculture business were always something of a mystery. Some of the company's own executives have admitted that they did not understand how it was done. Food is basically a well-established low-margin business, yet Polly Peck managed to obtain margins of 37 per cent in 1985, falling to a still high 22 per cent in 1989. Mr Nadir has often said that the margins were obtained because of the group's control over the whole agriculture chain. But the company need not have bothered to obtain such control. It could probably have obtained such margins merely by accounting for the business in these high-inflation economies in a particular way.

Since Polly Peck's Turkish lira profits were not fully adjusted for inflation while they were being calculated, an adjustment had to take place when they were being translated into sterling. The Turkish lira was rapidly depreciating against the pound throughout the 1980s due to the huge difference between the inflation rates of Turkey and the UK. At the end of 1985 there were 830 lira to the pound; by the end of 1990 there were over 5500 lira to the pound. The translation of Polly Peck's Turkish and Cypriot assets into the sterling accounts each year resulted in what is called an 'unrealised translation loss'.

This loss was not set off against the company's trading profits in its profit and loss statement; rather, it was mentioned in a footnote to the accounts and deducted straight from the reserves in the balance sheet. SSAP 20, today's UK accounting standard for dealing with foreign-currency business, gives no clear guide-line on accounting for areas of high inflation. All it says is that 'Local currency financial statements should be adjusted . . . to reflect current price levels before the translation process is undertaken.'

In its 1987 accounting year the translation loss that Polly Peck passed through its reserves amounted to £84 million (although in its 1988 accounts, which gave the previous year's figure for comparison, the £84 million had been adjusted to £50 million). If Polly Peck had passed the 'loss' through its 1987 profit and loss account it would have almost exactly equalled its reported pre-tax profit of £86 million.

In the next accounting period (the sixteen months to the end of 1988) Polly Peck's translation losses were a massive £182 million, compared with reported pre-tax profits of £144 million. As one accountant said in commenting on these Polly Peck accounts: 'The scale of overall translation losses suggests that it may have presented a fairer view to take these through the profit and loss account rather than via reserves, or at least to provide loss details in a prominent note in close proximity to reported earnings figures.'

There was, however, a compensating factor to these translation losses, and that was that the value of Polly Peck's assets in northern Cyprus and Turkey was increasing by large amounts each year due to inflation. In 1987 the extra arising from revaluing these assets was £45 million. In 1988 it was £123 million. These sums were also passed straight through the company's reserves, and went a long way to compensate for the translation losses.

Nevertheless, they depended crucially on the value put on property in northern Cyprus and in remote parts of Turkey (such as Niksar and Manisa). The market for these assets was, to say the least, thin. Some of the revaluations were done by chartered surveyors, but some were done by Polly Peck's directors. In 1987, freehold and leasehold properties in the Near East were revalued by the directors. In 1988 the directors revalued the company's plant and machinery on the basis of 'appropriate indices'. This was the first time that Polly Peck had revalued its plant and machinery, and the revaluation accounted for £43 million of the £123 million revaluation surplus.

If the translation loss of £182 million is taken from the £144 million profit for the sixteen months to the end of 1988, there was a loss of £38 million. If the revaluation surplus of £123 million is added back then Polly Peck's profits rise to £85 million. From its pre-tax profits that year the company paid £24 million in tax and £26 million in dividends. That left the company with retained profits of £35 million, all of it (and more) effectively arising from revaluations by the directors of plant and machinery, much of it in Turkey and northern Cyprus.

Polly Peck has been heavily criticised for tucking its translation losses away in a footnote. But analysts like Peter Jones of L. Messel say that the market always took the footnote into account. It was part of the reason for the company's lowly P/E ratio throughout the mid-1980s. Its reported earnings were not being taken at face value. For much of that period the company's P/E ratio was around 40 per cent of what it might have expected to have been. That could mean that the market was assuming that Polly Peck's 'real' profits were as little as 40 per cent of its reported profits.

Stoy Hayward's senior partner says the firm carried out an internal review of its audit of Polly Peck's 1989 accounts and found nothing to reproach itself for. But the fact remains that accounting is an impressionistic art that can make the Styx look like the Thames in Henley Regatta week. Those who lend money on the basis of details in a company's accounts without looking very closely at the canvas are asking for trouble.

CHAPTER EIGHT

HOMES SWEET HOMES

LIKE Polly Peck, Asil Nadir himself got the buying bug. He bought expensive things, and they were usually beautiful things. 'He wanted the best – he always wanted the best of everything,' said a close friend. However, unlike most Turks and Cypriots, he seems to have had little eye and even less time for a bargain. Dealing in huge figures with Polly Peck and insulated from routine day-to-day shopping, his awareness of what things ought to cost became blurred. But even the best has its price.

The thing that Mr Nadir bought most was his own company's shares, which he did with the voracity displayed by shopaholics in Harrods or Marks and Spencer. Houses he had when married, but they did not interest him as collectables. After his divorces he lived 'above the shop' with his mistress in the mews house adjoining 42 Berkeley Square. When he bought and restored an old Turkish village house in Lapta, northern Cyprus, in the late 1980s it was the only home he himself owned at the time.

Helped by Ayşegül, however, he learned to enjoy being surrounded by beautiful things, but he was not particularly avaricious about them. He had neither the time nor the inclination to become 'cultured' enough to be a true 'collector'. He had no consuming interests other than business, despite his early flirtation with music and despite the fact that his nephew Tolga Kashif was carving out a career in England as a conductor. Tolga, who worked with both the London and Liverpool philharmonic orchestras, said that his maternal uncle was less of an influence than his paternal grandfather, a man who had once been a *muezzin*.

Mr Nadir's most conspicuous consumption was not for himself but for Polly Peck's headquarters at 42 Berkeley Square, which he furnished in the style appropriate to an eighteenth-century English town house. This seems to have been done less to suit his own personal taste than to conform with an idea he had (or that had been given to him) of what that taste should be. 'This is how he saw himself,' said Lady Middleton, a director of the auctioneers Phillips, as she took curious visitors on a tour of the house just before Phillips sold the contents in 1991. His office was certainly the place where Mr Nadir spent the largest part of his life, and in so far as possessions speak for their owner, the furnishings of 42 Berkeley Square speak for Mr Nadir.

The headquarters was a stunning example of what can be achieved with an ample cheque-book and some good advice. Even when Polly Peck was still based in the grim Commercial Road, Mr Nadir's office was a delight to the eye, furnished with Chinese porcelain, oriental rugs and a huge light-brown chunky oak table.

When the company moved to the West End in 1987 it was not going to be to some back-street 1960s identikit monstrosity equipped courtesy of Habitat. The Berkeley Square house that Mr Nadir plumped for was built in 1740, a fine example of a late Georgian town house, used by the aristocracy when doing the London season.

Mr Nadir asked Gülderen Tekvar, the wife of Armağan Tekvar who was effectively Polly Peck's in-house architect, to put together the furniture for the house. This she did over a three-year period from 1985, and by most accounts she did an excellent job. Paul Viney, Lady Middleton's boss at Phillips, said that it was 'the best single-owner collection [of Georgian furniture] to come to market for five years'. Geraldine Norman, the doyenne of English auction-house critics, suggested that 'While everything is English and old, it does not look like an old aristocratic collection – none of the furniture is falling apart. It looks more like Madison Avenue – the Americans like their old furniture to look new and, since American millionaires are the biggest buyers of English furniture, that's the way the smartest dealers turn it out.' So restored were some items that one cynical dealer at the auction was heard to say that a George II wall lantern was 'no more George Two than my arse'.

Nevertheless, the well-restored collection was catholic in taste and the items carefully chosen. Some pieces were sent to Berkeley Square and returned after a few days when it was decided that they did not fit. The majority of the items were bought in London through the four or five dealers who dominate that particular corner of the antiques market (Hotspur, Partridge, Mallett and

John Keil). The unimpressed said that with these dealers and an open cheque-book anybody could put such a collection together.

Much of the furniture had originally stood in great English country houses, such as Ditchley Park in Oxfordshire, a haunt of Winston Churchill during war-time weekends, or Holme Lacy in Herefordshire where had hung one of the prizes of the collection – a George I giltwood and gesso chandelier which appears in the authoritative *Dictionary of English Furniture*. It hung in Polly Peck's ground-floor boardroom encircled by ornate silk brocade wall-hangings and equestrian paintings. These included such masterpieces of Englishness as John Ferneley's early nineteenth-century depiction of '*Captain Anderson's Grey Pony in a Stable Yard*'.

It was all terribly English, the apogee being a painting hanging above the fireplace in the dining-room. This was a portrait by Sir William Beechey of his daughter Harriet. She is seated, wearing a simple Empire-line white dress, and looking for all the world as if she has stepped straight from the novels of Jane Austen – which were being written at much the same time as she was being painted. Harriet Beechey has a bemused look about her as if to say, 'What on earth am I doing here, amid these discussions of borrowed money and the movement of fruit?'

Unlike the luxury that can be found in other British companies' headquarters, Polly Peck's was not confined to the boardroom and the corridors of power. The receptionist sat at a 'fine and rare George III mahogany partner's pedestal desk' which fetched £26,000 at the Phillips sale. Her chair was a George III mahogany Bergère upholstered in green leather. It was sold for £4200.

Mr Nadir, of course, was merely following a long line of English merchants who have made it, and who have subsequently bought themselves good taste and respectability not far from Berkeley Square. Some of those who scoffed at the pretentiousness of it all may well have been descendants of such people.

The feeling that it was the home of a rich merchant was emphasised by the globes (Georgian, of course) which stood around the building, one of them tracing Captain Cook's voyage of discovery. Books scattered on low tables amidst large bowls of pot-pourri included a *History of the Turks*, leather-bound volumes of the works of Jonathan Swift, and a paperback edition of *Bonfire of the Vanities*, the cult novel about physical and mental violence on Wall Street. A gentle reminder of the origin of the merchant's trade came from the prints and water-colours depicting views of Constantinople and Turkish figures. Some of these were by Amadeo, Count Preziosi, a much-in-demand nineteenth-century Levantine painter.

But the star of the collection was an oil painting by the French Orientalist Jean-Léon Gérôme. The Orientalists were a group of enormously popular nineteenth-century painters. They were Europeans who travelled to the Near East and then played on Europe's fascination with the opulence and eroticism of the region. They frequently depicted (strictly from their imagination) scenes from the harem that were liberally scattered with naked women. They could paint such things and avoid censure because they set their subjects in exotic faraway places. One Gérôme, for instance, shows a snake entwined around a naked boy who is being watched by a wide-eyed group of oriental males. This was not a scene that the prudish nineteenth-century salons of Paris and London would have stomached had it been set in Toulouse or Birmingham. With their depiction of strange customs and even stranger costumes, the Orientalists added to the Western world's sense of alienation from the odd creatures of Cairo and Constantinople.

Polly Peck's Gérôme was not an erotic sample of the genre. Entitled *Harem Ladies Feeding Pigeons in a Palace Courtyard*, it is a beautiful painting of pigeons suspended in flight, dappled by the light through the courtyard roof. A group of ladies is watching from one side, their only visible flesh their hands and the eyes seen through slits in their headgear. The painting was sold at Phillips for £315,000.

But it was not the first Gérôme that Mr Nadir had owned. A Turkish friend found him one day looking at another painting by the artist that was hanging in his office. Next to the painting on a stand was a book about Gérôme, open at the page where the picture was reproduced.

'It's a good copy,' joked the visitor. 'No,' said Mr Nadir, 'it's the real thing.' The visitor then flipped through the pages of the book until he found the painting of the harem ladies and the pigeons. 'This', he said, 'is my favourite.' 'Funny you should say that,' replied Mr Nadir. 'It's coming next week to replace this one.'

Mrs Nadir had furnished their home in Belgravia's Eaton

Square herself, and she preferred French to English furniture. It was again done with great taste, and mingled with the Turkiquity that Ayşegül loved to collect. Even those people who found her little more than a determined social climber admired the way she taught herself about Ottoman and Arabic artefacts. She had a wide knowledge of Islamic calligraphy and, with the help of a Turkish antique dealer and a former Christie's employee called Oliver Hoare, she created what is now a lively market in the exquisite scroll-work of the ancient Muslim scribes.

Mrs Nadir loved to throw parties, and there were many in Eaton Square. Champagne (vintage Krug) and caviar were almost obligatory – even for casual visitors who called in for a drink. The guests were usually an assortment of hangers-on and more influential people who would all too rarely invite the Nadirs back. Turks and Cypriots are generous hosts who get upset when there is not even a token attempt to return their hospitality, or, if there is, when it is of the parsimonious English variety which reeks of obligation. The Nadirs had plenty of that.

Sometimes Mr Nadir lived at Eaton Square and sometimes he didn't. The marriage was an unconventional one. Although never officially divorced in Turkey (where they were first married), the Nadirs were divorced twice in England. After their first divorce in the 1970s, they continued to live together occasionally. When Ayşegül became pregnant with their second son in 1976 they remarried in England to make sure that the son (Serhan, who was sent by his parents to Eton) was fully legitimate. Then they divorced again, and if rumours are to be believed both had no shortage of affairs. Mr Nadir has three other sons by two different women.

Mr Nadir would joke about how most men get rid of their wives with one divorce, but he had not been able to get rid of his with two. Something kept bringing them back together, and it was not sex. Neither of them had much difficulty finding that elsewhere. Asil Nadir's money, power and good looks attracted many women, and he would talk in a schoolboy fashion about whether they were or were not a 'good lay'.

Ayşegül is reputed not to have been highly sexed despite an alleged string of lovers who were the source of much gossip in the Turkish press. She probably returned to Asil again and again because he gave her what she really wanted: status, the entrée into a rich social life, and the ability to pursue her expensive hobby of antiques. He would also indulgently make time to attend her parties, which were not his scene.

To him Ayşegül brought a woman's instinct, a sound intelligence, and an understanding of Turkey and the Turks. For years she was his ambassadress in Turkey, where he remained virtually unknown long after he was a household name in the City of London.

She gave him straightforward opinions undiluted by any feeling of what he might want to hear. It was difficult for someone who had known him cooped up in the family house in Romford to have many illusions about him. In an interview she gave after his arrest she confided to the interviewer that her ex-husband had told her, 'If you had been next to me as my wife all along none of this would have happened.'

People say he always loved her, and the two certainly remained good friends. But their tastes were very different. His were simple and had less need of money. Many of the people around him at the time of Polly Peck's success probably now have more money than he has. After Polly Peck collapsed he said that his ambition was only to have 'a small garden somewhere, either in Turkey or Cyprus, with fresh bread, a few olives and one tomato. Could there be anything better than that?' Ayşegül's reply would be an emphatic yes.

Ayşegül compensated for her husband's shyness with a certain haughty cheek which brought her the attention of gossip columnists and photographers. She could attract attention in a remarkable way. At a party in London given in the mid-1980s for the visiting Turkish prime minister Turgut Ozal and attended by countless dignitaries, all eyes were on her. She was dressed in simple black, wearing a Cartier diamond brooch and a bracelet in the shape of a panther.

It helped that she is a beautiful woman (though far from being, as she has been described in the English press, 'the most beautiful woman in Turkey'). She has dark black eyes and soft Tatar features, not all of them any longer quite how God intended. She is always impeccably made-up, and likes expensive clothes – particularly original garments by long-gone designers such as Madame Grès. She would often wear several different outfits in the course of a day, and has been known to turn up at parties with a change of clothing which she dons half-way through. In everything she wore and did she paid great attention to detail.

Ayşegül also loved jewellery. She would spend days searching for art-deco items that were made in exactly the same year as the old gown that she was to wear for a particular occasion. Among her large collection was a 20-carat solitaire diamond, a great rock of a thing. Her husband bought her much of this jewellery, and after he had given it to her she would sometimes go to the jeweller to find out how much he had paid for it.

Mr Nadir was dressed by Bijan, the Beverly Hills designer who helps multi-millionaire film stars decide what to wear. He had a sort of standing order with Bijan's New York shop which sent him so many suits that he scarcely had time to wear one lot before the next arrived. Visitors would sometimes be offered a choice from the racks of unworn garments that he owned. The *Financial Times* once said that his preference for hand-tailored blue blazers, grey flannel trousers and Gucci loafers was the style of dress of 'international café society rather than of the chairman of a large British quoted company'.

Mr Nadir did not dine out much, but when he did he liked Scott's, a fish restaurant in Mayfair; Efes, the best Turkish kebab house in London; and Mark's Club, the ever-so-exclusive annex of Annabel's discotheque just around the corner from Berkeley Square. In his office he preferred to eat olives and the white cheese beloved by Turks. All the time he chain-smoked cigarettes, usually Silk Cut.

'I genuinely haven't got a social life,' he told a journalist in 1989. 'I don't go out and about. Why would I want to go to a night-club? You can't have a conversation, the food is nothing. So why go? I'd rather be at home so that the next day I'm fit. People don't realise that an international businessman's life is such that you have to be as fit as an athlete.'

He loved cars, and had done so since before the day that his red MG had caught Ayşegül's eye. In London he favoured a Bentley; in New York a Cadillac; and in Istanbul a Mercedes. His cars in England – including the Bentley and a Ferrari Testarossa – had personalised number-plates such as AN 6, AN 11, and PP 11.

In the latter years of Polly Peck's expansion Mr Nadir spent a lot more time in the company's jet planes than in his cars. There were two of them, a G-IV Gulfstream and a Jetstar. These were not bought or hired capriciously. Mr Nadir was once advised by the Turkish authorities that the Greek Cypriots might try to kidnap him on a scheduled flight and take him to Athens to stand trial for theft in northern Cyprus. Fact or fantasy, this threat may have contributed to Polly Peck's expansion. For the corporate jets certainly made it easier for Mr Nadir and his top executives to swan around the world. Indeed, Mr Nadir may have been happiest in the stateless solitude of his plane, speeding at 33,000 feet in the hands of a man who had once been the pilot of Kurt Waldheim, the former UN secretary-general.

At one stage Mr Nadir also owned a couple of houses in the English countryside, both in the good hunting county of Leicestershire. Baggrave Hall was a listed mansion with 2000 acres, two herds of pedigree cattle (which won prizes at the Royal Agricultural Show) and 1500 sheep. He bought a few race-horses, which he liked more than the cattle. One of them, Golden Freeze, came second in the prestigious Mackeson Gold Cup in 1989.

Mr Nadir spent very little time at Baggrave Hall, but (whether he liked it or not) it added some of the trappings of an English country gentleman to his public persona. He sold the house in early 1991 for just over £3 million, more or less what he paid for it, but not taking into account the considerable sums he spent on improvement.

The other Leicestershire house, Burley-on-the-Hill,was more of a business proposition than a home. It had been falling to bits for some time and was bought in April 1990 for a reported £7 million by Vemak (Jersey) Ltd, a company controlled by Mr Nadir. Burley-on-the-Hill has 750 acres of land and 250 rooms, and is described in official guides as 'a baroque/palladian masterpiece'. It became a source of controversy as Mr Nadir sought planning permission to convert it into a hotel with a thirty-six-hole golf course. A planned annex at the front of the house was described by conservationists as the most horrific of its kind ever seen.

When they were in Istanbul (where they were not officially divorced) the Nadirs lived in rented accommodation, in one of the few remaining magnificent *yali*, the wooden seaside houses built by the Ottoman courtiers along the shores of the Bosphorus. Theirs was called the Sa'dullah Pasha *yali*, and is a russet-coloured two-storey beauty on the Asian side of the seaway. Although originally occupied by a sultan's chief barber, the house took its name from Sa'dullah Pasha, a nineteenth-century Ottoman ambassador to Berlin, and its owner after 1872.

Inside it is a gem of its type with an octagonal central hall and rooms branching off. The floors are marble and around the walls are niches in which are painted *trompe-l'oeil* landscapes. In line with Islamic custom there is no figurative representation on the murals. Under the windows are long sofas from which can be viewed the Bosphorus on one side and lush gardens on the other.

When they took the lease on the property the Nadirs promised to complete a restoration of the house that had already been begun. After completion the house looked magnificent and appeared in a number of glossy magazines. In one photograph Mrs Nadir had chosen to sprawl across the floor like a Hollywood starlet in her hillside mansion.

To this house came some influential guests. Henry Kissinger, the former American secretary of state, was a visitor on one of his trips to Turkey in the 1980s. Princess Margaret stayed with Mrs Nadir on more than one occasion, and Queen Elizabeth's cousin, Prince Michael of Kent, was also a visitor. The Bosphorus right in front of the house provided these guests with some protection from the Turkish *paparazzi* who besieged them during their visits.

The Nadirs had come to know Princess Margaret through the charities they were both involved in. There was also the horse connection; the Princess was the guest of honour at the Windsor Horse Show which Polly Peck sponsored in May 1989. When in Istanbul Princess Margaret would attend discreetly arranged parties around town, ferried back and forth in the Nadirs' extra-terrestrial speedboat. But the best parties were invariably *chez* Ayşegül.

As in London, she loved to throw parties, and she gave them all the attention and effort of a theatrical performance. Every summer there would be one grand thematic party at Sa'dullah Pasha *yali* that would be the talk of the town for the whole season. The gardens and the house would be wonderfully lit and decorated by professional stage designers. One year the party was a Venetian masked ball and Ayşegül imported masks for all those who had difficulty finding them locally. The guests were a mixture of local tycoons, artists and celebrities, plus a few international jet-setters and a royal or two as guest of honour. At the Venetian party the British ambassador was a guest, and so was Mark Birley, the owner of Annabel's in Berkeley Square.

Another year the theme was red, black and grey. Everything down to the chairs, tablecloths and even the food was in these colours. Ayşegül was the centre of attention, her antique jewellery, as always, a sure topic of conversation. In the early hours she put on a dancing act in which she drew gasps as she removed her long skirt – only to reveal a short one underneath. Guests stayed for breakfast the next day and the party finally ended about noon.

As Ayşegül climbed the social ladder, her old friends felt left behind. One of them once spent all day searching for the biggest lobster in town to honour her with at dinner that night. On his way home with the forlorn crustacean he saw his putative guest disappearing to another party for the evening.

By the end of the 1980s pollution and over-crowding were forcing Istanbul's rich pleasure-seekers away from the city and its surrounding waters. The south was the new chic playground, and especially the islands around Göçek on Fethiye Bay. The Nadirs bought an island in the bay where Princess Margaret and Prince Charles had already enjoyed summer holidays on other Turks' boats.

Anybody believed to be as wealthy as Mr Nadir inevitably gets plagued with requests for money. These come from many directions, but the most irresistible are probably those from political parties and from charities. In Turkey there were regular requests for money from Mr Ozal's Anap (Motherland) Party, and in Britain Mrs Thatcher's Conservative Party soon identified Mr Nadir as a potentially generous donor to their cause. He was invited to many gatherings of industrialists that were thinly disguised fund-raising occasions.

Although Polly Peck was a phenomenon of the Thatcher years, Mr Nadir was no blind admirer of the Iron Lady. He had spent too long in the East End of London where he had grown familiar with the local politicians. They were invariably members of the Labour Party. He felt more comfortable with them than with the snobbish county types who still permeated the Conservative Party organisation and who, he believed, would treat him very differently had he been a Caucasian from Eton and Trinity College,

Cambridge. (He did, notably, send one of his sons by Ayşegül to Eton.) Polly Peck, which as a UK company has to declare its donations to political parties, declared that it gave nothing to the Conservatives in the 1980s.

The company did, however, make public the hundreds of thousands of pounds it gave to charities to help under-privileged children. Mr Nadir could be moved to tears by the sight of a spastic boy or by the story of an orphan. The office of his personal holding company in Istanbul was in what was once the grandest apartment block in town. Although now gone to seed (on the floor below Mr Nadir's are the offices of Transendental Meditasyon) the block still boasts a lift that would thrill fans of pre-war Vienna. In pride of place on the walls of these offices were some of the medals Mr Nadir received for donations that enabled handicapped Turks to take part in things like the World Paraplegic Games. He also sponsored orphans, and flew sick Turkish children to London for medical attention.

Ayşegül also liked the charity scene. There were lots of parties and balls where she could meet the royal and the famous. On Tuesday 11 December 1990 – just four days before her ex-husband was arrested at Heathrow airport – she attended (without him) a £150-a-ticket charity ball at London's smart Park Lane Hotel sponsored by Nina Ricci and Adler, the jewellers. The *Sunday Times* said that the ball 'must have been the most elegant dance London has seen in many a year'. Among the 'regiment of tycoons and tax exiles' who joined Princess Michael of Kent for the evening were a number of Greek shipowners. In an ironic twist, a Turkish member of Mrs Nadir's party won the main raffle prize – a weekend in Greece!

But the charity work for which Mr Nadir became most famous was his much-publicised promise of a multi-million pound gift to Britain's Spastics Society. In May 1987 he saw a programme on television which described the work of a Spastics Society school called Beechtree where severely handicapped children were trained in a novel way. A psychologist on the programme said that there was a desperate need for a similar school for over-sixteens.

Deeply moved, Mr Nadir rang the Society almost immediately and said that he wanted to help. 'It was one of the most emotional, moving programmes I had ever seen,' he recalled later. The Society was divided at the time in its opinion of the effectiveness of Beechtree, and Mr Nadir's offer lay dormant for over a year. Then, in the summer of 1988, when Polly Peck was buying companies all over the world and Mr Nadir was personally buying some of Turkey's biggest daily newspapers, he was reapproached about his original offer to the Spastics Society. The Society was not to know that its delay was to have cost it almost £5 million.

It took some time before plans for the new project, which was to be called Oaktree, could be drawn up, and Mr Nadir's involvement agreed upon. He wanted it to be funded by an offshore family foundation. But the Spastics Society, which hoped to obtain local authority finance for some of the running costs of the school, urged him to set up an onshore UK foundation. The local authorities could not disapprove of that.

Mr Nadir instructed his personal accountants, a firm called Rawlinson & Hunter, to work on drawing up heads of agreement for the deal. The Spastics Society was somewhat surprised that he should use accountants for work that was normally carried out by solicitors. Eventually a firm of solicitors was brought into the picture.

In November 1989 the Society publicly announced that Mr Nadir had pledged £5 million to the Oaktree project, the largest private donation to charity in Britain for ten years. Mr Nadir is 'surely one of the most endearing and charismatic industrialists of our time', said the then chairman of the Spastics Society. The details of the deal were left to be tidied up by South Audley Management, a company set up to look after Mr Nadir's personal empire of houses, newspapers, banks and offshore companies.

Another surprise for the Society was South Audley's plan that Mr Nadir's foundation (to be called the Nadir Health and Education Foundation) should retain ownership of the buildings of the school, while the school itself was actually to be run by the Spastics Society. This was not the sort of donation they had had in mind.

Negotiations continued, although there was never much put in writing by South Audley. Meanwhile a number of people had agreed to be trustees of the Nadir foundation. They included Sir John Batten, a former physician to the Queen, Sir Brian Rix, the comedy actor involved in work for the handicapped, and William Grosvenor of Mr Nadir's personal public relations company, Wheatsheaf. Armağan Tekvar, the architect, was given the job of representing the foundation and working on the building of the school which, it had been decided by now, would be in the new town of Milton Keynes, some sixty miles north of London. However, Milton Keynes was never to see Oaktree. It was felled in 1990, along with a host of other Nadir plans.

CHAPTER NINE

THE BARONS OF BABIALI

THE biggest purchase that Asil Nadir ever made for himself was a bunch of newspapers in Istanbul. In the summer of 1988 he bought, through offshore trusts, two national Turkish daily papers: *Günaydin* (Good-day) and *Tan* (Dawn). By the end of the year he had bought a third, *Güneş* (Sun). When he bought the papers *Günaydin* had a circulation of about 220,000, *Tan* 130,000 and *Güneş* 120,000. At the time only *Günaydin* was making money. The others were losing millions of dollars a year. It was not only Mr Nadir's biggest purchase, it was also his biggest mistake.

For these newspapers, and for *Gelişim*, a group of once-pioneering magazine titles that had seen better days, Asil Nadir probably paid around $70 million, more than half as much as Polly Peck handed over more than a year later for the publicly quoted Japanese electronics firm Sansui. *Gelişim* published *Nokta*, a magazine that had built a reputation for fearless reporting on police and army brutality. It also published *Panorama*, an economic weekly which curiously used *The Economist*'s logo on its cover.

The purchases were surprising for several reasons. It was a huge amount of money to pay for entrée into a business of which Mr Nadir had very little knowledge and which he had always viewed with suspicion. He avoided journalists as much as possible, although on occasions he could charm them as easily as he could other groups of less threatening people. He felt uncomfortable with them and, after press conferences that he could not avoid, he would often have to change his shirt because it was drenched in sweat. In an interview in Cyprus in December 1990 he explained his feelings about journalists:

> 'Whatever you say, they are always negative. If you say that you've come to Cyprus they ask if you came here

> because there's no extradition with Britain. There are two options – you can either try to find that ounce of dignity in those people, or you just don't see them. That way they can't say, "That is what he actually told us." I can say subsequently that I never spoke to them and I can do something about it.'

There was some justification for this animosity. For many years the English press could not take Polly Peck seriously. It was either a 'Turkish delight', or it was at its 'nadir'. The Turkish press was no better. In its wilder moments it could say the silliest things.

Shortly after he had been arrested in December 1990 Mr Nadir was interviewed on BBC television. The interviewer was Peter Jay, a former British ambassador to the United States and once the son-in-law of a prime minister. Mr Jay's very first question was, 'Mr Nadir, are you in this matter a crook?'

What sort of answer did Mr Jay expect from a man who had just been charged with serious offences but who was still (presumably) presumed innocent? Was this to be trial by television? Mr Nadir's answer was the right one: 'I think the question is an odd question.'

In Turkey the press was more hysterical. In June 1989 a magazine called *Ikibin'e Dogru* (Towards 2000) published a cover story called 'Asil Nadir: the Finger that Stirs Turkey.' It was a rambling, unsubstantiated theory of conspiracy that embraced the Rothschilds, the Bilderberg Club (a group of internationally prominent people who meet infrequently and in secret), the CIA (always central to any good conspiracy theory), ITT, drug-runners, the Greek banker-turned-fugitive George Koskotas and Asil Nadir.

Mr Nadir brought some twenty different legal actions against the magazine as a result of the article, and won many of them. Turks, perhaps because of their Byzantine heritage, are great believers in the conspiratorial theory of history. Many of these conspiracies are designed, they believe, specifically to disadvantage them. Mr Nadir did not help to dispel their suspicions by his own veiled references to a 'dirty foursome' (the United States, Greece, the UK, and certain circles in Turkey) who were out to destroy him.

Try as they might, people close to Mr Nadir could never persuade him to open up to journalists. His few recorded interviews (there have been more since his arrest at Heathrow in December 1990 than there ever were before) have been studies in gamesmanship, a subtle mix of verbal chess and shy politeness. Since Mr Nadir was at his most winning when enthusing small groups of bankers or investors, why could he not be the same with journalists? Perhaps because they asked too many questions about things which he considered to be his private affairs, and he was never one to wallow in self-analysis. What he considered to be his private affairs stretched wide. When asked how his newspapers in Turkey were doing, he answered, 'We're not going to discuss my accounts today.'

Despite his reasons to be nervous of journalists, Mr Nadir did include a couple of them among his close entourage: Metin Munir, a Turkish Cypriot and former *Financial Times* correspondent in Ankara, and Nuyan Yigit, an older journalist from Istanbul who had been London correspondent of the Turkish newspaper *Hürriyet* for many years. *Hürriyet* was owned by Erol Simavi, the younger brother of Haldun Simavi, the man who sold *Günaydin* to Mr Nadir.

Of working journalists in England he came to trust only one: Michael Walters of the *Daily Mail*, the man who had caused such a stir in 1981 when he had reported from Famagusta on the 'bullet-scarred shed' that was Uni-Pac's factory. Michael Walters subsequently changed his mind about Polly Peck. In 1987 he wrote:

> In the early days, when Polly shares were flying, I questioned the crazy optimism [behind the price rise]. Later I became a convert, just as the real business began to grow and the share-price to wilt. I take back nothing . . . Give it another year or two and there will be much more than Turkish delight in Polly.

So complete was Michael Walters's conversion from sceptic to believer that *Private Eye*, which had been uninterruptedly sceptical about Polly Peck, came to refer to Mr Walters's paper as the *Daily Nadir* and to the Polly Peck chairman as Asil Mail.

When he bought into the industry of these prying people, Mr Nadir did so in no half-measure. He started with a small company in the UK called the Mercury Newspaper Group which published free weekly papers around Bristol and Stroud. Few of the folks in Stroud who read these local rags can have realised that the ultimate owner of their papers was a trust on the faraway Cayman Islands.

In Cyprus Mr Nadir started one new paper, called *Kibris*, and then for some strange reason launched two more. These came to dominate the local market, but they were small fry compared with his foray into Turkey in the summer of 1988, at a time when there seemed to be nothing that he was not prepared to buy, and no price that he was not prepared to pay. He handed over a hefty sum for Gelişim at a time when it was almost on its knees because of strikes and increases in newsprint prices. If he had waited a few months (and followed traditional publishing practice) he might have picked it up for next to nothing from the liquidators.

He even toyed with the idea of buying the prized and profitable *Hürriyet* in partnership with Robert Maxwell. But the deal, which could well have cost over $100 million, fell through.

For the $70 million or so that he did pay for his papers and magazines, Mr Nadir also got some property (particularly through *Güneş*), a place among Turkey's small band of press barons, and a headache whose intensity he could never have envisaged. By 1990 his three publishing companies were losing money almost as fast as their presses were printing papers. Industry estimates in Istanbul put his losses at one stage as high as $30 million a year.

Two questions come to mind at this stage. How did Mr Nadir raise the money to buy these newspapers in the same year that he paid out some £9 million buying Polly Peck shares and over £15 million to come up with half of his share of Polly Peck's rights issue in October 1988 – not to mention the £3 million or so that he paid for Baggrave Hall, his country estate in Leicestershire? And what on earth induced him to spend so much money on such a load of commercial rubbish?

It is easier to answer the first question: he paid for almost all these things with borrowed money. Just as banks in London were pestering Polly Peck to borrow, so they were pestering Mr Nadir to do likewise. He could not resist because it was so easy. All he had to do was to cross the road and give his Polly Peck shares as security for personal loans that at one stage might have been as high as £100 million.

How this system works became a crucial factor in the subsequent fate of Polly Peck. Banks which lend money against the security of shares usually lend up to a certain value of the shares, rarely more than 60 per cent. In the middle of 1988 Polly Peck's share price was at a level that valued the whole company at some £600 million. At the time Mr Nadir owned 25 per cent of the company, a stake that was worth £150 million. If he borrowed to the 60 per cent limit that the banks might have allowed he could then have borrowed some £90 million. By early 1990, when Polly Peck had bought the fresh fruit business of Del Monte and was worth over £1.5 billion, Mr Nadir was worth over £400 million. Against that share value he could have borrowed up to £240 million.

The problem with this sort of borrowing, using shares as security, comes if the shares fall in value. For then the amount that the banks have lent can rise above the set limit of 60 per cent of the value of the shares. When this happens the banks call upon the borrower to repay enough to make his loans fall below the set percentage. Mr Nadir had been convinced for many years that the London stock-market was failing to reflect the full value of Polly Peck's shares, and he spent much time and effort in trying to make the Exchange appreciate what he saw to be their full value. It probably never occurred to him that one day his shares might not be worth enough to cover the value of his loans.

This form of lending has several implications. First, the borrower has a double interest in seeing that the share value does not fall – both for the sake of the value of his shareholding, and to avoid having to come up with ready cash for his lending banks. This became the smoke behind the allegations that in 1989 and 1990 there was an organised attempt artificially to boost Polly Peck's share price. Second: it means that if the borrower cannot meet the banks' 'call' for cash, then the banks can sell the shares that they hold as security. This was behind the dramatic fall in Polly Peck's share price in September 1990. By then, so many of Mr Nadir's shares were held as security by banks that when they sold the shares to recoup their loans, they brought about the collapse of the company.

The reasons why Mr Nadir bought the expensive Turkish newspapers are less clear. Obviously, he did not believe at the beginning that they would not sooner or later make money. The Nadir magic could surely be wrought in much the same way as it had been elsewhere? He would cast his favourite phrase, 'Don't worry', at the furrowed brows of frantic lieutenants, less out of a desire to pacify them than out of a conviction in his own supreme ability to solve any problem.

In February 1990 he was still insisting to sceptical colleagues in Istanbul that the papers would have a circulation of 3 million by September that year. The extent of that ambition can be gauged from the fact that the first Turkish newspaper ever to achieve a circulation of over 1 million (*Sabah*) only did so in early 1991.

The reality was that the circulation of Mr Nadir's two main newspapers (*Günaydin* and *Güneş*) was under 400,000 in September 1990. That completely destroyed any chance of reaching another target that he mentioned to a colleague in early 1990: a profit of TL100 billion (almost £20 million) from his publishing businesses in 1990.

In an interview in January 1991 Mr Nadir said that he bought the publishing businesses for three reasons:

1 to be closer to the people;
2 in time, to correct certain mistakes in Babiali (Istanbul's Fleet Street); and
3 to keep the Cyprus issue warm and as close to the truth as possible.

Significantly, he did not include making a profit as a reason. Just as well, because by then the newspapers and magazines were in difficulties, with editors and staff leaving at a rapid rate. Babiali was chattering away about who had and who had not been paid among the Nadir employees. Advertisers were being beseeched to pay in advance for the advertisements that they were planning to run in the papers.

Mr Nadir, however, stoutly insisted that nothing was for sale, despite approaches from a number of interested parties, including the French group, *Figaro*. In January 1991 he gave a charge over the newspapers to his personal creditors – the brokers Barclays de Zoete Wedd and Lehman Brothers, to whom he owed £22.1 million; Merrill Lynch, to whom he owed more than £5 million; and Carr Kitcat Aitken to whom he owed £20 million. This was in return for the creditors dropping a bankruptcy petition against him until he could raise the cash to pay them off.

If Mr Nadir had really believed that the newspapers were such a good investment, why had he not been able to persuade the board of Polly Peck to buy them? He had tried. The media was then a 'hot' sector. Diversification into it would not have been unthinkable for Polly Peck. It could have been embraced under the leisure leg of its tripod of businesses – leisure, agro-industry and electronics.

But Polly Peck had too many other fruits to digest, and the company was not at all sure that being a baron in Babiali was as rewarding as it had once been. Whereas owning Turkish newspapers had for long been a licence to print money, competitive pressures were changing the whole structure of the industry. For a start, the price of newsprint had been almost doubled overnight by the pro-free market government's removal of long-standing subsidies on the industry's raw material. This, of course, had not encouraged Babiali to see the government or the then prime minister, Mr Ozal, in a particularly favourable light.

At the same time the readership of the newspapers was changing and broadening. For as long as they were heavily subsidised the papers were so cheap that the educated urban Turk would think nothing of buying three or four a day. With a number of price increases that took account not only of inflation but also of the newspapers' own rising costs, that changed very quickly. Educated readers became much more selective, and the newspapers had to move down-market to maintain their circulation.

That meant appealing to the hundreds of thousands of Turks who were drifting from the countryside to the cities, and to Istanbul in particular, in search of streets paved with gold. The method devised to appeal to these people was to turn the newspapers, in effect, into lottery tickets. Every day, cars, houses or holidays were given away to the person who collected the right coupons from the paper. If one day one paper gave away five cars, then the next day another would give away ten.

The strategy worked in terms of increasing circulation. But few people were buying the papers in order to read them. As soon as the expensive lotteries were stopped, the newspapers' circulations plummeted. They had got themselves in a bind, more especially as advertisers were wise to the fact that an increasingly large part of the newspapers' 'readership' was actually illiterate.

At the same time the press barons were moving their offices

out of cramped Babiali, near where tourists teem into the famous covered bazaar, and where traffic honks incessantly in one of the busiest parts of a city that threatens to become the world's largest traffic jam. An area near the airport was being designated as the new Babiali. Both *Sabah* and *Hürriyet* had grandiose plans for new buildings in the area. Although the move and some of the reasons for it were not dissimilar to those that had pushed London's Fleet Street to the south and east of the British capital only a few years earlier, the cost savings were by no means so great.

So the lottery-ticket printers were under heavy financial pressure. They had managed to find some relief in regular increases in the cover price of their newspapers. These could conceal real price increases under the veil of the country's massive and unpredictable inflation rate. But in 1989 the Turkish Cypriot newcomer incurred the undying wrath of the barons of Babiali by unilaterally holding back on increases in the cover price of his newspapers. Everybody had to follow his example.

Why did Mr Nadir make this strange decision when his newspapers were already losing money hand-over-fist? Did he really believe that he could gain a competitive advantage over his rivals? Or did he just hate them so much (as he sometimes seemed to) that he was set on dragging them down, convinced that the depth of his own pockets would enable his papers to outlast theirs? Or (as has been suggested) was Mr Nadir persuaded by somebody in government that this could make a real contribution to reducing irritatingly high inflation?

If he was so persuaded, it was probably the only favour he did to the government in buying the Turkish newspapers. Byzantine minds had been convinced that Mr Nadir had bought the papers as a favour to Mr Ozal. At the time Mr Ozal, and the ruling Anap (Motherland) Party that he founded, were being treated roughly by the press. Their popularity in the opinion polls was waning, and few kind words were being written about them in Babiali.

It is not inconceivable that Mr Ozal's son Ahmed, who acted as a sort of go-between between the government in Ankara and the commercial and industrial community in Istanbul, suggested that Mr Nadir might like to make an offer for *Günaydin*. But Mr Nadir knew Haldun Simavi, the owner of *Günaydin*, very well. Haldun's wife Cigdem, who was previously married to Rahmi Koç, was a close friend of Ayşegül's. The two men needed nobody to introduce them or to recommend a business deal between them. The fact that Mr Simavi got the better of the deal (between TL40 billion and TL60 billion in cash) probably had more to do with Mr Nadir's frame of mind at the time than with political persuasion.

Coincidentally, Mr Nadir's newspapers did become much more supportive of the government and of Mr Ozal. Mr Ozal held Mr Nadir up as a model of a patriotic press baron, an attitude that infuriated the other barons of Babiali, particularly Erol Simavi who on one notorious occasion lambasted the Cypriot for his presumptuous claim to be a Turkish patriot.

But at the time the balance of favours between Mr Ozal and Mr Nadir was the other way round. If anything, Mr Ozal still owed Mr Nadir. To much of western Europe, Mr Nadir and Polly Peck were the face of investment in Turkey. When *The Times* of London said (as it later did) that Polly Peck was 'pukka', it effectively said that investment in Turkey was pukka too. For Mr Ozal and for Turkey, such an opinion, created almost single-handedly by Asil Nadir, was without price.

So we have to look elsewhere for the reasons why Mr Nadir burdened himself with a cash-hungry newspaper empire in Turkey. One reason, suggested by himself, is that the first money he ever earned was from selling newspapers on the streets of Cyprus forty years earlier. That was not like selling newspapers on the streets of London, where both the newspapers and the customers come to the vendor. Mr Nadir says that he had to run around all the time, first to get hold of the newspapers and then to sell them. He says that it taught him an important lesson: keep moving to make money. Business does not come to those who stand and wait.

What greater thrill, then, for a man who earned his first sou as a newspaper boy, than to own newspapers in a country that had been a vast unpredictable power on the edge of his childhood horizon? Such emotional reasons could well have played a part in the decisions of an emotional man who was reaching an age and a status where strategy and business plans counted for less than the pure desire to do something. Nevertheless, there probably was some strategy behind the move. In many ways it followed a similar pattern to what had happened in northern Cyprus.

There (in the words of one of his close advisors) Mr Nadir had been persuaded that 'to build a castle you need two towers'. Those towers were banks and newspapers. In northern Cyprus he had built a two-towered castle by setting up the Cyprus Industrial Bank, and by subsequently publishing three local newspapers. In Turkey he set about building similar 'towers'. He bought a bank which had been called Titibank and wisely changed its name (to Impexbank), and he bought the newspapers.

But in Turkey he bit off more than he could chew. It was a country of over 50 million people, compared with the 170,000 of tiny northern Cyprus. Castles built there were of a different order of magnitude. In northern Cyprus Mr Nadir's publishing empire was not a huge financial commitment nor a particularly complicated operation to run. His newspaper *Kibris* was considered a success with a circulation of 8000.

On the Turkish mainland there were many more complicated factors to take into account. The Babiali barons liked to hunt as a pack, and Mr Nadir was not a pack-man. Among the top managers of his newspapers there, were three former employees of Erol Simavi's *Hürriyet*. They flattered their new boss into believing that by confronting the establishment he could become an even bigger baron than their former employer.

Mr Nadir made Metin Munir editor in chief of *Güneş* and he made Nuyan Yigit managing editor of *Günaydin*. Metin's brief was to produce 'the best-quality newspaper in Turkey'. It is likely that by this time Mr Nadir believed that all he had to do to make money was to introduce quality into any industrial sector in Turkey, almost regardless of cost.

Güneş set out to be a sort of Turkish version of the *Independent*, the critically acclaimed British daily newspaper launched in October 1986, and the first new quality daily paper to be launched in Britain for over fifty years. Like the *Independent* itself, *Güneş* was a bold attempt to create something fresh in a stale and smug market. It was bound to take time and money to succeed. In the event it did not have enough of either.

Asil Nadir has admitted that he now knows that 'newspapers cannot be managed like an industrial enterprise. They need more attention and effort.' And certainly his Turkish newspapers needed more attention and effort than he was able to give them. He was sometimes not available by telephone for days on end, and he gave little indication that he ever read memos, however short and to the point the author made them. His lieutenants in Istanbul had to be content with the promise that Mr Nadir would soon be spending several months in Turkey and that everything would then be all right.

His absence might not have mattered if the businesses had been put in the hands of competent managers, backed up by foreign advice and skills – as had been the pattern with previous Polly Peck investments in Cyprus and Turkey. Mr Nadir did bring in Bruce Matthews, an experienced publisher who had implemented Rupert Murdoch's historic and bitter removal of *The Times* and the *Sunday Times* from old-fashioned Fleet Street out to Wapping and high technology. Mr Matthews had been introduced to Mr Nadir by Peter Hetherington, a former chairman of Express Newspapers in England, and the senior partner at Rawlinson & Hunter, Mr Nadir's personal accountants and the auditors of his sister's company Noble Raredon. Rawlinson & Hunter had handled the affairs of the Beaverbrook estate (which owned Express Newspapers) and was expert at setting up offshore trusts to own things like newspapers.

Mr Nadir's reluctance to impose discipline on the big business that his private empire had rapidly become meant that it degenerated into a series of power-pockets fighting against each other. There was no attempt, for example, to gain economies of scale by forcing the newspapers to share printing facilities.

By the time a single managing director for all the publishing interests was appointed, it was too late. Mehmet Bayraktarlar took the job in August 1990 and lasted less than four months. By that time he had the impossible task of forging the diverse bits together without any money to do the job.

For most of the time the only unifying force was Fahri Görgülü, a former governor and head of security who had been working with Mr Nadir in Turkey for some years. A man who had little business (let alone publishing) experience until he joined Mr Nadir, Mr Görgülü was on the board of all three newspaper companies. He handled many of Mr Nadir's affairs in Turkey and acted as his mouthpiece, telling both Metin Munir and Nuyan Yigit when they were fired. As he had with others, Mr Nadir offered the sacked men alternative jobs. Mr Munir refused a call to come to London to help with public relations, but Mr Yigit (who had kissed Mr

Nadir's hand in public and said 'I am your dog') accepted an offer to run a small billboard business that Mr Nadir owned in Turkey.

In his hey-day as a newspaper baron Mr Nadir seemed to think that he was running some sort of charitable institution. The purse-strings were untied and there were plenty of hands ready to dip in. The papers paid generous salaries that in many cases were unnecessarily out of line with the market, and there was very little control over expenses run up by the staff. Deeply reluctant to lay anybody off, Mr Nadir did not try to trim costs and increase efficiency and productivity. While the top-selling paper *Sabah* had some 500 employees, *Güneş* had over 850 at one time, and *Günaydin* over 1500. *Cumhuriyet*, the best 'quality' Turkish paper, which would have been *Güneş*'s main rival, had a staff of under 400 on salaries far below those at *Güneş*.

The extravagance extended to the newspapers' printing facilities. *Günaydin* set up a printing operation in Frankfurt that could only be justified if (and when) it got a major contract to print something like the European edition of the *Financial Times*. It was as if Mr Nadir wished to indulge his own staff in the sort of wild generosity that had been to some extent restrained within the corporate structure of Polly Peck. If he had such a wish, it was in the end a death wish.

THE reality was that Mr Nadir was juggling with so many balls at the time that he did not have the capacity to watch them all with his usual intensity. Superior information and a hands-on will to succeed had always been at the heart of his commercial successes. Now he was sometimes not getting the information, or not absorbing what he was getting. And his deep mental determination, which had had an almost physical power in the early days of Polly Peck, was diffused in too many directions.

He tried to set up new structures and systems within Polly Peck to cope with the increased work-load. The company recruited some new senior managers and called in the management consultants McKinsey. Companies like to call in management consultants when they can't make awkward decisions themselves. It gives them some protection should their plans go wrong – 'I knew those bloody consultants were idiots as soon as they walked through the door.'

The success of managing a big public company (as opposed to a small family company) depends on choosing the right people for various tasks and then giving them the right balance of freedom and control. On both these counts Mr Nadir seems to have failed. When choosing employees, he was probably not a very good judge of character. But, like many before him, he also had no intention of appointing anyone who might steal his limelight. When Norman Tebbit, a man whom Mr Nadir said he admired, resigned from Mrs Thatcher's government, it was suggested that he be invited on to the Polly Peck board. 'What,' said Mr Nadir, 'and have me stand in his shadow?'

On the other count, Mr Nadir seemed to have no idea about the right balance between freedom and control for his managers. On one occasion he demanded that all Polly Peck's mail, regardless of whom it was addressed to, should pass through his office. On the other hand he would allow a few people whom he trusted extraordinary freedom to do as they wished. The inexperienced managers of a satellite television channel for Turkish workers in Germany, for example, went very much their own way. The channel was closed down a few months after it began transmitting.

Within his private empire there was even more freedom than within Polly Peck. The Turkish newspapers' bosses were left very much to their own devices. So was South Audley Management (SAM), the company set up by Mr Nadir in London to run his own non-Polly Peck affairs.

SAM, said Mr Nadir, 'is a private company owned by a trust and is responsible for providing management services to such interests as I, my family, and family trusts, have in this country.' SAM was owned by some trusts in Jersey, the beneficiary of which was Asil Nadir's mother, Safiye Nadir.

SAM got its name from South Audley Street in Mayfair where it had offices briefly before moving to 24 Berkeley Square, just across the square from Polly Peck. Mr Nadir recruited Elizabeth Forsyth from Citibank to be the head of SAM, and with a staff of three she started to run Mr Nadir's fast-growing private empire. At the beginning the whole thing was a family affair. The directors of SAM were people like Armağan Tekvar, the architect who had been close to Asil for decades, and Arseven Gümüş, an old Cypriot friend and an accountant who resigned from SAM when he became a director of Noble Raredon (née Gnome Photographic), the company of Asil's sister Bilge Nevzat.

People popped in and out of South Audley. Bilge Nevzat shared the offices for six or seven months until SAM moved to Berkeley Square. Mrs Nevzat, who had worked for Polly Peck until 1986, stayed on at South Audley Street, and the office became the headquarters of Noble Raredon. Like her brother, she liked to work in lavish surroundings. 'Such is the grandeur of the curtains in her personal suite,' wrote one interviewer, 'that it would seem out of place to do anything so vulgar as pull them. Visitors lounge on luscious couches and the table is shiny enough to make the mirror redundant.'

Anil Doshi, a consultant who had been Asil's finance director in Wearwell days, also popped in and out of SAM's offices. When Tim Wood, the tall lanky stockbroker's analyst taken on as Polly Peck's treasurer, fell out with David Fawcus, Polly Peck's finance director, he was sacked. But Mr Nadir found him a job at South Audley. He stayed there for some months until Polly Peck invited him back with the promise of a directorship.

There were never very many people working for South Audley. But as Mr Nadir's personal empire grew, so did their responsibilities. Mrs Forsyth has said that 'SAM never bought shares.' Mr Nadir's shares in Polly Peck, held through the Jersey company Restro Investments, were managed by a Zurich company. SAM was 'purely a property management company and consultant to the newspaper companies of the Nadir family'. That was the basis for Mrs Forsyth's claim that she had built up the company from three employees to 3000 – which included the employees of Mr Nadir's newspapers in Turkey.

The head office backing to run all this was scarcely ever more than ten people. It included Elizabeth Forsyth's loyal and down-to-earth assistant, Barbara Jackson-Smith, and was backed up by a bevy of Mr Nadir's private advisors, such as the accountants Rawlinson & Hunter (who were also SAM's auditors) and William Grosvenor, a public-relations consultant.

One of the key people at South Audley was Jason Davies, who had met Mr Nadir's son Birol when they had both been stockbrokers at Giles & Overbury, a small City firm that had gone bankrupt in 1986, one of the first casualties of Big Bang.

At SAM Mr Davies was a jack-of-all-trades. For example, one of Mr Nadir's Cypriot publishing ventures had been the magazine *Turquoise*. Beautifully printed in Britain, *Turquoise* carried some first-class articles about the eastern Mediterranean, along with the occasional glowing 'family' profile of people like Bilge Nevzat.

When it first appeared, *Turquoise* listed its London advertising manager as Jason Davies, whose address and telephone number were those of South Audley Management at 24 Berkeley Square. At SAM everybody could turn their hand to anything. Even stockbrokers could become advertising managers. They could also become property experts. Jason Davies and Elizabeth Forsyth were both directors of Baggrave Hall, Mr Nadir's country house in Leicestershire. Mrs Forsyth was largely responsible for its renovation and for stocking the estate with prize-winning cattle.

Although they had such wide responsibilities, the staff at South Audley was never short of confidence in its own ability to carry out all the jobs required. One person who had many dealings with the company says that 'most of them were babies; insubstantial yuppies with no real experience. There was no sense of depth in them.' Another recalls that few of them seemed to do much except drink coffee and eat late breakfasts. Mrs Forsyth has denied that they had in-house breakfasts, although they did have in-house lunches 'because we did not have time to go out'. By all accounts, whatever they were busy doing, it did not involve writing many letters.

Mrs Forsyth was the daughter of an accountant from Grantham in Lincolnshire, the market town where Margaret Thatcher was born and bred. At eighteen she had become a secretary in a bank, rising to become a personal assistant and then a fully fledged banker with Citibank at 41 Berkeley Square. There she handled private clients' affairs and was introduced to Mr Nadir, she says, by a man called Ted Petropoulos.

Jason Davies, who was in his twenties, had had an even less auspicious career. The son of a builder, he had gone into the City as a clerk at the age of seventeen. He moved around doing back-office paperwork for various brokers until he joined Giles & Overbury. There he was promoted, and became a real broker – a not dissimilar career path to that of many of the 'boys from the Essex marshes' who were at the time making City fortunes beyond their wildest dreams.

On leaving Giles & Overbury Mr Davies joined another broking firm called A. J. Bekhor. But again he did not have much luck. A. J. Bekhor got caught out by the stock-market crash in October 1987, and by November Mr Davies was out of a job. He has described how miserable it was on Bonfire Night that year. His wife was pregnant, he was jobless, and he owed £230,000 to A. J. Bekhor for dealing that he had been doing on behalf of a Scottish punter who wouldn't pay.

By Christmas 1987 Mrs Forsyth had helped to ease his problems, offering him £30,000 a year to be a consultant to SAM. At the same time Mr Davies was able to continue as a broker by becoming a commission agent for the broking firm of Paul E. Schweder Miller. Apparently Mrs Forsyth was so impressed with his work that she soon made him a director of SAM.

By the end of 1989, however, not only had all Turks and Cypriots resigned from the board of SAM, but so had all males. The all-female board then consisted of Elizabeth Forsyth, Sharon Marsh (of Grantham), Patricia Phillips (of Reading), Janet Pullinger (of Nuneaton), Sabire Djamgoz (of Hounslow) and Shirley Evennett (of Sidcup).

These inexperienced people from modest backgrounds were suddenly whisked into the glamour of Berkeley Square, country estates and foreign travel. Mrs Forsyth always seemed to be travelling. She was often in Switzerland and lunched there with Mr Nadir on the day before he launched his bid to take the company private in the summer of 1990. When the Serious Fraud Office raided SAM's premises in September that year she was again abroad. She bought a derelict house on Cyprus and spent a lot of time in Turkey.

On some occasions Mrs Forsyth would brag that she controlled everything at Polly Peck; on other occasions she would say that SAM had nothing to do with Polly Peck. The truth was probably somewhere in the middle. For sure, the two were not entirely separate. For example, in February 1989 Mr Nadir decided to raise some money for Polly Peck through a Swiss franc bond issue. The preparatory work for the issue was done between Tim Wood, who was working for SAM at the time, and Polly Peck's bankers in Switzerland, the S. G. Warburg subsidiary Soditic. Polly Peck's finance director David Fawcus was presented with the issue more or less as a *fait accompli*.

In addition, Jason Davies spent a lot of time dealing in Polly Peck's shares. Some of these deals were on behalf of Middle and Near Eastern investors he had met through Birol Nadir. Others were on behalf of a number of 'letter-box' companies in Switzerland called Gateway Investments, Riverbridge Investments, Forum and Tristan. Between them, Tristan and Forum alone dealt in over 4 million Polly Peck shares in 1988.

The links between these companies and Nadir family interests raised suspicions that they were merely fronts for Nadir family dealings in Polly Peck shares. Tristan's address was the same Zurich building as the Swiss address of Fairweather Investments, the Cayman Island company through which Mrs Nevzat had bought Gnome Photographic. This was 'no surprise,' said Mrs Nevzat, because 'the place is owned by Citibank. There are thousands of companies registered there.' Like Fairweather, Tristan was actually a Cayman Island company and is alleged to have had some shareholders in common with Mountain Dew, the Cayman Island company which Birol Nadir used in 1988 to buy his stake in Harland Simon, a UK company that made computer systems for the newspaper industry.

Many of the instructions for these share deals came to Jason Davies through a Swiss-based company called Rhône Finance. Roger Hunziker, the chairman of Rhône Finance, is a rare animal: a Swiss with both a British and an American accountancy qualification. He trained with Price Waterhouse in London and has a Welsh wife. He was also once associated with Rawlinson & Hunter, the Nadir family's private accountants.

When Rawlinson & Hunter had opened an office in Geneva in 1982, Mr Hunziker had become a director and shareholder of their local firm. In 1987, however, Mr Hunziker and Rawlinson & Hunter went their separate ways. The London accountants say that they had no dealings with Mr Hunziker or with Rhône Finance after that date. Mr Davies has said that he asked Rhône Finance whether there was any connection between these deals and the Nadir family: 'Rhône said there was no connection.' Mr Nadir has also said that share dealings by the Swiss letter-box companies 'had absolutely nothing to do with me'.

CHAPTER TEN

NOBLE HOUSE

MR Nadir's personal fortune was increasing in parallel with the fortunes of Polly Peck. Although he claimed that his wealth was not all tied up in his Polly Peck shares, there is no evidence that he had any substantial assets that had not been bought in one way or another with these shares. If he got carried away by his own spending power, it was in part because Polly Peck itself was again being carried into the stock-market stratosphere.

One vital ingredient in Polly Peck's second stock-market coming, in 1987 and the years after, was the new management team brought in to guide the company's strategy. In early 1987 Mr Nadir had been advised by some of Polly Peck's institutional shareholders, led by the Legal & General insurance company, that he should get more faces that would be respected in the City of London among the ranks of his top executives. Polly Peck was still seen as a maverick, and needed to increase its stature in the eyes of investors and bankers. The company's long-serving finance director, Anil Doshi, was known to have a good financial brain, but he had repeatedly failed to impress at presentations of the company's results. Mark Ellis, the managing director, had risen from a fairly junior level in a merchant bank to become a Polly Peck board member at the ripe young age of twenty-nine. Not only was he young, he was also perceived as mercurial.

So Mr Nadir appointed head-hunters to find him a team with clout. Head-hunting was another service industry that had flourished in the peculiar commercial compost of the 1980s. Whereas merchant banks got fees for shuffling companies about, head-hunters got fees for shuffling executives about. With the utmost discretion they would poach high-flyers from one company and persuade them to join another. For a long time their most rewarding ground was the City itself, where whole teams of over-paid bankers and brokers would switch allegiance at a head-hunter's hint of another 20 per cent.

The most important new appointment for Polly Peck was that of a chief of day-to-day operations. He would release Mr Nadir for more strategic thinking about the company's future. For a company like Polly Peck, however, to recruit such a man from outside was not easy. The fact that the company had been a one-man band for so long, run by a strong-willed chairman, meant that potential recruits knew they would either be in his shadow or constantly fighting against his steely will. Moreover, the fact that the company had for long been seen as an outsider meant that anybody moving in to take over one of the top jobs was taking a risk by leaving the mainstream of corporate management. On a manager's CV, Polly Peck did not yet sound like Unilever or Sainsbury.

By September the head-hunters had found Anthony Reading to spearhead the new management team. He was another British accountant who had been a senior executive with the conglomerate BTR, in charge of its engineering and manufacturing division. He had been one of the few senior executives at Thomas Tilling (of Crewe House fame) to survive its stormy takeover by BTR in 1983.

Thomas Tilling had an oblique connection with Polly Peck. Its most famous product was Pretty Polly, the brand of women's stockings that most men-in-the-street assumed were made by Polly Peck. As late as 1989, the Hong Kong-based *South China Morning Post* could still describe Polly Peck as 'known in Britain for its women's stockings'.

Mr Reading's four years working for the spartan BTR, reknowned as a tightly run ship that was particularly strong on financial controls, was thought to be the ideal experience to bring to the rather loosely controlled Polly Peck. Mr Reading was to be 'group managing director for operations', and one of a triumvirate of equals who reported directly to Mr Nadir. (Mark Ellis and David Fawcus, who had joined in 1986, were the other two.)

Anthony Reading had a classic career dilemma. If he stayed at BTR he was very unlikely to get the top job there. So to become a chief executive he would have to move. The job on offer at Polly Peck held out the promise of the top post in a major quoted company, and that for him was something worth moving for.

While he was an honourable manager, Mr Reading was still relatively young and he may not have had what it takes to outwill

Mr Nadir. He was to leave Polly Peck after less than two years, in June 1989, to become managing director of Pepe Group, a fast-growing fashion company. His tenure there, however, was to be even shorter than his stay at Polly Peck. After nine months, and after announcing a 20 per cent fall in Pepe Group's full-year profits, he left to become a divisional director of F. H. Tomkins, a quoted industrial conglomerate where his main responsibility was for the group's Smith & Wesson firearms division. That was no more than he had had at BTR more than three years earlier.

On his arrival at Polly Peck Tony Reading set about consolidating the new team. David Fawcus, the finance director, was already there, a professional manager trained in the schools of Unilever and Guinness. To him was added John Clayton, a solicitor and Cambridge rugby blue who had worked with Fisons; Malcolm Fenner, an accountant from the stockbrokers Phillips & Drew, who was in charge of corporate finance; and Vi Jensen, a management accountant who had been enticed away from Guinness by David Fawcus.

This team set about imposing tighter internal disciplines and putting Polly Peck's case more strongly to the City. It began to run Polly Peck more like a British public company than an entrepreneurial fiefdom. The string of purchases in 1988 was one visible sign of its efforts. Another was the pre-tax profits of £144 million reported for the sixteen months to the end of 1988. The new team grew in confidence and began to feel that the new success was in large part its doing.

It was not, however, an entirely happy ship. Mr Nadir resented the City's perception of Tony Reading as the man who mattered. After Mr Reading had left Polly Peck, Mr Nadir revealingly said that 'Tony Reading came into the company as managing director of operations. There was a perception that he was chief executive. I have always been chief executive.'

Tim Wood, the company's ambitious treasurer, fell out with David Fawcus, and their relationship became so strained that the two could scarcely bear to be in the same room together. Mr Nadir was persuaded by Mr Reading and Mr Fawcus to fire Mr Wood. But in a rebuff to his two top managers, Mr Nadir immediately found a job for Mr Wood with South Audley Management. Mr Wood was later to return to Polly Peck as head of investor relations.

Another clash came over Mr Nadir's external public relations consultant, William Grosvenor, whose firm Wheatsheaf was on the other side of Piccadilly in smart St James's Street. Mr Grosvenor could be somewhat impulsive. On one occasion a Scottish newspaper rang Polly Peck to ask for the company's comment on rumours that the Stock Exchange was investigating suspected insider dealing in Polly Peck's shares. The firm answered the query in the normal way: 'We don't comment on market rumours.'

It was unlikely that the company itself would know whether there had been insider dealing in its shares (dealing by an investor on the basis of privileged access to information), or whether there was a Stock Exchange investigation. The Exchange would no more tell it about its investigations than it would an enquiring journalist. However, Mr Grosvenor rang the Scottish newspaper right back, saying that Polly Peck categorically denied the rumour and that if the Scottish paper printed anything about it, 'the consequences could be serious'. He went on to blame the Greeks for the rumour, and the Scottish newspaper went on to report his outburst.

Anyway, Wheatsheaf's services were dispensed with, even though Mr Grosvenor was a devoted admirer of Mr Nadir, and Mr Nadir was a devoted admirer of Mr Grosvenor's connections. He was a cousin of the Duke of Westminster, Britain's richest man.

Wheatsheaf was reinstated later by Mr Nadir, and Mr Grosvenor was charged with making the company's corporate video – an expensive production that whipped around the world in a celebration of Polly Peck's 'commitment to growth on a global scale' and to its 'proper husbandry of resources'.

At times Mr Nadir suspected the new team of plotting to take the company over through a management buy-out. One of the things that the Reading team had been busy doing was improving the company's records of who its 13,000 shareholders were. Malcolm Fenner had obtained the board's approval (under section 212 of the Companies Act) to get behind the many nominee names on the company's share register. Such an exercise could have been seen as a plot to enable somebody at a later stage to woo the then more accessible shareholders with an offer for their shares.

It could also have been seen as a way of finding out if anybody was trying to build up a big stake in the company (disguised behind a number of nominee names) in order to mount a takeover. Mark

Ellis subsequently said that the section 212 search had thrown up nothing of sufficient concern to be reported to the board.

A conspiracy was more easily imagined because Mark Ellis, the longest-serving member of the top-management triumvirate, had moved to New York in the summer of 1988. That had left the two newcomers, Tony Reading and David Fawcus, in charge in London, and the two of them might have hoped to get the City's support for a deal that would have put Mr Reading in the chief executive's chair and Mr Nadir out of it. In any case suspicions were aroused, and for a period in early 1989 Mr Nadir demanded that all the company's mail pass through his office, run with rigid efficiency by his personal assistant Aisling Daley, a tall, stylish dresser who drove around in a white GTi company car.

The simmering hostility came to a head on a warm day in May 1989. Polly Peck was sponsoring a three-day show-jumping event at Windsor, attended by Princess Margaret. Although Mr Nadir was fond of horses, and the company had sponsored a dressage event at Goodwood the previous year, the strongest horse connection was through David Fawcus whose daughter was a show-jumper close to getting on the national team. Elizabeth Forsyth, the head of South Audley Management, was also a keen horsewoman. Her office was filled with pictures of the animals and she enjoyed riding around the grounds of Baggrave Hall.

Mr Nadir had decided not to attend the Windsor event. But as the Polly Peck executives were about to sit down to lunch with the 150 guests that had assembled to impress, word came through that Mr Nadir had asked the company's personnel officer to fire a number of key executives. These included a couple of British executives of Sunzest, Polly Peck's Cypriot fresh fruit operation, and Vi Jensen, the financial controller. Also dismissed (without his knowledge) was David Fawcus's secretary.

Tony Reading drove straight back to Berkeley Square where he had a stormy meeting with Mr Nadir in which he demanded that the sacked staff be reinstated. Mr Nadir refused. When news of the row between the two most powerful men in the company became known to the press, a company spokesman said, 'There is no boardroom split, and it seems to us that too much has been made of these internal rearrangements.'

Anybody fooled by these semantic niceties was put right just a month later when Mr Reading resigned. He said he was leaving because 'My responsibilities are going to be shared among more people. My job is being diluted.' A number of other members of the Reading team left soon after, including Malcolm Fenner. Although David Fawcus stayed, the team designed and put together to boost Polly Peck's credibility was in shreds.

Inevitably, the company's share price fell on the news of the management departures. To Mr Nadir at the time this could have been either good news or bad news. It was already being suggested that he wanted to take the company private. His sister has said that he was talking about this as early as 1988.

'Going private' would have involved Mr Nadir in buying all the Polly Peck shares that he did not already own, thus removing the company from the Stock Exchange altogether. This would also have removed the hassles of being constantly in the public eye, the need to placate investors and to answer the impertinent questions of financial journalists.

It would not have been a totally novel thing for a man in his position to have done. Other entrepreneurs such as Richard Branson, who started the Virgin record and airline group, and Andrew Lloyd Webber, whose Really Useful Company owned the copyright of such Lloyd Webber compositions as *Cats* and *Evita*, had done the same. Having turned their entrepreneurial creations into public companies, they had decided that the benefits of being a public company (in particular, greater access to the markets for capital) were outweighed by the disadvantages of being constantly accountable in public for everything that they did. In effect they had second thoughts about selling the family silver for a handful of betting slips called share certificates.

In order to take Polly Peck private, Mr Nadir would have had to offer shareholders a premium on the price for which they could sell their shares on the stock-market. The lower the share price, therefore, the less he would have had to pay to take the company out of the prying eyes of the City.

But that was not in fact the strategy that Mr Nadir was intending to pursue in the summer of 1989. For even as Tony Reading resigned, Polly Peck was planning the biggest and best deal in its history. 'If anything, the pace at Polly is set to quicken now,' wrote the converted Michael Walters in July 1989. 'There are deals galore on the boil, perhaps in fruit. Polly is so much smarter than the average company.' The excitement generated inside the smart Polly by just one of those deals was more than enough to shrug off the loss of Mr Reading and his followers.

However, ambitious deals are expensive and require lots of money. Financing the major deal that the company was cooking would require turning to its shareholders yet again, scarcely a year after the last big rights issue had raised £133 million from them. The higher the company's share price, the better a rights issue would be for Mr Nadir. He would have to issue fewer new shares (and therefore dilute his stake less) in order to raise a given sum of money for the intended purchase.

Fortunately for Polly Peck, its share price soon began to rise again following the fall immediately after Mr Reading's resignation. This rise was helped by considerable buying of the shares by Mr Nadir himself. The day after the announcement that Mr Reading had resigned he bought 2 million shares at a price of some £2.70 a share (i.e., at a cost to him of £5.4 million). A month later he bought a further 1.5 million shares at an average price of almost £3.02 (costing £4.5 million). Presumably the nigh-on £10 million with which he bought these shares was borrowed from banks. It must have made the banks feel warm to see that the money they were lending was helping to push up the Polly Peck share price. For the higher the share price, the greater was the security to back their loans.

Anyway, the mammoth deal that was on the boil was indeed in fruit. The world's biggest fresh fruit and vegetable growers and distributors are in the United States, companies like Castle & Cooke (which produces Dole fruits), United Brands (which owns Chiquita), and Del Monte. In 1989 Del Monte was part of a huge conglomerate called RJR Nabisco. It had been bought by the group a decade earlier in order to diversity its profits away from tobacco. (RJR stood for R. J. Reynolds, the manufacturer of Winston cigarettes.) Cigarettes produced huge profits for their manufacturers, but stock-market investors had been reading more government health warnings than profit and loss accounts.

Del Monte had acres and acres of banana and pineapple plantations in Guatemala and Costa Rica. It imported almost 50 per cent of the pineapples and 20 per cent of the bananas consumed in North America. It sent almost one million tons of bananas around the world every year, and the little yellow boomerangs accounted for over 80 per cent of its profits. Del Monte also had a huge food-processing operation which made its canned fruits the most famous name in the business. With its advertising slogan – 'The man from Del Monte says yes' – it had become a household name from Los Angeles to Liverpool.

In the autumn of 1988 RJR Nabisco became the victim of the biggest leveraged buy-out (LBO) in all financial history. Wall Street firms had fought tooth and nail for the privilege (and for fees of hundreds of millions of dollars) of putting together a $25 billion deal that would buy out the company's shareholders and put in new management. One of the Wall Street firms vying to do the deal was Shearson Lehman, the company which had bought L. Messel, Polly Peck's long-standing London broker. The chief executive of RJR Nabisco, put in after the LBO, was Lou Gerstner, a stocky senior manager with American Express whose signature adorned the company's famous travellers' cheques. American Express owned Shearson Lehman.

The LBO left RJR Nabisco paying $3 billion a year to service the debt used to buy it out. There was no way that could go on indefinitely. Lou Gerstner's first job was to sell the company's bits and pieces as fast as possible in order to service its debts. It looked more like a sell-out than a buy-out.

One of the first things that Mr Gerstner sold was seven of the company's eight executive jets. The feeling of remorse at the break-up of a great company was tempered by a feeling that the crude extravagance of its management (described in vivid detail in the best-selling book by Bryan Burrough and John Helyar, *Barbarians at the Gate*) had brought about the break-up. As in the City of London, so on Wall Street: the lackadaisical greed of corporate America had played into the hands of the avid greed of Wall Street.

Del Monte was a prime candidate for sale, and early in 1989 Goldman Sachs, the New York investment bank charged with finding a buyer for it, sent a prospectus out to more than 100 potential purchasers. One of them was Polly Peck, and the mooted purchase price was £1.5 billion. David Fawcus later described how Polly Peck had 'had a day with the managers of all the Del Monte businesses in June'. That was after the Windsor Horse Trials but before Tony Reading's resignation. It must have been all the harder for him to resign knowing that Polly Peck stood a chance of becoming one of the greatest names in the fresh-fruit business.

During the summer the contenders for Del Monte were whittled down to single figures, including the great American firms of United Brands and Castle & Cooke. Mark Ellis, Polly Peck's director in New York, was closely involved in the negotiations, as were David Fawcus and Anil Doshi, Mr Nadir's faithful accountant. Asil Nadir himself was also deeply involved with the deal, and that summer there were plenty of rumours that he was putting together something 'very big' in New York.

Brian Haycox, the British-born boss of Del Monte's tropical fruit operation, made no secret of his preference for Polly Peck. 'When I got the list of companies wanting to buy Del Monte, Polly Peck was the one which made a perfect fit,' he said later. 'Polly is strong in citrus and in Europe, the Middle East and the Comecon countries. Del Monte is world leader in pineapples and number three in bananas, and strong in America and the Far East.'

By August the deal was done. The final problems were to do with the fact that Polly Peck did not want the whole of Del Monte, tinned fruit and all. It just wanted the fresh fruit business. RJR Nabisco was not happy about this because it wanted to sell Del Monte as a single chunk. But it realised that the big American firms that were the most likely buyers of the whole lot could be tied up for ages with anti-trust authorities in America. The authorities would look closely at the near-monopoly that Del Monte could give to an American buyer in certain American markets. At the end of the day the 'trust-busters' could simply veto the deal.

So RJR Nabisco played safe and accepted Polly Peck's offer of $875 million in cash for Del Monte's fresh fruit. It later sold the processed food businesses to a group of the company's managers for $1.5 billion. Polly Peck had bought a great name for a price which was a mere twelve times the company's earnings. The shares of Del Monte's rivals in America (United Brands and Castle & Cooke) were selling on P/E ratios of almost 20, and its rivals in the UK (Geest and Fyffes) were selling on multiples of over 15. RJR Nabisco made no secret of its disappointment at the price obtained for Del Monte.

The press had a field-day with its headlines – 'The man from Del Monte says yes'; 'the stock-market goes bananas' – as the market pushed Polly Peck's share price up by more than 20 per cent. As the company's stock-market value rose above £1 billion it became a candidate for the FT–SE (Footsie) index, the main UK stock-market index which embraced all the largest companies in the land. It was duly included in the index in October 1989. That opened Polly Peck to a number of big new investors who did no more than put their money in the constituent parts of the index. Their investments then performed no better and no worse than the index itself, which gave them the security of knowing that they could not be criticised for 'under-performing the market.'

The City's calculators set to reworking Polly Peck's figures. A P/E ratio of 15 (which, for a major fruit business in the FT–SE index, was not unreasonable) would shortly give the company a value of £3 billion, making it bigger than Midland Bank and its old mentor Thorn-EMI. The man who owned over a quarter of that was almost a billionaire. By the end of 1989 Mr Nadir was reckoned to be the thirty-sixth richest person in Britain; thirty-fifth was Tiny Rowland, the entrepreneurial chairman of Lonrho, owner of the *Observer* newspaper that had been almost perpetually hostile to Polly Peck. Lonrho was also a company with considerable industrial and trading interests in remote parts of the world. Like Polly Peck, it too understood the complexities of converting accounts from rapidly depreciating currencies into more stable sterling.

There were a few problems about the Del Monte purchase, but how to pay for it was the least of them. Polly Peck had arranged that the $875 million would be raised in a mixture of loans and equity (i.e., another rights issue). The rights issue was to be for £283 million. In his customary way Mr Nadir said that he would take up half of his rights, a gesture that would involve him in finding £35 million of cash. At the time he was well advanced in discussions with the Spastics Society about his £5 million donation to the charity.

The loan, of £330 million, was being put together by the London investment bank of Credit Suisse First Boston. This would increase Polly Peck's gearing unpleasantly, but it was not as bad as it looked. Del Monte was building nine ships – for tax reasons, it was said, rather than for basic commercial reasons. If Polly Peck could sell these for the £120 million that they were said to be worth, then it could cut what it needed to borrow for the deal by more than a third. In May 1990 Polly Peck did indeed sell these ships – to a Norwegian consortium, for £141 million.

Del Monte also promised to bring an unexpected bonus to Polly Peck's equity that would, in turn, improve the company's gearing ratio (of debt to equity). This was through the value of the Del Monte brand name, which Polly Peck said was worth £250 million.

Valuing brand names became a fashionable thing to do in the late 1980s. The absurdity of not valuing them had been made most apparent by Nestlé's purchase of Rowntree in 1988. Nestlé had paid £2 billion or so for something that did not appear in Rowntree's balance sheet at all. This 'something' was the fact that Rowntree's brands (such as Polo mints and Kit-Kat chocolate bars) were so well known that the company could charge much more for them in their distinctive wrappers than for exactly the same products without the name and without the wrapper.

Valuing this 'something' was not easy, but companies like the drinks and hotels group Grand Metropolitan had had a go. It was worth trying because the sums involved could be enormous. Grand Metropolitan had put a value of £500 million on just a few of its recently acquired brands, such as Smirnoff vodka. This was more than just a mere exercise in book-keeping, because the value of these brands went into the balance sheet and increased the company's equity by the same amount. Inserted into the crucial gearing ratio, that also increased the amount of debt that gearing-conscious bankers would let the company have.

A slight flaw about Del Monte was that most of its business came from commodity-type fruits like bananas and pineapples. They are mature businesses with little scope for expansion in developed countries, and Del Monte's profits from them had peaked in 1986. The biggest profit margins were to be found from the new fruits appearing in Western supermarkets: kumquats, mangoes and rambutans.

Polly Peck, however, was in a position to offer new markets for Del Monte's mature fruits. Turks eat hardly any bananas or pineapples, and the opening up of eastern Europe presented a huge population hungry for a banana, but a long way off acquiring a taste for a rambutan. Polly Peck had some entrée into eastern Europe, and had had for a while. Some years earlier one of its temperature-controlled plants in Mersin, in the south-east of Turkey, had been built by Polish contractors. In return Polly Peck shipped citrus fruit to Poland. Noble Raredon, the quoted company of Mr Nadir's sister Bilge Nevzat, once had plans to build a cardboard box factory in Poland.

In another deal, indicative of some of the complexity of Polly Peck's business and of Asil Nadir's commercial mind, the company had shipped oranges to Hungary. There they were consumed and the (Uni-Pac) boxes in which they had been shipped were re-used to package Hungarian apples bound for Finland. Finland then sent paper to Cyprus for use in Uni-Pac's cardboard box plant. Given the right quantities, there was no need for money to change hands.

On top of this there was, by the late 1980s, much promise for the future in a huge barter deal that Turkey had negotiated with the Soviet Union. In return for large quantities of Soviet natural gas, the Turks were to send products (many of them agricultural) to the Soviet Union.

When the Del Monte deal was almost complete, but before it was announced to the public, Polly Peck unveiled its new post-Reading management structure. Mark Ellis was recalled from New York to head up a new corporate development team. His sojourn in the Big Apple had been almost exactly as long as Mr Reading's in Berkeley Square.

At the heart of the new management structure was the appointment of four executive board directors to head each of the company's main businesses: a Turk, Radar Reshad, was in charge of the about-to-become-enormous food division; Joe Harris was in charge of the about-to-be-sold textiles division; Norbert Wirsching, a German who had come to the company through its purchase of Capetronic, was head of the electronics division; and Tahsin Karan, who had built up the most remarkable of Polly Peck's new businesses, the electronics operations in Turkey, was shunted sideways to head the leisure division. 'In the event that something happens to me,' said Mr Nadir, 'any of the divisional heads is eligible to take my role.' By the time something did happen to Mr Nadir – his arrest and charges against him of theft and false accounting – Joe Harris had left the company, Radar Reshad was persuaded by the administrators to resign, and the other two (who were very much operational managers) stayed out in the field and away from the flak.

'This effectively gives us four managing directors,' said Tim Wood at the time of the appointments. Mr Wood had just returned to Polly Peck from South Audley as investor-relations supremo, with the promise of a seat on the board. There were a number of other new appointments that added to the younger team being groomed for succession to the four managing directors. Among them was Dominic Henry, who had been a senior manager with BP in Turkey, and Peter Compson, who had been in charge of personnel at the Sedgwick Group, where Neil Mills, a long-serving Polly Peck non-executive director, had once been chairman.

The new team had hardly had time to draw breath and digest the Del Monte acquisition before Mr Nadir was pulling in yet more headlines with another sensational deal. But this time it was at the opposite end of the earth, and it was not so obviously the great deal that Del Monte had been.

Sansui was one of a bevy of Japanese electronics companies whose products provided home video and audio entertainment to much of the Western world. It was well known for its audio products, particularly its amplifiers, which accounted for almost all its turnover. But it was an example of something that Japan-struck Europe could scarcely believe existed: an unsuccessful Japanese electronics company. It had failed to move quickly enough from old-fashioned audio equipment into the new digital technology that a rapidly changing industry demanded. By 1989 it had made a loss for four consecutive years, and the Japanese were at a loss as to what to do with it.

To the outsider, however, Sansui had one hidden asset, and that was its quotation on the Tokyo Stock Exchange. The Japanese were being increasingly criticised in both America and Europe for the way in which their companies were free and able to buy publicly quoted companies on Anglo-Saxon-style stock-markets (for example, Sony had bought America's recording giant CBS in 1987), while Western companies were not free to do likewise in Japan.

By and large, Japanese companies are protected from takeover by the general Japanese distaste for hostile bids, and by the large number of any Japanese company's shares that are owned by those with a vested interest in avoiding a change of ownership – i.e., by the company's suppliers, its banks, and the people it supplies. For example, Matsushita, Sony's great rival and the manufacturer of JVC products, has significant stakes in over 300 different companies.

Japanese companies close ranks against foreign takeovers even more tightly than they do against domestic ones. A nation which values its traditions highly believes that foreign financiers are fickle, flighty folk. In the end, Polly Peck was not able to prove them wrong.

Polly Peck's interest in Sansui was stimulated by the company's well-known brand name. Written with the characters for 'mountain' and 'water', it was still worth something, although Polly Peck said that it was not going to put a value on it in its balance sheet, as it had with Del Monte. It saw Sansui as a label to stick on to all its electronics goods, in the same way that Del Monte was a label to stick on to all its fruits. After Sansui, all it would need would be a label to stick on to its hotels. When the Japanese bought the Intercontinental hotel chain, Mr Nadir turned his attention to the Sheraton hotel group for that purpose.

To the Japanese, Polly Peck's desire to purchase Sansui seemed rather strange. But they realised that they could use it to demonstrate that their Stock Exchange was not closed to foreign takeovers, without actually allowing a significant company to be taken over to make the point. At the announcement in Tokyo of Polly Peck's purchase of 51 per cent of Sansui for £69 million, the Japanese finance minister Ryutataro Hashimoto said that the acquisition 'demonstrates the open nature of the Japanese market'. Some indication of the significance of the deal for the Japanese came when Mr Nadir appeared as the main item on the evening television news that day.

Polly Peck made much of the way in which Mr Nadir had succeeded in breaking into the Japanese market where others had failed. Although the company frequently asserted that it was the first foreigner to take over a Japanese quoted company, in fact it was not. Both British Oxygen and the American pharmaceuticals group Merck had done so (though with lesser companies) in the early 1980s.

Polly Peck claimed that its success in getting Sansui was due to Mr Nadir's empathy with the Japanese. Mr Nadir himself said that 'There is a lot of similarity between Turkey and Japan. The concept of family; behaviour towards elders; respectfulness; losing face being the worst thing. And they are industrious.' After the deal, the chairman of an American company that had also been trying to buy a Japanese company rang Mr Nadir to ask him how the hell he had done it. His questions were full of thinly disguised hostility to the Japanese, and peppered with racist remarks. Mr Nadir told him that he had succeeded because his attitude was different. He respected the Japanese, and treated them with respect.

This may have been somewhat sanctimonious, especially since the apparently mild-mannered Mr Nadir could swear like a trooper in private and pepper his comments liberally with derogatory remarks about the English or the Turks. But he was right to say that his attitude was different. Unlike the brash American, he did not approach the Japanese (or anybody else) with an assumption of superiority. A shy person from a scarcely existent state of 170,000 people does not easily presume superiority over anybody.

The reaction of the City of London to the Sansui deal was mixed. Polly Peck's share price slipped slightly and Mr Nadir talked widely to the press to persuade them of the merits of the deal. The original intention had been to finance the purchase from the company's own resources, but that pushed its gearing ratio unacceptably over 100 per cent. So six weeks later the company issued some convertible shares to pay for Sansui. These were largely sold to Japanese investors.

But the gearing ratio was still high, and the financial pressure to sell some assets was so strong that it forced Polly Peck out of the business which had been its foundation and the basis of all its fortunes. In November most of its textile businesses were sold to a Hong Kong company called Brave Dragon for a net sum of £27.5 million. That left Polly Peck with virtually no textile business for the first time in its life. It also left the newly promoted Joe Harris with virtually no job. He retired in May 1990, but remained as a consultant to the company.

There were plenty in the City who had seen the Sansui deal as a coup. Peter Jones, the Messel's analyst who had said sweet things about Polly Peck for years, said, 'There's no question that by Christmas 1990, Polly Peck's shares will be trading at around £5 [they were then at £3.25], given both the Del Monte and

Sansui deals.' By Christmas 1990 Polly Peck's shares were virtually worthless; Mr Jones's long career with L. Messel had come to an end in the summer of 1990.

There was one last significant event for Polly Peck before the 1980s came to a close. Despite the respectability gained from the Del Monte and Sansui deals, and after all the excitement had calmed down, Polly Peck's share price was still based on a P/E ratio of only 7. That put a value on the company of about £1.4 billion. Yet analysts were estimating that if the Del Monte bit alone were to be valued on the same basis as its American rivals, United Brands and Castle & Cooke, it would be worth £2 billion.

Polly Peck was not unique in this situation. Many other conglomerates found themselves worth much less than the sum of their parts – a sort of inverted synergy. One answer to the problem of how to realise the full potential value of these companies – a problem that had vexed Mr Nadir deeply for many years – was to de-merge them. This meant splitting up the conglomerate and getting separate stock-market quotations for different bits of it.

Mr Nadir was planning to do this by bundling all Polly Peck's electronics businesses into Sansui, which would have retained its stock-market quotation in Tokyo, and by putting all its fruit business into Del Monte, which would have then been floated on the New York Stock Exchange. The rest of the businesses – basically leisure – would remain in the parent company with its London quotation.

The key to the whole plan was to get a quotation for Del Monte in New York, and Polly Peck assumed that this would be straightforward. But it was not. The company was sent away and told to come back later on the grounds that it was too soon after the splitting of Del Monte from RJR Nabisco for Del Monte to be separately quoted.

To Mr Nadir, accustomed (as he saw it) to Greek persecution for his help to northern Cyprus, this excuse smelled of Greek lobbying and political pressure in Washington. The Greeks could have had a reason for not wanting a quotation in New York. For if the Turkish Cypriot businesses of Polly Peck were to be swallowed up by Del Monte, a New York quotation would put America's seal of approval on Polly Peck's ownership of the orchards around Güzelyurt (formerly Morphou) which was still contested by the Greek Cypriots.

The failure of Polly Peck to get a separate New York quotation for Del Monte was a serious setback. It cut the company off from sources of finance which would have reduced its burrowing and its gearing, and which might have enabled it to survive the cash crisis that was to put it into the hands of administrators a few months later. If Mr Nadir's suspicions about the Greek lobbying were correct, then it can be argued that, in a way, his old enemies did finally bring about his company's downfall. For all its diversification into the furthest-flung markets of the world, Polly Peck never escaped from its Cypriot origins.

As the end of the 1980s approached, statisticians started churning numbers to find the best-performing shares of the decade. Polly Peck came way out on top. Its 126,590 per cent increase compared with an increase of 480 per cent for the main London stock-market index – not bad for a company which had once lost a quarter of its stock-market value in just twenty minutes. This made it not only the best-performing share in Britain in the 1980s, but also the best-performing share on all the major stock-markets of the world: the United States, Japan and West Germany.

The extent by which it beat its nearest challenger was even more extraordinary. In Britain second place went to a company called Albert Fisher which was also in the food business. Albert Fisher's share price had increased by a modest 8360 per cent in the 1980s. There was nothing that could match either of these two in the United States, Japan or West Germany.

But if Polly Peck's story was extraordinary in the 1980s it was to become even more so in the 1990s.

CHAPTER ELEVEN

THE BRIDGES COLLAPSE

AS Polly Peck entered the 1990s the company was at its peak. At its annual general meeting on 22 May at the Grosvenor House Hotel, on London's posh Park Lane, champagne corks popped as shareholders drank to the health of their miraculous chairman. Stockbrokers like Barclays de Zoete Wedd (BZW) were reckoning that the company would be worth £7 a share if it were broken up, even though its shares could be bought on the stock-market for just over £4 each.

There was still some tidying-up to be done after the purchases of Del Monte and Sansui. In the eyes of the City, Polly Peck had only one fault – its gearing was too high. In the eyes of Mr Nadir, the company's fault was the usual one – its stock-market valuation was too low. So the tidying-up was designed to rectify these two failings.

In the first half of 1990, while he was trying in vain to obtain a New York quotation for Del Monte and the company's other fresh fruit businesses, Mr Nadir was wrapping up the electronics businesses. In June it was announced that Sansui would buy Polly Peck's Hong Kong subsidiary, Capetronic, and its Italian subsidiary, Imperial, for £307.5 million. The purchases were financed by an issue of Sansui shares that was almost all taken up by Polly Peck.

On the Tokyo stock-market companies have, on average, a much higher P/E ratio than they do in London or New York. This is partly because Japanese companies pay much lower dividends than do British and American companies. Investors depend more on capital gain than on earnings for the return on their investment.

Since Japanese companies reveal as little as possible in their balance sheets, the price of their shares is determined as much by rumour and sentiment as by their actual earnings (and ability to pay dividends) or by their underlying value. The Tokyo stock-market is a bit like a fairground on the periphery of the corporate market – fun, but not to be taken too seriously.

This bundling of Polly Peck's electronics businesses meant that Capetronic and Imperial would be more highly valued as a subsidiary of a company quoted in Tokyo (i.e., of Sansui) than they would be as part of a quoted company in London. This was particularly true since, as a group, their earnings were far from sparkling, and that would have affected their share price more in London than it would in Tokyo. Capetronic made a pre-tax profit of £14.8 million in 1989, but Imperial made a loss in the same period of £5.6 million – although by May 1990 Polly Peck was saying that 'Imperial has begun to trade profitably.' Sansui made a loss in 1989 of £24.5 million on sales of £85.5 million.

The other main part of Polly Peck's electronics business was the Turkish company Vestel. It was not packaged with Sansui but rather, in June 1990, was floated on the resurgent Istanbul Stock Exchange. Some £70 million was raised by the successful sale of 15 per cent of the company to the Turkish public. This money was used to reduce Polly Peck's debt, and it put a market value on Vestel of some £460 million. That was said to give the company a P/E ratio of almost 16, about twice the ratio of the Polly Peck group in London.

But all this tinkering with P/E ratios was not helping much with Polly Peck's other problem – its debts. At the end of 1989 the company's net debt had stood at £804 million; by the end of June 1990 it had risen to £864 million. According to the company's accounts, the interest charge for the half-year was a mere £18.3 million. The *Independent* newspaper said this meant that Polly Peck was earning 36 per cent on its deposits and paying 15 per cent for its loans. 'Would that we all could do this,' was the newspaper's wry comment. In 1989 the company had reported receiving £12 million more in interest than it had paid out.

The company's debt was rising partly because it was set on a £200 million investment programme in the leisure industry. This included a considerable investment in hotels and holiday villages in northern Cyprus. The lavish Jasmine Court was opened in September 1990, and money was pouring into the even more lavish Crystal Cove. The showpiece of the expanding leisure business was Polly Peck's $60 million Sheraton Voyager hotel on the Turkish Riviera. It was opened with great fanfare at the end of August.

Turkey's tourist industry had been booming for a number of years. Visitors to the country had increased from 2.4 million in 1986 to 4.2 million in 1988. There was the suggestion that more and more of northern Europe's packaged travellers, bored with familiar Mediterranean resorts in Greece and Spain, would come to lie on Turkish beds.

The main focus of their interest would be teeming Istanbul, with its bazaars and minarets, and the south-west coastline stretching from the sea port of Bodrum (once called Halicarnassus and home of one of the seven wonders of the ancient world) to Antalya, the largest town in the region. Polly Peck had plonked its wedding-cake of a Sheraton on the edge of Antalya, not far from the city's international airport. Like earlier Polly Peck projects in Turkey, it brazenly challenged all around to rise to its standards. On the hotel's ninth floor was a magnificent penthouse which was reserved for Mr Nadir's use. He may have dreamed of retreating there much as the reclusive unkempt Howard Hughes had to his hotel penthouses in Las Vegas. Howard Hughes was a man who fascinated the retiring Mr Nadir.

The hotel had a sort of double opening. One weekend there was a United Nations conference attended by the Turkish prime minister, Yildirim Akbulut, the president, Turgut Ozal, and his wife Semra, together with a bevy of foreign dignitaries. Mr Nadir was there too, a dispossessed soul from Cyprus mingling with the mighty. Dressed in some of the world's most expensive clothes, he gave a speech which could not match his appearance. His nervously tapping foot and hunched shoulders indicated a man ill at ease.

The second opening was for 'the trade'. Travel agents and tour operators flew in for the occasion from all over Europe. So too did bankers and brokers to whom Mr Nadir was eager to show off Polly Peck's latest asset. Down from Istanbul was a sprinkling of society, including Sakip Sabanci. The Turkish minister of tourism attended. And so did Rauf Denktash, president of the small piece of land fifty miles off the Turkish coast where Mr Nadir's heart belonged.

When the chairman of Polly Peck arrived among the dazzling floodlights, the assembled Turks and Cypriots stood up to applaud him. It was as if some demi-god had descended among mere mortals in a reincarnation of the mythology which infuses almost every rock in those parts. Los Paraguayos played, and not a Turkish wail was heard. It was thrilling, if expensive. The hotel's opening cost something in the region of $1.5 million.

The attending 'trade' was impressed by the professionalism of it all. It was a hotel that could sit comfortably in any sophisticated international resort anywhere. Polly Peck's reputation as a 'class act' was enhanced. One guest who stayed there said he would give it five stars, and the Sheraton in Istanbul only three and a half.

Back in London Mr Nadir's diary was being filled with similarly glamorous appointments. In the autumn he was to be the star of the high-society Harley Street Ball, held every other year at the Grosvenor House Hotel. The ball was being organised by Lady Anna Brocklebank, a Harley Street physician and close friend of Mr Nadir's public relations advisor, William Grosvenor. At the ball Mr Nadir was to be the auctioneer of a number of goods to be sold for charity.

But he was never to attend the ball. By the time it took place he was desperately trying to shore up a crumbling empire. The Iraqi invasion of Kuwait in early August made investors nervous about a company with so much business in a place which had a border with Iraq. They were right to be nervous. No sooner had Mr Nadir flown back to London from its opening than the Sheraton Voyager was deluged with cancellations. It was not alone. So were all hotels in the region, including the large number that Polly Peck was developing in northern Cyprus.

Meanwhile Mr Nadir had been increasingly moving his personal affairs to secretive Switzerland. In 1989 he had bought a small Swiss computer company called Alptech. This was making losses, and partly in return for buying it through his private Swiss company, Nadir Investments, Mr Nadir obtained the right to reside in Switzerland. He already held both a British and a Turkish passport, but Swiss residence could have been an extremely valuable addition.

Mr Nadir had been involved for a long time in discussions with the British tax authorities over his tax bills, and in particular over the huge capital-gains tax liabilities which arose from buying and selling Polly Peck's shares as they climbed steeply after the stock-market crash of 1987. If he could arrange his affairs to spend most of his time living outside the UK, his personal tax liability might be considerably reduced.

Jason Davies, who was already living in France and working for Sipa Press, the Paris photographic agency of which Mr Nadir owned 49 per cent, was despatched to Switzerland. There he was put in charge of Nadir Investments, a family company which had been set up in May 1989. Mr Davies lived in a five-bedroomed house in the village of Founex which was rented for him by the company. It was a far cry from the small flat in Saffron Walden which had been his home before he met Mr Nadir. It was not, however, a far cry from Lake Geneva and the village of Givrins where Nadir Investments had bought a farmhouse. Mr Davies set out to convert the farmhouse into the corporate headquarters of the Nadir family's Swiss company.

It was tempting to speculate that this was part of a plan to make Switzerland the repository of what was left of Polly Peck after the New York flotation of Del Monte and the Tokyo flotation of Sansui. Such a move could have been helped by the fact that Polly Peck was already quoted on the Zurich Stock Exchange.

But the plan may have been slightly different in view of what Mr Nadir came up with in the middle of August 1990. Perhaps Nadir Investments was designed as a vehicle to shift a privately owned Polly Peck out of the UK. Both Elizabeth Forsyth and Jason Davies have denied that it was, but Nadir Investments may well have had some role in Mr Nadir's August plans.

At the beginning of the month Polly Peck's share price was 434 pence, a bit down on its high for the year (and the highest price it ever reached) of 464 pence. But on 2 August Saddam Hussein invaded Kuwait and the stock-market started to mark down the share prices of companies that had business in the Near or Middle East. By 10 August Polly Peck's share price was down to 393 pence, a fall of almost 10 per cent in ten days. Over the same period the FT–SE index had fallen by less than 5 per cent.

Over the weekend of 11/12 August Mr Nadir put into effect his plan to take the company private, a plan he had discussed 'on and off' with his family and close advisors for at least two years. Elizabeth Forsyth remembers that she had lunch with Mr Nadir on Friday 10 August at his offices in Switzerland. 'At 7 p.m. he told me of the approach he intended to make to the board. He had been thinking about it for a long time. I asked him whether he was serious and he said he thought the timing was right. I said it was fine and we would need to assemble his advisors the following morning.' Mrs Forsyth must have wondered what her position would be if Mr Nadir took the whole of Polly Peck into his private empire.

Back in London on Saturday 11 August Mr Nadir talked with his personal accountants Rawlinson & Hunter and decided to call a board meeting for the following day. Polly Peck's executives were used to being expected to work during weekends; Mr Nadir himself rarely took days off. 'In my case,' he said, 'the seven days are all similar. A Sunday is no different from a Monday.'

On Rawlinson & Hunter's advice Mr Nadir called S. J. Berwin, one of the best-known firms of City lawyers but not a firm that Mr Nadir had ever dealt with before. During the Saturday afternoon he met Robert Burrow of S. J. Berwin in order to draft a letter to the Polly Peck board setting out his intentions. That same afternoon David Fawcus rang Mr Nadir to tell him that two Sunday newspapers (the *Observer* and the *Sunday Times*) were expected to publish articles the following day about the UK tax authorities' investigation of dealing in the company's shares by Swiss 'letter-box' companies that they suspected could be a veil to enable UK residents to avoid paying tax. During the telephone conversation Mr Nadir told Mr Fawcus of the next day's board meeting and of his intention to make an offer for the company.

Besides a lawyer, Mr Nadir needed a merchant bank for his proposed deal. On the Saturday afternoon Mr Burrow contacted George Magan at his home. A qualified accountant like so many others, Mr Magan was a founder/director of Hambro Magan, a small specialist merchant bank. He spoke briefly to Mr Nadir and advised him that a good deal of work would need to be done before he would be in a position to make an announcement of his intention to take the company private. Mr Magan was not told that a board meeting had already been convened for the next day.

The most vital thing that Mr Nadir needed in order to make the offer was money, and he told Mr Burrow that he was totally confident that financing would be available to him. In the Stock Exchange's subsequent description of the events surrounding the offer, it claimed that Mr Nadir had said that 'such funds would be available from Turkey.' Now since the deal would require

Mr Nadir to raise over £1 billion, it was most unlikely that all of that would be available from Turkey, or that Mr Nadir could ever have believed that it would be. Mr Nadir himself subsequently said that the Stock Exchange's version of events was inaccurate, claiming that he had said that 'Part of the financing would come from Turkey'. Mark Ellis said that financing would have come from at least eight countries. Given the way that non-Turkish banks had been lending Mr Nadir money in recent years, it was not unreasonable for him to believe that they might come up with what was needed for the buy-out.

On Sunday 12 August David Fawcus met Mr Nadir before the 1 p.m. board meeting and tried in vain to persuade him not to present his proposal in haste. At the board meeting six of the eight executive directors were present (including Mr Nadir) and two of the five non-executive directors. Only two directors who were not present were not consulted by telephone. Mr Nadir presented his letter to the board in which he stated his intention to make an offer. He explained that he was writing at an early stage in order to avoid creating a false market in the company's shares. By which he meant that anybody who caught wind of the deal might buy the company's shares knowing that an offer from Mr Nadir would be (as Mr Nadir later confirmed) at the conventional premium of some 20–30 per cent above the company's then share price.

Mr Nadir withdrew from the meeting, and the deputy chairman, Sir Michael Sandberg, took over the discussion with the company's own advisors: the lawyers Clifford Chance and the merchant bank Chartered WestLB. The redoubtable Sir Michael had joined the board as deputy chairman less than three months earlier. A tough chairman of the Hongkong and Shanghai Bank from 1977 to 1986, he had retired to homes in Nice and Knightsbridge. Like several other Polly Peckers he was a horse-racing fan.

The board was advised that it needed to make an immediate announcement of the offer, naming Mr Nadir as the person making the approach. An announcement that it had received 'an approach which may lead to an offer for the company' was duly made late that day.

Berwin's, Hambro Magan and Lehman Brothers, the company's brokers who had not attended the Sunday meeting, were all surprised to see the announcement in the papers the next day.

Naturally it was enough to send the Polly Peck share price up: on the Monday it jumped by 47 pence to 450 pence, thus counteracting any negative effect that might have been expected from the stories which had duly appeared in the *Sunday Times* and the *Observer* the previous day.

Monday and Tuesday were days of meetings, with Mr Nadir seeing his advisors (including Citibank Private Bank from 41 Berkeley Square and Rawlinson & Hunter). The company appointed the top merchant bank Morgan Grenfell to work for it alongside Chartered WestLB. Mr Nadir had not formally appointed a merchant bank advisor for himself. In the end he never did.

By Thursday 16 August Mr Nadir was beginning to express concern about the negative reactions to his proposal that he was receiving from shareholders and from some of the company's managers. For his bid to be successful he would need the acceptance of 90 per cent of the shares that he did not already own – at the time he owned some 26 per cent of Polly Peck. So any indication that his proposal (which at no stage was described in any detail) might not be acceptable to shareholders could scupper the deal. Daunted by the financing needed for the deal, the stock-market had taken the company's share price back down to 405 pence.

On Friday 17 August Mr Nadir told Berwin's Mr Burrow that he was proposing to withdraw his intention to make an offer. He said that this was as a result of being approached by shareholders representing some 15 per cent of the equity. His sister Bilge Nevzat said that he had received letters from small shareholders begging him not to go private, and that they had brought tears to his eyes. Mr Nadir subsequently gave the Stock Exchange the names of three of these shareholders. No shareholders had approached the company's brokers to say that they would not accept any offer from Mr Nadir. The company's biggest institutional shareholder, Friends Provident, said that it definitely did not put pressure on Mr Nadir to withdraw the offer.

But Mr Nadir was adamant at a lunchtime meeting on the Friday that it would be futile for him to continue. At 3.27 p.m. that day the board made public his letter formally notifying them of his intention to withdraw. Polly Peck's share price duly fell by 19 per cent in ninety minutes, back down to 324 pence, way below what it had been a week earlier, before the buy-out had been proposed.

The haste and the degree of preparation behind the proposal were most unusual. They were also disruptive to the market (which was something that Mr Nadir had said his public announcement had been designed to avoid). The market's expectations had been raised on a Monday only to be dashed by Friday. The London Stock Exchange's Quotations Panel subsequently looked into the events behind the proposal and the withdrawal. Its conclusions were published at the end of August, and it criticised several aspects of the events:

1 The lack of preparation to normal standards by Mr Nadir prior to advising the board of his intention to make an offer for the company.
2 Mr Nadir's apparent decision to ignore advice received, albeit on an informal basis, from Hambro Magan, that any formal notification of his intention to make an offer for the company was premature and should not be made.
3 The convening of the board meeting by Mr Nadir to consider his proposal for 1 p.m. on Sunday 12 August at only twenty-four hours' notice with no evident need to hold a meeting with such urgency.
4 The terms of the announcement made by the board did not highlight, to the extent that they should have done, the fact that the proposals were still at a preliminary stage.

Mr Nadir reacted vehemently to the Quotations Committee's report, saying that his reputation had been 'dragged through the mud' by a 'flippant report'. He objected to the suggestion that he had not made adequate preparations, arguing that his talks with Berwin's and Hambro Magan on the Saturday were sufficient in view of the tentative wording of his letter to the board. He was also angry that the report had been passed on to the Department of Trade and Industry and the Serious Fraud Office as a matter of course.

Later, Mr Nadir admitted that he might have acted 'a bit too fast' in presenting his buy-out proposal. But, he went on to add, 'Whatever I do, it's in my nature to think and act fast.' His behaviour is more explicable in the light of his tendency to think of things as born from the moment they are conceived. In his state of mind at the time, it may well have been enough for him to announce the buy-out for him to believe that it had happened.

In the event, the unsuccessful attempt succeeded in destroying in less than a week any confidence that the City of London had that Polly Peck was no flibbertigibbet – confidence that it had taken years of painstaking effort to build up. From the day that Mr Nadir called off his intention to buy out the company, Polly Peck's shares fell sharply. It is no wonder that he did not look a happy man when being fêted at the opening of the Sheraton Voyager hotel in Antalya at the end of August.

To try to restore some of the lost confidence, the company brought forward the announcement of its interim results to 3 September. These showed a growth in pre-tax profit from £64.4 million in the same half year of 1989 to £110.5 million (which included an exceptional gain of £40.5 million from the flotation of Vestel in June). The interim dividend was increased to 5.5 pence per share, although shareholders were never actually to receive it. By the time it was due (15 January 1991) the administrators had blocked it.

But the shining interim results could not stop the share-price slide. Nor could Mr Nadir's heavy buying of Polly Peck's shares. On 5 September he bought 4 million shares at a cost of more than £11 million. 'His faith in the company continues undiminished,' said his public relations consultant William Grosvenor. By then the price of a Polly Peck share was down to 290 pence.

'None of us here has any idea why the hell this is happening,' said Dominic Henry as the slide continued. Mr Henry was Polly Peck's head of investor relations, a job he had taken on when his predecessor Tim Wood had abruptly left Polly Peck earlier in the year. No reason for his sudden departure had been given, but he may have felt that Mr Nadir was not going to fulfil yet another promise – to make him a main board director. Shortly after Tim Wood left, his old foe David Fawcus was promoted to deputy chief executive of the group, and a new finance director, Reg Mogg, was brought into the company.

By 20 September Polly Peck's share price had fallen to 243 pence. That was 38 per cent less than on the day before Mr Nadir's buy-out announcement, and nearly half of its highest value in the year. As the share price fell, banks which had lent money to Mr Nadir on the security of his shares wanted either more shares to back their loans, or cash to make the value of their loans no more than 60 per cent of the value of the shares. In cases where a borrower cannot meet these so-called margin calls, banks have the right to start selling the shares they hold as security. The bankers who had lent money to Restro Investments, the holder of Mr Nadir's stake in Polly Peck, started to sell the shares they held as security as early as the last day of August.

The final straw came on 20 September. On the previous day the offices of South Audley Management had been invaded by the Serious Fraud Office (SFO). The SFO's investigators had arrived first thing in the morning and had shut Barbara Jackson-Smith and several of SAM's female staff in a room for several hours. The SFO say they followed normal police practice, but the Turkish press reported that the women had been denied access to their lawyers and a lavatory. The SFO's sleuths left the building with a pile of documents and a number of computer discs.

The SFO had received the Stock Exchange's report on the aborted buy-out of Polly Peck, and it had also received information that the Exchange had gathered about suspected insider-dealing in Polly Peck shares over a prolonged period of time. But earlier in the week the SFO had been contacted by Polly Peck's former head of investor relations, Tim Wood, who had talked to them at length about things he claimed had happened at SAM. The SFO invited Mr Nadir to come to their offices for an interview on 20 September, the day following their visit to SAM.

The SFO was a new animal designed specifically to deal with complicated fraud cases involving sums in excess of £1 million. Towards the end of the 1980s the British government had become increasingly concerned at the growing number of cases of large-scale fraud and white-collar crime that were coming to the public's attention. These included the Guinness case where a concerted share-rigging scheme had helped the company to buy the Distillers group; and the Ferranti case where the electronics company had found allegedly fictitious contracts for hundreds of millions of dollars at ISC, an American defence company which it had bought in 1987. These cases were in danger of turning the public against the Conservative Party policies of free-market economics and deregulation, policies that were believed to spawn large-scale crookery.

The SFO brought together accountants, lawyers and police investigators to look, as a team, into suspected cases of substantial fraud. There was a feeling that without the professional help of accountants and lawyers, the police were not sufficiently skilled to investigate complex cases. The SFO was actually set up by the Criminal Justice Act of 1987, and in the Act was given draconian powers (under section 2) to force witnesses to talk. Anybody served with a section 2 notice loses the right to silence. That right is still available to common murderers or rapists, but it was not available to Mr Nadir on the September day when he went to the SFO's offices on London's Elm Street for a three-hour interrogation. Section 2 gives the SFO more power to abuse civil liberties than any other body in Britain, with the possible exception of the Customs and Excise authorities.

It is an awesome responsibility for such a young organisation, staffed by lawyers and accountants who have chosen a career in the civil service rather than in private practice, where they could probably earn twice as much. Any of the forty-or-so accountants and lawyers on the SFO's staff can issue section 2 notices and many firms of solicitors have expressed concern that section 2 notices 'fly around like confetti', and that investigators who issue them seemed to go on 'fishing expeditions', giving the interviewee little clue as to what charges are being investigated. In normal criminal cases (again like murder or rape) suspects have the right not to co-operate if they are not told what it is they are accused of.

When he arrived voluntarily at the SFO's offices for his 'nightmare on Elm Street' on 20 September Mr Nadir was served with a section 2 notice. After a three-hour interrogation by an SFO accountant, David Morrison, and a solicitor, Robert Wardle, Mr Nadir complained that the SFO's questioning 'lacked direction'. He appealed to the courts to demand that the SFO give details of the transactions which were under investigation. This legal pursuit was dropped after Mr Nadir was arrested in December and the specific nature of the charges against him were made known. The courts thus lost the opportunity to rule on the extent and nature of the SFO's powers.

Almost more disturbing than the SFO's methods of investigation, however, was the fact that the investigation rapidly became known to the public. On the morning of 20 September a banker in the City of London received confirmation that Mr Nadir was to be interrogated that afternoon. Throughout the day the SFO confirmed to callers that it had visited SAM's offices the previous day, but there was no public announcement of the fact. That allowed wild rumours to fly around, including theories that Mr Nadir had been killed, kidnapped and arrested.

Over the Nadir affair the SFO appeared to be as leaky as a sieve. The press received so many tit-bits of suspicion that the Turkish ambassador in London eventually maintained that Mr Nadir could not have a fair trial in Britain. At Mr Nadir's second court hearing at Bow Street in January 1991 his lawyer complained that he had first learned of what the SFO was proposing in court in the previous day's Sunday papers. The magistrate stressed that leaks from the SFO must cease. The SFO denied that they had ever taken place.

Banks that held Mr Nadir's shares as security for his loans on that morning in September when the Polly Peck music stopped, rushed to find a chair. In some cases they ruthlessly crushed each other as they sold shares in order to get something back for the Nadir loans that they must have thought were doomed. A Citibank office in Switzerland started the rush by selling 7.9 million shares at 10.20 a.m. The unlucky buyer was UBS Phillips & Drew, a London broker owned by Union Bank of Switzerland, which eventually stood to lose some £14 million on the deal.

The share price fell from 243 pence to 108 pence before dealing in Polly Peck shares was suspended in the middle of the afternoon. Over 30 million Polly Peck shares changed hands on that day, and the value of Mr Nadir's stake fell by over £160 million in under five hours. Even on the next day, S. G. Warburg's Zurich office was able to sell a further 2.6 million shares before Polly Peck's quotation was suspended in Zurich as well as in London.

Mr Nadir has said that he was not notified about the sales of his shares by his personal bankers until 20 September and the days following. Had he not been asked previously by the banks to meet margin calls arising from the fall in the share price of Polly Peck? It is not clear whether the banks jumped the gun in selling Mr Nadir's shares, or whether they had followed all the necessary processes and were perfectly within their rights to sell at the first hint of bad news.

Polly Peck's shareholders were left bothered and bewildered by their losses. This was the most dramatic corporate collapse that Britain had ever seen. But how could something that had been worth over £1.5 billion one month be worth next to nothing the next, simply because its chairman had been questioned by the SFO? There had been no sudden disclosure of hitherto unknown trading losses in the group's operating units, nor of huge foreign exchange losses in the company's treasury department – more usual causes of a helter-skelter fall in a company's share price.

At this stage Mr Nadir himself had not even been charged with anything, let alone found guilty. But even if he were about to be frog-marched off to serve an indefinite term in jail, surely Del Monte and the electronics businesses were worth well over £1 billion, with him or without him? As the Lex column on the *Financial Times* put it: 'Polly Peck's market price has lost all contact with fundamentals. At 108 pence, the prospective P/E is 2.3 and the gross yield 19.8 per cent, a death-bed rating that companies reach only when nearly bust.' It was the most bizarre destruction of a corporation that anybody had ever seen.

Creditors and shareholders were not the only ones to lose from the collapse. Representatives of the Spastics Society had flown out to Turkey in the summer to see how they might develop services for severely handicapped children in rural areas there. While in Istanbul they heard of Mr Nadir's abortive attempt to buy out Polly Peck and began to wonder about the fate of Oaktree, the special school that was to be financed by Mr Nadir's £5 million donation to the Society. On their return to London Mr Nadir sent them a fax saying that, God willing, he would make every endeavour to ensure that the project went ahead. Shortly after, Oaktree was abandoned.

There had never been any doubt in anybody's mind of Mr Nadir's desire and intention to make the project work. Some of his small staff at South Audley also seemed to be genuinely seized by it. But in the end the much-publicised charitable gift that was to have come from Mr Nadir's own pocket amounted to little more than £200,000. This had been sent to cover some of the operating costs of setting up the project, and had been received by the society in lumps at irregular intervals. Cheques would arrive with no more than a compliments slip attached. They were Polly Peck cheques, and Mr Nadir (who had the authority to sign company cheques on his own) was the sole signatory.

As the Stock Exchange waited for a statement from Polly Peck that would restore confidence and enable trading in the company's shares to recommence, banks began to get nervous about the credit facilities that they had extended to Polly Peck. The longer the stock-market waited for the statement, which had originally been promised for the next day, the more nervous the banks became.

They were able to withdraw their loan facilities to the company the more easily because Polly Peck had been in the process of tying up its loans in the form of longer-term commitments, but had failed to complete the process. Mr Nadir later identified this as one of his biggest mistakes as a manager. Too many of the company's loans (some 20 per cent of them, he estimated) were recallable on demand, i.e., the banks could withdraw them whenever they felt like it. After the events of 20 September, many of them felt like it.

In olden days they would have acted together in such circumstances, cemented either by the company's closest bank (its 'lead bank') or by the central bank, the Bank of England. But Polly Peck had been able to shop around for its loans and it had no lead bank as such. And the Bank of England was no longer in a position to exert influence over the far-flung foreign banks which had been Polly Peck's most ardent supporters.

Faute de mieux, Standard Chartered bank took the initiative. It was not Polly Peck's biggest creditor (that honour was probably reserved for a Scandinavian bank), but it was half-owner of Chartered WestLB, a merchant bank which had done a number of deals for Polly Peck, including the rights issue to finance the Del Monte purchase. Standard Chartered had also lent in its own right some £55 million to Polly Peck, and it stood to lose £30 million of that should the company never pay its creditors another penny.

Standard Chartered chaired a meeting in early October attended by most of the 100-or-so banks which were Polly Peck creditors. At the meeting it was agreed that the banks would give the company a week or so to find the cash it needed to stay afloat. The meeting was fairly amicable, although one banker said that it was 'a bit light on information'.

Late in the evening of 1 October Polly Peck had finally come out with a statement about the events of recent weeks. It said that it was seeking to find a solution to its liquidity problems (the first official notification that it had such problems), brought about by the banks' withdrawal of their loan facilities. It also said that it was not able to provide enough information for dealing in Polly Peck's shares to resume. The statement added that 'The chairman has been in contact with the government of Turkey and the board draws considerable encouragement from the degree of interest shown by that government.'

That led to speculation that Polly Peck was going to be bailed out by the Turkish government, which was clearly annoyed by the treatment of Mr Nadir by the SFO and the British media, and by the implicit assumption of his guilt. Although not a Turk, Mr Nadir had a Turkish passport, and he had met the Turkish president, Turgut Ozal, in New York on the weekend before the company issued its statement. That was just before Mr Ozal also met Mrs Thatcher in New York – a meeting at which the Polly Peck affair was discussed. Had Mr Nadir been given reason to hope that the Turkish government would ride to his rescue? Mr Nadir has said that he needed $250 million to tide Polly Peck over its liquidity crisis. That might not have been beyond the capacity of the Turkish government and its bevy of state-owned banks.

But he was to be disappointed. First, because he had few friends among the Turkish banking community. They still felt they had been snubbed by Polly Peck when they had offered their services in earlier years. Second, Mr Ozal's free-market policies had left troubled local companies free to go bust. As in Britain, the days of automatic state rescues were over in Turkey. The president would have been heavily criticised if he had supported a foreign company while leaving locals to go under. His political position was not so strong that he could easily brush such criticism aside. Mr Nadir later told Turkish television viewers that 'our [sic] president' looked on the request for help favourably and promised his support, but 'I believe that the attitude at the top did not filter through to the lower ranks as sensitively.'

In a later interview, also on Turkish television, Mr Ozal was asked why he 'abandoned' Polly Peck. The president replied that he had not exactly abandoned Polly Peck, but 'Asil Nadir's condition was not clear to us.' The Turkish word he used for 'condition' (***durum***) could also be translated as 'situation'.

If salvation did not lie in Turkey, then Polly Peck had only its own resources left. At one time Mr Nadir claimed that his personal wealth was worth several times the value of his stake in Polly Peck. 'I have a lot of assets in Cyprus and Turkey,' he explained. If these assets were only his newspapers, banks and properties, then they alone could not add up to the nigh-on £1 billion that he had occasionally indicated was the value of his non-Polly Peck assets. However, if they were worth even as much as a few 100 million then perhaps he could sell them to tide Polly Peck over its short-term liquidity problems? But no. At the meeting of the company's bankers in early October Mr Nadir had made it clear to them that he was not going to dig into his own pocket, however deep it might or might not be, to help the company out.

Why could the company not dig into its own cash flow, often said to be handsome, to get itself out of trouble? Part of the reason lay in the fact that in the late 1980s Polly Peck's trade debtors were increasing more rapidly than its trade creditors – i.e., it was extending more credit to people who supplied it with goods (such as fruit or electrical components) than it was getting from people to whom it supplied goods. By the end of 1989, for example, the company had given £260 million more in trade credit than it had received. This was effectively a loan financed out of the company's own cash flow.

Could the company not, then, make a quick sale of some of its assets to give it a life-saving injection of cash? It tried, and managed to sell its 24 per cent stake in a Hong Kong manufacturer of domestic appliances called Shell Electric. This raised a fairly insignificant £5.5 million. The government of northern Cyprus was said to have paid $12 million for the 93 per cent of the Salamis Bay hotel that it did not already own. But the most promising place for a sale – Turkey – threw up no eager buyers. The Koç and Sabanci groups insisted that they were not interested.

There was, however, talk of the Çukurova group taking a majority stake in Vestel. Çukurova was a large conglomerate which had become involved with Mr Nadir earlier in the year when it had announced a joint venture with Polly Peck and Peugeot to set up a car-manufacturing plant in Turkey. At the same time Çukurova was also trying to buy the merchant banking arm of the British & Commonwealth group, a large UK financial conglomerate which had fallen into the hands of administrators. To buy the bank it needed to gain the confidence of the British financial authorities.

However, despite its links with Mr Nadir and its need to curry favour in the UK, Çukurova's offer for Vestel was not forthcoming. 'We are not interested because we do not have the resources,' said the group's chairman, Mehmet Karamehmet.

The last hope of salvation from its increasingly impatient bankers lay in Polly Peck's own cash. At the end of 1989 its accounts had stated that the group had £249 million of cash. This amount had risen rapidly from £21 million at the end of 1987. Since only £7 million of the £249 million was held by the parent company, most of this cash can be presumed to have been in Turkey or Cyprus, although the accounts give no hint of its geographical location. By June 1990 there was an even larger amount of cash. It should have been enough to get the company out of its liquidity crisis. But it never became available.

Court injunctions in northern Cyprus had prevented Coopers & Lybrand, the accountants appointed by the company to do a review of Polly Peck's operations, from gaining access to the company's local accounts. But they were told that much of the cash held locally had been spent between the end of June and the end of September 1990 in developing a number of holiday projects in remote parts of the island.

Mr Nadir returned to London on 23 October after ferrying between Istanbul and Cyprus in a last attempt to find the cash to tide Polly Peck over. But he returned empty-handed. On 24 October Polly Peck held a board meeting at which the directors expressed concern about their personal liability if the company were to carry on trading. They felt that they were left with no option but to call in administrators. At the meeting Mr Nadir was quiet but clearly shocked.

Less than a week earlier the shares of Noble Raredon, the company run by Mr Nadir's sister, had been suspended after two banks withdrew facilities of more than £2 million from the company. Noble Raredon's share price had fallen from 100 pence in early 1990 to 26 pence at the time of its suspension. The company said that it felt that the fall was entirely due to market sentiment relating to Polly Peck's suspension and the Nadir–Nevzat relationship.

Administrators are a fairly recent creation in British corporate history. They are usually accountants and are appointed by the courts at the request of a company. They give a company relief from its creditors and thus buy it time in which to be reorganised in the hope of surviving and of eventually trading normally again. Not dissimilar to the protection given under so-called Chapter 11 in the United States, administration is a sort of half-way house between insolvency and normalcy. It is a process, however, that can take many years to complete and be very expensive.

The three chief administrators appointed to Polly Peck were the biggest names in the business: Michael A. Jordan (known to his colleagues as Major Dan) and Richard Stone of Coopers & Lybrand's insolvency practice Cork Gully; and Christopher Morris of the accountants Touche Ross, the man who had handled the break-up of the maverick Laker Airways in the early 1980s. Michael Jordan's office is tucked away in a small street in the City of London called, ironically, Noble Street.

The administrators lost no time in getting down to business. They met Mr Nadir the next day and then flew back and forth to Turkey and Cyprus to try to find information about the company's businesses in those two places. In that they were frustrated by an injunction brought by a group of orange-growers in northern Cyprus which effectively kept them out of Polly Peck's operations on the island.

The administrators decided early on to put the Georgian furnishings in Polly Peck's headquarters up for auction. They sacked seventy of the head office staff of 120, and they got rid of a number of the company's advisors. Later on, in January and February 1991, most of the old-timers still on Polly Peck's board resigned: Mark Ellis, David Fawcus and Radar Reshad left with three non-executive directors. 'The services of these directors are no longer required,' said Richard Stone. Reg Mogg and John Clayton remained as executive directors, and Larry Tindale and Sir Michael Sandberg remained as non-executive directors. Despite several offers from Mr Nadir to resign, he remained as chairman of the company.

Scarcely had the administrators begun their work than the SFO sent its sleuths into Polly Peck's headquarters at 42 Berkeley Square, the first time they had used their powers to raid the offices of the company itself. Yet another firm of accountants, Peat Marwick, had been looking through Polly Peck's books (with the company's permission) for some weeks on behalf of the SFO. But they had been working in a basement room and felt they were not getting access to all the documents that they needed. So in swept the SFO with a search-warrant; police officers stood guard outside the front door while handbags, briefcases and documents were examined.

The administrators described the raid as 'disruptive', but the SFO was under pressure to come up with charges relating to Polly Peck itself, and not just to South Audley Management over which most suspicion hung. If there were no charges relating to Polly Peck, then the SFO would have to answer some very tricky questions about who was responsible for all the losses to Polly Peck's shareholders, creditors and employees.

All these raids and all these accountants combing through the company's books raised a worrying question in many people's minds: how many company chairmen, in Britain or elsewhere, could swear with their hands on their hearts that if accountants and detectives pored over their books for weeks on end they would not find something to charge them with?

By mid-November Mr Nadir was off to Turkey and Cyprus again, but this time it was on his own behalf, not the company's. Some of the banks which had lent him money to buy Polly Peck shares in the days just before the company's collapse had brought a personal bankrupty suit against him for non-payment of their bills – amounting in total to some £50 million.

While in Turkey Mr Nadir sold some of the property owned by *Güneş*, one of his newspapers. And in mid-December he sold his Turkish bank, Impex Bank, to Reşat Karamehmet and Hasan Karamehmet, breakaway members of the family which controlled Çukurova – the group which had declined to come to Polly Peck's rescue on Mr Nadir's previous visit to Istanbul.

On Saturday 15 December Mr Nadir flew back to London on Polly Peck's Gulfstream jet. He was returning for a meeting with Michael Jordan, the administrator, but he already thought that 'in all likelihood' he would be arrested when he arrived in England. With him were his brother-in-law Fehim Nevzat, and Çetin Kurşat, a Cypriot who had sold his Pearl Construction company to Polly Peck in 1987.

When the Gulfstream came in to land at Luton airport, its usual destination some thirty miles north of London, the pilot was told to divert to Heathrow because of fog. On landing there the plane was diverted to a quiet corner of the busy airport which rarely has spare slots for private jets. A convoy of eight or nine police cars was waiting on the tarmac nearby. Police officers swarmed on to the plane. 'You're all under arrest,' they screamed. 'You would have thought I was Che Guevara at his peak,' said Mr Nadir later.

CHAPTER TWELVE

LOOSE ENDS

AFTER his arrest, Mr Nadir was detained for two nights at Holborn police station in central London. Fehim Nevzat and Çetin Kurşat were released after being questioned. On Monday 17 December Mr Nadir was driven the short distance from Holborn police station to Bow Street magistrates court where he appeared on fourteen charges of theft and four of false accounting. They were that he:

1 On or about 10 June 1988 stole £6 million belonging to Polly Peck International (PPI).
2 On or about 10 June 1988 stole £8 million belonging to Uni-Pac Packaging Industries Ltd.
3 On or about 8 September 1988 stole £2 million belonging to PPI.
4 On a day between 8 September 1988 and 31 December 1988 'dishonestly and with a view to gain for yourself or another, or with intent to cause loss to another' falsified a document required for an accounting purpose, namely a PPI cash-book, by making an entry therein which was or may have been misleading, false or deceptive in a material particular in that it concealed the destination of a payment of £2 million on 8 September 1988 by PPI.
5 On or about 7 June 1989 stole £4 million belonging to PPI.
6 On or about 8 June 1989 stole £4 million belonging to PPI.
7 On or about 9 June 1989 stole £8 million belonging to Uni-Pac Packaging Industries.
8 On or about 16 August 1989 stole £3 million belonging to Uni-Pac Packaging Industries.
9 On or about 19 December 1989 stole £1 million belonging to PPI.
10 On or about 21 December 1989 stole £500,000 belonging to PPI.

11 On or about 22 December 1989 stole £1.1 million belonging to Uni-Pac Packaging Industries.

12 Between 22 December 1989 and 31 January 1990 'dishonestly and with a view to gain for yourself, or with intent to cause loss to another', falsified a document required for an accounting purpose, namely a PPI cash-book, by making an entry therein which was or may have been misleading, false or deceptive in a material particular in that it concealed the source of a payment of £1.1 million on 28 December 1989 to PPI.

13 On or about 8 January 1990 stole £750,000 belonging to PPI.

14 On or about 8 January 1990 stole £700,000 belonging to Uni-Pac Packaging Industries.

15 On a day between 8 January 1990 and 20 September 1990 'dishonestly and with a view to gain for yourself or another, or with intent to cause loss to another', falsified a document required for an accounting purpose, namely a PPI cash-book, by making an entry therein which was or may have been misleading, false or deceptive in a material particular in that it concealed the source of a payment of £700,000 on 8 January 1990 to PPI.

16 On or about 18 July 1990 stole £2 million belonging to PPI.

17 On or about 20 July 1990 stole £950,000 belonging to Uni-Pac Packaging Industries.

18 On a day between 20 July 1990 and 20 September 1990 'dishonestly and with a view to gain for yourself or another, or with intent to cause loss to another', falsified a document required for an accounting purpose, namely a PPI cash-book, by making an entry therein which was or may have been misleading, false or deceptive in a material particular in that it concealed the source of a payment of £950,000 on 20 July 1990 to PPI.

Lorna Harris, who was leading the prosecution on behalf of the SFO, told the court that these were 'sample charges'. Although the amounts involved added up to over £40 million, the SFO said later that only £25 million was involved because some of the charges were alternatives. Some were of theft from a company (Uni-Pac) which is based in a territory (northern Cyprus) not recognised by anybody in Europe other than Turkey.

The magistrate at the December hearing, Sir David Hopkin, said that he would remand Mr Nadir on bail on condition:

1 that he lives and sleeps at his London home in Mayfair;
2 that he reports to Savile Row police station between 7 p.m. and 9 p.m. every day;
3 that he surrenders all his passports, British or otherwise, to the police; that he does not apply for any fresh travel documents, including air or rail tickets;
4 that he does not interfere with or contact or communicate with any witnesses in the case which, Sir David said, 'means no third parties, no messages, no telephones, no letters – nothing, no contact whatsoever, third party or yourself';
5 that he deposit £2 million with his solicitors, Vizards, to the order of the chief clerk of Bow Street justices, the deposit to be irrevocable, and find up to five sureties totalling £1.5 million.

Despite frantic calls by Mr Nadir's family and friends from mobile phones in the court-house, they were not able to get together that day the £3.5 million bail, believed to be the highest ever imposed. Mr Nadir had to spend a further three nights in detention, this time in Wormwood Scrubs prison in West London. A British boxer, Terry Marsh, who was in Wormwood Scrubs at the same time, said that the first thing Mr Nadir had noted about the prison was that it had two towers. It was his belief that 'to build a castle you need two towers' (the ownership of banks and newspapers) that had been the beginning of Mr Nadir's downfall.

In prison he shared a cell with a young black man accused of stealing goods worth £17. He had to take a shower in full view of four guards, and his lavatory at night was a bucket. Later he told one of his own Turkish newspapers of this time in prison: 'In British jails they pay prisoners who are awaiting trial £1.45 a week to spend at the canteen. I was also given the money. At the end of twenty-three hours in my cell, I was allowed to go to the canteen. I asked for two packets of cigarettes, a pack of sweets, two colas, a bottle of soda and a box of matches. The canteen man told me, "You must be joking. You can only buy thirteen cigarettes with that money. Try next week for the matches."' For a life-time chain-smoker, that must have been torture.

To the Bow Street magistrate Mr Nadir's ex-wife Ayşegül put up one surety for him of £500,000, and Ramadan Güney, a Cypriot funeral director who claimed to own 'the largest cemetery in Europe' – 460 acres in Surrey – put up another for £1 million.

Finding the £2 million deposit to be lodged with Vizards and S. J. Berwin, Mr Nadir's solicitors, was more difficult. The money could not come from Mr Nadir himself or from any of his blood relatives. The Turkish government tried to persuade Turkish banks to come up with the money, but they were not keen. After much fuss Menteş Aziz, Mr Nadir's Cypriot lawyer who was also chairman of his bank in Cyprus, handed over £450,000 in cash. A letter of credit for £1.55 million came from a group of Turkish banks, some of it almost certainly courtesy of the Turkish government. On the Thursday afternoon at 3 p.m. Mr Nadir left Wormwood Scrubs by a side door.

The bail conditions were relaxed slightly in January when the SFO was given until April to bring more charges against Mr Nadir. By August no further charges had been forthcoming.

In February the contents of 42 Berkeley Square had been sold. The administrators had instructed Phillips, the auctioneers, to get rid of the lush Georgian trappings carefully collected by Mr Nadir and Gülderen Tekvar. The auction created the type of media sensation reserved for Elizabeth Taylor's jewels or Van Gogh's mad canvases. Phillips (very much London's third auction house after Sotheby's and Christie's) scarcely had room to house the bidders and the hangers-on.

Television crews jostled with buyers who demanded to know whether they were watching a sale or a soap. Part of the reason for the extraordinary coverage was Phillips's fear that the sale would be a flop. Rarely did the firm get a chance to hit the front pages in the way that Sotheby's and Christie's were accustomed to. This – their one chance in years – could make or break them. But the extraordinary coverage was also a reflection of the way in which the Polly Peck and Nadir stories had gripped the nation.

For February is not the traditional month for such events. And what a February it was. The Gulf War and threats of terrorism had stopped people flying – Americans in particular – and the freezing cold in London made the casual buyer think twice about turning up. But Phillips had gone to unprecedented lengths to publicise the sale, playing on the Nadir factor, and on the panthers and tigers which were depicted in a number of rooms in 42 Berkeley Square, and which were said to be part of 'how he saw himself'.

Mr Nadir, with his sleek black hair (the grey held at bay with the help of liquid from a bottle), was hurriedly analysed as having some sort of psychological symbiosis with the panther and its menace. But in the early 1980s he had sported an entirely different hairstyle, frizzy like a poodle. And he also had another collection of animals which most people failed to notice, but which adorned his desk in Istanbul: a bunch of tortoises, one of which hid a bell used to summon people to the chairman's office. Nobody, surely, could have proposed that there was a psychological symbiosis between Mr Nadir and the crawling tortoise, or a decade earlier between him and the pampered poodle? The media had gone wild.

Phillips need not have worried about the sale, for in its own terms it was a great success. The auctioneers had put extremely conservative estimates on the prices they reckoned that the furniture would fetch, and the ultimate tally of £3.8 million (before tax and commissions) was well in excess of what they had expected. Less than 4 per cent of the chattels were left unsold, although that included a strangely out-of-place Turner water-colour. It had been estimated to fetch between £150,000 and £250,000, but was withdrawn when the highest bid that the auctioneer, Christopher Hawking, could extract was a mere £95,000.

Anyway, some of London's top furniture dealers were there and there was a generous sprinkling of rich private buyers such as Susan Sangster, the wife of a racing enthusiast who had inherited a football pools business, and Uri Geller, the famous fork-bender. The telephone lines were busy to New York and to Gstaad, and plenty of items were sold to the absent rich. The Gérôme was bought over the phone by a Swiss dealer.

From the very first few items it was clear that all was going to be well. The early lots included some tapestry cushions which had been scattered across Polly Peck's sofas so liberally that it had been almost impossible to sit down. One lot of four of these cushions had been estimated to fetch between £300 and £400. They went for £3200. Mrs Sangster paid £1900 for three cushions depicting swans which had also been estimated at £300 to £400.

Mr Nadir was not present at the sale, although a group of Turkish Cypriot friends bought a memento for him – a striking Paul Jouve ink drawing of a black panther on a background of gold leaf. The Nadir family, however, was represented.

With the auction well underway, in swept Ayşegül in the same dramatic black coat she had worn for her ex-husband's appearance at Bow Street Magistrates' Court two months earlier. She was accompanied by Semiramis Pekkan whose sister Ajda is Turkey's best-known *chanteuse*. The photographers present immediately found Mrs Nadir more appealing than the Gérôme or the re-covered sofas.

At first she could only find a seat on the third row, and the photographers had to snap her across buyers who would inconveniently lean forward to bid just as the cameras flashed. Before long this problem was solved by the appearance of a spare seat on the front row. Ayşegül moved to it with alacrity, and was rewarded with the appearance of her photograph in almost every English newspaper the next day.

She bought nothing and had turned up, she said, 'out of curiosity'. The event was not distressing, she claimed, 'It's only the office furniture.' She reported that her ex-husband, whom she was seeing almost every day, was not distressed by the sale either.

Many of Polly Peck's shareholders, however, were distressed at the thought that so much of their money had been spent on 'the office furniture'. There was much speculation about how much the collection had originally cost. Mr Nadir was rumoured to have paid £234,000 for the Turner water-colour which was withdrawn from the sale. The whole lot was reliably said to have cost some £7 million.

So Polly Peck's shareholders lost over £3 million on the sale. Why so much when Sotheby's index of English furniture prices had gone up by some 70 per cent over the period during which the collection was being put together? One possible explanation is that in the second half of the 1980s, when their business was booming, the antique dealers' price tags altered at the approach of a buyer with more money than discretion.

But shareholders are a rum lot. They can get upset about the loss of £3 million on beautiful furniture bought by a company that was at one time worth over £1 billion, yet they will not raise a squeak when a similar sum is paid to get rid of a useless chief executive who has brought their company close to ruin. And they don't bother to question sums many times that size paid by loss-making banks and brokers in the City of London for the building of self-aggrandising glass palaces.

Was Mr Nadir himself really not distressed by the sale? He certainly kept some of the items from his office which were his personal property, including some rather muddy oil paintings of Istanbul seascapes which had hung behind his desk, and an eighteenth-century musket which had sat to one side, behind the always-at-hand VDUs. At the last minute he sent a fax to the administrators contesting the ownership of some of the lots up for sale, including a pair of the globes which Mrs Nadir said was hers. The lots were withdrawn just before the auction began.

In an interview she gave shortly after the sale, Mrs Nadir said that 'material things are not the most important things' to her ex-husband. 'Things come and go. We are the temporary keepers of objects. They remain. When we're dead and gone the objects will still be around and someone else will look after them.'

At the time Mrs Nadir was also getting rid of some of her own material things. She sold a chunk of her jewellery in Geneva, and friends were invited to Eaton Square to buy things they fancied. In a classic cliché, people say that the more money she had, the less happy she was. A sweet, kind girl had become a tortured, self-conscious woman. The ending of her time as 'the temporary keeper' of these objects may have come as a relief.

At Mr Nadir's third court hearing in April the faithful Ayşegül was again in attendance, and so was the by now familiar crowd of Nadir supporters standing outside the Bow Street building with banners declaring 'We have faith in British justice'. No new charges were brought, and the bail conditions were further relaxed to allow Mr Nadir to travel outside London. He emerged from the court waving and smiling.

There had been one other piece of good news for Mr Nadir. His personal bankruptcy had been postponed by handing over shares in his newspapers and in his airline, Noble Air, to his creditors. The shares were held against instalments of cash to be paid in tranches later in the year.

South Audley Management had almost disappeared. Its English

lady directors had all resigned and it had retreated to the same small Mayfair office as Mr Nadir. The sorting out of its complicated affairs was left in the hands of one man, a Cypriot called Çetin Mehmet.

There had been little indication of when Mr Nadir's trial might be expected to begin. The roll-call of post-Thatcher fraud trials was lengthening: 1991 was to see the trial of employees of County NatWest, a City merchant bank, who were accused of manipulating a rights issue for the employment agency Blue Arrow; the trial of Peter Barlow, of Barlow Clowes, a financial company which had collapsed in the summer of 1988, having taken in hundreds of millions of pounds from mainly elderly investors; and part two of the Guinness trial, which had been postponed because one of the defendants could no longer afford to pay lawyers to defend him. Other fraud trials were waiting in the wings. Mr Nadir's would join the queue.

The administrators continued with their work. Although they finally got access to all Polly Peck's companies in Turkey, including 'to a limited extent' the fruit and vegetable businesses of Meyna, they were continually frustrated in northern Cyprus. Menteş Aziz, Mr Nadir's lawyer, obtained more injunctions on the island, based on increasingly complicated technicalities, to prevent the administrators from getting their hands on Polly Peck's businesses there. 'We are concerned at the unwarranted interference of Menteş Aziz in the affairs of Polly Peck in Turkey and northern Cyprus,' said Richard Stone.

Mr Denktash, the Cypriot president, said that he was concerned about 'people' who wanted to get hold of Polly Peck's Cyprus assets simply in order to close them down. If they were not 'worked', he said, they would be nationalised.

The administrators had been due to present a proposal to Polly Peck's shareholders and creditors at the end of January 1991. That deadline was extended to the end of March, and the proposals were finally presented in May.

Creditors were urged to be patient. The administrators argued that they would get more money back by allowing the group to continue to operate than by forcing it into liquidation. If Polly Peck were liquidated, the administrators reckoned that creditors would get between 15 and 30 pence for every pound that they had lent to the company.

How much they finally do get back will depend on how much lies behind the smoke-screen in northern Cyprus and Turkey. According to Polly Peck's books the company's leisure and food and packaging subsidiaries in the Near East owed the parent company £959 million at the end of June 1990. The administrators suggested that the best chance for the parent company to get that money might be for the Near East interests to be separated (with a role there possibly for Mr Nadir) and for the rest of Polly Peck to be run by a new chairman and chief executive.

The document spelt out the beginning of the end of Mr Nadir's connection with Polly Peck – except as one shareholder among many – and it also signposted a divorce between the British company and most of the Turkish and Cypriot businesses on which it had been built. That divorce threatened to strain Anglo-Turkish relations beyond an immediate Turkish hostility to Britons involved in returning Kurdish refugees to the safe zone in northern Iraq. In his downfall, Turkey took Mr Nadir more to its heart than it had ever done in his days of glory. The formerly hostile industrial establishment, which until then had rarely said a word in his favour, rallied round. 'I wish there were ten to twenty people here doing business like Asil Bey,' said Sakip Sabanci, scion of one of the two leading Turkish industrial families.

The Turks, shocked by the way the English had treated a still-innocent white-collar suspect, saw in the manner of Mr Nadir's arrest (and in the almost simultaneous release of ten Irishmen imprisoned for over a decade on unsubstantiated charges of terrorism) a chink in the armour of a self-righteous nation which had rarely hesitated to criticise Turkey for its harsh treatment of suspected terrorists.

In Britain, where the 1990/91 recession was causing companies to collapse at a frightening rate, Polly Peck became an object-lesson in corporate failure. 'It is often the corporate mavericks, with highly individualistic entrepreneurial management, that expose the cracks in the system,' said the *Financial Times*. 'We can learn from past collapses of all types,' added John Redwood, the minister for corporate affairs in John Major's first government.

But the lessons from Polly Peck were not easily grasped. It was not the sort of fly-by-night operation that disappears into thin air once its owner/manager is detained at Her Majesty's pleasure; a financial shell that when the accountants and lawyers move in is found to have nothing in it. And it was not some asset-stripping operation that merely took over existing companies in order to dress them up like trussed chickens ready for market.

'The role model of success to many in British industry has been Hanson and BTR,' said Mr Redwood in a key-note speech on corporate governance. 'Often loved by the stock-market, [these industrial conglomerates] have combined industrial skills with an instinct for acquisition that have rapidly increased shareholder value. Fewer have tried to emulate Glaxo or Pilkington, building businesses on in-house ideas and technology.' And more's the pity. For only in financially besotted Britain would increasing shareholder value be seen as a more desirable aim than inventing a new way of manufacturing glass, or a new pill to sooth ulcers. When in 1991 Hanson tilted at ICI, it promised rapidly to increase shareholder value yet again. But apart from Hanson's (relatively few) shareholders, *cui bono*?

In some ways Polly Peck was both a Hanson and a Pilkington. On the one hand it increased shareholder value like never before, but on the other it built up from nothing some extraordinary businesses. Vestel, the group's electronics operation in Turkey, was a great achievement, a profitable enterprise with quality plant and managers which should be an example to every businessman in that country. The citrus fruit in Cyprus was genuinely rotting on the ground until Polly Peck found a way to export it and to create wealth for the people of an area who had little else going for them. In Istanbul Mr Nadir's Mediaprint factory stands out as a handsome oasis amidst a tatty desert of concrete. Even the hotels in southern Turkey and northern Cyprus are inspiring projects. There are plenty of people who cannot believe that these hotels could ever make sufficient returns on the capital invested to justify their cost. But those same people probably used the same arguments against Vestel seven years earlier.

Business plans always require an element of fantasy and dreaming. Figures can be rigged to show that almost any project will work in terms of return on capital, or whatever the ultimate numerical criterion for its success is. Or, put another way: any set of assumptions behind a particular project can be assumed to suit the project. The business plan then creates targets which ambitious, hard-working people set out to achieve. Some are reached, and some are not.

Mr Nadir's business plans set highly ambitious targets, towards which he demandingly drove himself and his staff. Human nature is such, perhaps, that the harder the targets, the more tempting it is to take short cuts. To hard work and ambition at Polly Peck was added an obsession with quality – almost regardless of cost. 'High standards of excellence are the hallmark of all Mr Nadir's ventures,' said William Grosvenor once, and he was right. Hard work, ambition and a close eye on quality should, surely, be enough to ensure financial success?

That was not the Anglo-Saxon way of looking at things. If anything it was more akin to the Japanese point of view: work away at business goals, like quality and market share, and from there all good financial things will flow. In the Anglo-Saxon tradition, maximising profit is the name of the game from the word go.

But that is turning means into ends. Charles Handy, a respected writer and former businessman, suggested in a little-noticed speech he gave at London's Royal Society of Arts at the end of 1990 that this confusion of means and ends is a dangerous fissure in the foundations of corporate Britain. The speech was entitled 'What is a company for?' Mr Handy put forward the controversial view that a company should not be merely, or even primarily, for making profit. The first lesson that he learnt at his American business school in the 1960s was, he maintained, wrong. The lesson was that the purpose of a company is 'to maximise medium-term earnings per share'. It was inscribed above the blackboard in every classroom.

In his real business life (as an executive with an oil company far up a river in Borneo) Mr Handy soon found that maximising earnings per share 'was very remote, very long-term, very intellectual, very unreal'. He came to believe that the principal purpose of a company is not to make a profit – full stop. It is to make a profit in order to continue to do things or make things, and to do them even better and more abundantly.

Anyway, what are profits when they can be doubled or trebled with the flick of a footnote? They are a creation of accountants, accused by Mr Handy of unintentionally skewing our view of the world. Accountants developed their art in an age when companies were little more than physical assets run by families who hired physical labour. Physical assets were measurable, and they could be bought and sold.

Nowadays, companies' most important assets lie in human brains. Can they be measured on a balance sheet? Accountants have found no answer to this practical question. Nor have they found an answer to the moral, and related, question: should these assets then be bought and sold? Mr Handy presents a view of the takeover business as a sort of slave market. 'Buying and selling people is wrong,' he rightly maintains.

To find out why Britain got itself into this mess would require a long search into the way its company law developed, beginning as far back as the South Sea Bubble Act of 1720. In essence the fault lies with the fact that British law does not recognise the rights of large groups of a company's constituency. In 1944 Lord Eustace Percy, a government minister for many years, eloquently summed up the situation:

> Here is the most urgent challenge to political invention ever offered to the jurist and the statesman. The human association which in fact produces and distributes wealth, the association of workmen, managers, technicians and directors, is not an association recognised by the law. The association which the law does recognise – the association of shareholders, creditors and directors – is incapable of production or distribution, and is not expected by the law to perform these functions. We have to give the law to the real association and to withdraw meaningless privilege from the imaginary one.

In Germany and Japan, the two most successful industrial economies in the world, that 'real association' is more properly recognised in law and in practice. It would have conspired to hold back a Polly Peck from flying so high, and also from falling so far.

Little has changed since Lord Eustace Percy's remarks, and there are no signs of change in the near future. Britain stands alone in Europe in opposing the European Commission's Social Charter, a document that goes some way towards recognising a company's wider constituency. And few have wondered why the era of the

1980s ended with the downfall of so many of those American, British and Australian companies that had been swollen to bursting by their nations' peculiarly Anglo-Saxon financial markets.

The only lesson that the British government seemed to draw from the excesses of the 1980s was that it needed to fight harder against white-collar crime, a fight demonstrated by the setting up of institutions such as the SFO. After the fall of Mrs Thatcher, John Major's government continued to apply band-aids to the existing system. In John Redwood's key-note speech mentioned earlier, he emphasised two points: 'The essence of shareholder democracy is eternal vigilance. The essence of good corporate governance is good corporate board-making.' True indeed, but it was ever thus. If vigilance and good board-making were not occurring before Mr Redwood's time, then the feeble list of things that he did 'as a result of recent [corporate] failures' would be unlikely to make any difference.

Polly Peck, like Mr Nadir himself, straddled this British corporate culture and that of the eastern Mediterranean. For most of its life in the 1980s Polly Peck did business in Cyprus and Turkey, and raised money for that business in Britain. It used occidental finance for oriental business. For some this turned Asil Nadir into a modern-day Robin Hood, borrowing money from the rich to give factories to the poor. But it also created a gulf of misunderstanding which was at times useful to hide behind, but which was ultimately destructive.

In all three places there were powerful forces willing the company to succeed. The London stock-market stands to make much more money from the turnover of a hyperactive stock like Polly Peck than it does from a staid mature company like ICI or Shell – until a Hanson bids for it.

Mr Nadir understood perfectly well that the London market was the indirect source of almost all the money that made Polly Peck and his own private industrial empire possible – the capital raised and the money borrowed with his shares as security. That was why he watched so avidly the flickering VDU which displayed his share price and other financial market details.

Only the stock-market could have limited his ambitions. And they knew few bounds, which is why he railed against the market so continually for failing to appreciate the 'real value' of Polly Peck.

His railing did sound somewhat hollow in view of the fact that his company was the best-performing share that the market had ever created.

The stock-market had become the centre of 'popular capitalism', and it was in no mood to rein him in. The British have a long tradition of hunting for their investment 'bargains' overseas, far from the all-too-evident dead hand of British industry. But they have more usually found them in former colonies where there were large British communities to interpret local customs. Although Cyprus had been familiar because Britain was a co-guarantor (with Turkey and Greece) of the 1960 treaty which set up a single republic on the island – a republic which lasted for all of fourteen years – the northern part of the island had effectively been cut off from the rest of the world since partition in 1974.

The Turkish economy was an almost equally unknown quantity in London. There were few Britons established in it, and for the British media the 'story' in the region was political, not economic. Investors relied on Mr Nadir to tell them where he was going to invest their money. He was both their principal and their agent.

Financiers in the City of London who backed Polly Peck did so on the scantest information. Niksar, the Anatolian town where Polly Peck set up a water-bottling plant, was as remote as the moon to the investors who put money into it. And if it had not been water-bottling, could it just as well have been crab farming or a nut cutlet franchise?

Mr Nadir well knew the importance of information as a source of power and control, even if his backers did not. When Polly Peck collapsed, both bankers and shareholders complained that they were not given enough information about the company. Mr Nadir kept things close to his chest, and many promises that he made were left unfulfilled. This was the way he had been left to run things in the good times. Why should it suddenly be different when, as far as he was concerned, nothing to do with the company's day-to-day operations had altered?

Anybody who has seen the Japanese diligently gleaning information about an investment proposal is forced to contrast it with the *laissez-faire* British assumption that a good gut feeling is all that matters. The Japanese would have crawled all over Niksar before they ever put a yen into water-bottling (or crab farming) in such a fantastic place.

What mattered to the British (and later to the Americans) had been not what Polly Peck did, or where, but the fact that it was Mr Nadir who did it. He had the sort of following a top jockey might get at the races. Punters did not back the horse he was riding, but rather the fact that he was riding it. They were encouraged to back the man, not the horse, by the Thatcherite promotion of the entrepreneur. New companies were being floated on the stock-market while scarcely out of their nappies. But they were full of entrepreneurial promise, and it was the entrepreneur, not the enterprise, that mattered.

These punters had also been drawn to the stock-market by the Thatcher privatisations. In the absence of any adequately competitive fiscal incentives to persuade individuals to spend their money on shares rather than on houses or pensions, the government had to seduce people to buy state industries with the help of give-aways and almost certain capital gains.

The barrenness of popular capitalism without fiscal incentives was demonstrated by the fact that throughout the 1980s individuals owned fewer and fewer shares. On one estimate, the last individual shareholder in Britain will sell his share in the year 2003. Yet even after Mrs Thatcher, the Conservative government still held dear the dream of wider share ownership.

The gamblers in this new world of people's capitalism liked something exotic. The ordinary and the familiar was never going to make the fast buck that their fast world demanded. At least one small shareholder bought Polly Peck shares because he felt sure that the London stock-market would under-value anything to do with Turkey. He was totally wrong. If anything, they over-valued it precisely because it had something to do with Turkey.

That was in the early days of Polly Peck. In its latter years the market had again changed in its favour. Mrs Thatcher's deregulation of the City of London (spotlighted by Big Bang in October 1986) had left gentlemanly bankers and brokers over-run by the 'boys from the Essex marshes' and a new Americanised affluent middle class. Both groups were fiercely competitive (after all, 'deregulation' was officialese for 'more competition'), and they set about selling money like it was a job lot of plastic dolls.

When twenty bankers try to convince you to borrow more money – an 'offer you can't refuse' – who are you to say that twenty bankers can all be wrong? So Polly Peck managed to borrow more than £1 billion from banks. And when competition is the name of the game, the wise businessman plays one banker off against another to get the cheapest plastic doll. Only in the end does this policy of divide-and-rule bear a high price – when banks with no loyalty rush to save their skins. But who ever believes that the end is nigh?

There was only one thing that these financiers demanded of their favoured entrepreneurial playthings, and that was a constant stream of rising profits. If this was not forthcoming they could be savage in their disappointment. Share prices would be marked down, and the plaything would itself be thrown 'into play', perhaps to be taken over by some new entrepreneur whose figures were more voluptuous.

Behind all these deals had been the king-makers of the 1980s – the accountants, the men and women who could produce the figures that could please the financiers. But the definitive measures that these people appeared to produce in companies' accounts were at odds with the flexibility that was available to them in drawing up the accounts. Gottfried Hoffmann, a retired Swiss banker who owned 700,000 Polly Peck shares, wrote to the British Institute of Chartered Accountants in 1987 to say that Polly Peck's reported profits of £61 million were 'really' only £35 million if the effect of the devaluing Turkish lira was taken into the profit and loss account, rather than being passed through the reserves. The Swiss banker was surprised at the legalistic approach of the profession, which maintained that as long as the accounts obeyed the law (and so-called 'reserve accounting' for foreign currencies was not against the law), they presented a true and fair view. So the great unspoken secret of the accounting profession is that there is no unique, single true and fair view of anything, least of all of oranges and lemons on the trees of Güzelyurt.

Accounts have to be interpreted, not read literally, and Polly Peck's accounts were not like the Rosetta Stone; their code was much easier to break. But for London's brokers and bankers, interpreting accounts had been fast falling down their list of priorities.

In the other main arenas of the Polly Peck story, Cyprus and

Turkey, the powerful forces willing it to succeed, were more political than commercial. Although Mr Nadir had a Turkish and a British passport, and the right of residence in Switzerland, he was first and always a Cypriot. 'If you look at the history of Cyprus you would appreciate what people like me have experienced. It is important to keep that in mind,' he once said. And on another occasion: 'Certain values in life are higher than commerce, profits or personal benefits. The issue of northern Cyprus in my mind should be valued that high.'

In his first years abroad he had little to do with the island. But as with other young émigrés, the older he grew, the closer he felt to the soil where he was born. The island's influence became more and more pervasive. He saw Greeks and Greek Cypriots behind almost every bad thing that ever happened to him. Greek Cypriots were subverting the media; they were influencing the SFO; and they were trying to take him to Athens to stand trial. He even noted that a Greek doctor was sinisterly brought to treat him for sleeplessness when he was in Wormwood Scrubs jail.

Being such a big fish in such a small pond, Asil Nadir inevitably got entangled in the intractable politics of the island. In such a small place it is hardly surprising that he was related to powerful politicians. The daughter of Dervis Eroğlu, the prime minister of the self-declared republic of northern Cyprus, married the son of Ilker Nevzat. Ilker Nevzat was a lawyer and the manager of Mr Nadir's companies in Cyprus until he resigned in October 1990. That was not a decision that can have been taken lightly since he was also the brother of Fehim Nevzat, the husband of Mr Nadir's sister Bilge.

Rauf Denktash, the former lawyer and long-serving president of northern Cyprus, encouraged Mr Nadir to do business in the island, and supported him throughout his troubles at the end of 1990. Çavlan Suerdem, who worked for Polly Peck from 1987 as special advisor to the chairman, had been, immediately before that, political advisor to Mr Denktash.

Mr Denktash was never an eager supporter of reunion between the north and south of the island. By bringing economic growth to northern Cyprus, Mr Nadir helped its 170,000 people to continue as an independent entity. The breakaway party formed by Necat Konuk in 1979 with the aim of creating some form of union with the Greek-speaking south shrivelled away. In the elections of 1985 it failed to get the minimum vote necessary for parliamentary representation.

The collapse of Polly Peck increased the likelihood that the northern part of the island would either become an even more indistinguishable part of Turkey (which is what the British fear most), or be forced into an uneasy accommodation with the Greek Cypriots in the south.

Although Mr Nadir often said that he was not political and had no political ambitions, he did on one notorious occasion meet Nelson Ledsky, the American administration official responsible for Cyprus. At the meeting, held in London in late 1989, it was suggested that life on the island might be easier if Mr Nadir were to take over from Mr Denktash. As a businessman he should be able to reach an accord with the Greek Cypriots. Their president, George Vassiliou, was also a businessman, and once a visiting professor at Cranfield school of management. Needless to say the Ledsky suggestion came to nought.

On mainland Turkey Mr Nadir also got embroiled in politics. As he was convenient to Mr Denktash in Cyprus, so he was convenient to Mr Ozal who, in the mid-1980s, grew worried that his free-market reforms were going unnoticed and unpraised in the rest of Europe. As in Mr Denktash's Cyprus, so in Mr Ozal's Turkey the relationships between business and politics are close. Like most of Turkey's top businessmen, Mr Nadir met and spoke with Mr Ozal frequently. While in prison in London, he received a telegram from the former prime minister, Bülent Ecevit, wishing him well. Mr Ecevit was a staunch political opponent of Mr Ozal.

The politics and business of Turkey mingled with that of Cyprus. Mr Ozal's son Ahmet was a good friend of Bülent Semiler, an American-educated young man who had returned to Turkey to head up a state bank. Mr Semiler was born in Cyprus, and was the leading figure in the attempt to raise the £2 million bail for Mr Nadir. He was at the time also an unofficial advisor to Mr Ozal. Mr Denktash himself was a frequent visitor to Ankara, where he was welcomed by politicians of all political complexions.

To say that he was not political was an over-simplification on Mr Nadir's part. He may not have harboured ambitions to be a politician, but that did not mean that he did not want to have an influence on the changing world about him. He just preferred to do it in an inconspicuous way. His newspapers and bank in Cyprus were the 'two towers needed to build a castle' – a castle from which he hoped to wield that influence.

But to build such a castle in vast Turkey was more expensive than even he could afford. His greatest success was in Turkey – the Vestel electronics business – but so was his greatest failure – the publishing empire he bought at crippling cost, and which he may have chosen to neglect because he did not want to face what he knew was a mistake. It was in Turkey that Mr Nadir's business ambitions over-reached themselves.

In the final analysis, however, the biggest influence willing Polly Peck to succeed was Mr Nadir himself. He was founder, chairman, chief executive, and largest single shareholder. Was he an overmighty boss whose own blind ambition brought about the downfall of a company whose fortunes were bound too tightly to his own? That is certainly one way of looking at things.

Mr Nadir had an obsessive determination to succeed, to show the business world that a poor disadvantaged boy from the streets of nowhere can achieve as much as anyone. ('I'm just a village kid,' he once said while shyly surveying the splendours of 42 Berkeley Square.) Such ambition is as old as the hills, and Mr Nadir's downfall will not stop others being similarly obsessed.

The spur to his obsession was a feeling of belonging nowhere that mattered, and of being properly appreciated by nobody who mattered. That is uncomfortable to live with, but anybody who is too much *à l'aise dans sa peau*, as the French say so beautifully, becomes a civil servant and remains one. While civil servants may be necessary, they are not sufficient.

Mr Nadir's chips were not without foundation. He was as much an outsider in Istanbul as he was in London. And he was not perhaps appreciated for what he did achieve, especially in Britain where few people are bred to be aware of the fact that at the root of everything that makes their life tolerable are the wealth-creators – men (and far too few women) like Asil Nadir.

Unbridled, Mr Nadir's ambition would have been harmless in a private company owned by himself and his family. And in Turkey, Cyprus or Newington Green that is what he would have run – a traditional Mediterranean family business. But in most of Britain family businesses can become public companies overnight, even though they carry on with all the relationships that a family business implies.

Becoming a public company provides much greater access to capital and greater opportunities to expand. But it is, after all, capital that comes from 'the public'. And that broadening of its constituency gives the former family firm a new responsibility, which implies a change in its management style. Did Polly Peck, which became one of the biggest public companies in a highly developed economy, change its style sufficiently to suit its changing status?

The main responsibility for that change lies in the boardroom. But the powers of the board in an individualistically driven British company are largely dependent on the non-executive directors, and they are too frequently chosen for flawed reasons, such as a friendship with an existing director. However, if it was Mr Nadir's personal borrowing against the security of his shares that brought the company down, there is little that the company's board could have been expected to do about it. Mr Nadir was always zealously private about his private affairs.

Nevertheless Mr Nadir did not encourage the appointment of directors of sufficient weight to counterbalance his own. In his charming, understated way he could mesmerise lesser souls into believing what he wanted them to believe, and it is easy to imagine that for most of Polly Peck's life the board was putty in his hands. But he was not an impregnable man of steel. With his constant smoking and his nervous twitches, he induced as much sympathy as fear. It would not have taken too much for a dissenter to cause a stir that would have reached the ears of the stock-market.

If Mr Nadir was over-mighty, then at the end of the day it was up to the company's shareholders, and especially the large institutions that held big stakes in Polly Peck, to insist on appointing heavyweights to the board. In 1987 they did insist. And Tony Reading was the result. But it was not long before he left and Mr Nadir was effectively in sole charge again. Did the institutions complain then, or did they keep quiet in the belief that their bread was buttered by Mr Nadir and by him alone? And why, when the company was collapsing because its chairman was being interviewed by the Serious Fraud Office, did they not insist to the board which was supporting him that he resign? Guinness had managed to isolate itself very successfully from the charges levelled at its chief executive Ernest Saunders by rapidly replacing him with a top-rank manager.

The task of all those willing Polly Peck to success was made easier by the personality of Asil Nadir himself. He was polite, intelligent, generous to a fault, immature in some respects, vulnerable and courteous. He was also unusually good-looking for a top businessman, with captivating eyes and a kindly smile. It is hard to find anybody who knew him well who did not find him charming and remembered him with some affection. The same cannot be said about many other more obviously over-mighty entrepreneurs. He is not like the Australian Rupert Murdoch, for example, whose Adelaide acquaintances of his youth remembered, when his media empire was in financial difficulties, that as a young man 'He had many words to say, but thank-you was not one of them'. Nor like Alan Bond, another Australian who once had pots of power, who personally cursed a young secretary at *The Economist* for ruining his 'reputation in the City of London'. *The Economist* had published an article describing how Mr Bond had been prosecuted in Australia for driving his Rolls-Royce with bald tyres.

Most people would prefer to work for a handsome charmer than for an overweight bully, yet Mr Nadir did not avail himself of the opportunity to gather first-class people around him. He preferred to work with family and old friends from Cyprus plus a few trusted long-serving advisors in England and Turkey. Rather like Mrs Thatcher, he seemed to surround himself with people who would not attempt to undermine his hard-won if still fragile self-confidence. He and Mrs Thatcher were not the first, and won't be the last, powerful people whose view of the world has been thus fatally distorted.

To his charm was added a Mediterranean ability to live amidst much greater uncertainty and complexity than the average Englishman can tolerate. The skein of trusts through which he held his private businesses could confuse the sharpest mind. Even the ownership structure of Polly Peck's assets was extremely complex and sometimes imprecise.

When asked questions about his affairs Mr Nadir could seem evasive and purposely vague. It may have been a skill he learned in Cyprus thirty-five years earlier when one false word could spell death for someone. However, it only aroused suspicion in the minds of the many people who, at different stages of his career and for different reasons, were not willing him to succeed.

In the end those people had their day, seeing his company on its knees and him in the court-house. But the ripples from the Polly Peck affair spread far – rocking political relationships, destroying dreams, and leaving thousands of people besides Mr Nadir very much the poorer.

CHAPTER THIRTEEN

WHERE ARE THEY NOW?

TWO and a half years after he had been first arrested in December 1990, Asil Nadir had still not been brought to trial. The fourteen charges that had been read out to him at Bow Street Magistrates' Court on that cold December day had been added to. In September 1991 he was rearrested and re-interrogated, and the following month another fifty-eight charges were brought against him. This machine-gun approach to prosecution left Mr Nadir accused of stealing £155 million under seventy-two different charges. At the same time John Turner, a former group chief accountant of Polly Peck, was charged on ten counts of false accounting. Two years later the prosecution dropped its case against Mr Turner.

The initial investigation by the SFO into the affair had led people to believe that charges would be brought in relation to insider dealing in Polly Peck shares through nominee companies in Switzerland. This was the line of investigation that had been pursued after the first suspicions had been aroused that Mr Nadir's personal affairs were not 100 per cent correct.

The suspicions had been spread by the Inland Revenue's special investigations department, which had informally swapped information with the Stock Exchange about trading in Polly Peck shares by a number of Swiss companies in the late 1980s. (It is illegal for the Inland Revenue to pass details of taxpayers' affairs to a third party without a court order.) The Stock Exchange had then passed the results of its investigations into these dealings on to the Serious Fraud Office. The Inland Revenue may also have had direct contact with the SFO over the affair.

The man who was in charge of the Inland Revenue's special investigations unit at the time was called Michael Allcock. In a peculiar twist to the tale he was suspended from duty in September

1992 pending an investigation. In July 1993 he and his wife were arrested and questioned in connection with allegations of bribery. None of the allegations has yet been related to the Nadir case.

In view of the nature of the Inland Revenue's investigation, it was always rather surprising that the charges which ultimately were made against Mr Nadir never had anything to do with insider dealing. Mr Nadir has claimed that the Inland Revenue investigation was concluded without there being any suggestion of impropriety.

By February 1992, when Mr Nadir was finally committed for trial at the Old Bailey, there were sixty-six charges still standing against him. In June 1992, however, forty-six of these were dropped at a hearing of the case held in Birmingham, a city some 100 miles north-west of London. Mr Justice Tucker, the judge in charge of the case, decreed that they should be dropped due to lack of evidence.

This was a considerable triumph for Mr Nadir and his advisors. But it was a devastating blow to the SFO in its prosecution of the case. On hearing of the verdict one SFO officer is said to have burst into tears. By May 1993 only thirteen charges against Mr Nadir remained, relating to the theft of some £30 million.

From the moment the first charges were made Asil Nadir devoted most of his time and energy to compiling his defence and clearing his name. He said he put in sixteen-hour working days, just as he had done when he was chairman of Polly Peck. He worked partly from his home in Mayfair's Aldford Street, where he continued to live for a while with his English mistress Joanna MacKay, and partly from a small office which he borrowed from his sister Bilge Nevzat.

At first he was forbidden to travel outside London, and he was not allowed to speak to anyone who worked for Polly Peck or who might take the stand as a witness in his trial. So broad was this condition that it took some time to determine whether he was still allowed to talk to his mother.

In one of the countless court hearings that followed the initial arraignment, the terms of his bail were relaxed slightly. He was allowed to travel throughout the United Kingdom, but he still had to report back to a London police station every Monday. He was not, however, at any stage allowed to travel outside the country, and his passports were never returned to him. This became a sore point, with Mr Nadir's lawyer claiming that his client needed to go to northern Cyprus to gather evidence vital to his defence. But the SFO had always been convinced that if allowed out of the country, Mr Nadir would never return. At every court hearing it opposed any relaxation in the terms of his bail.

Mr Nadir's eldest son Birol acted as a messenger between London and Istanbul where Birol had launched an illustrated sports magazine that had considerably more commercial success than any of his father's Turkish publishing ventures. At the same time as he was working on his defence against the SFO's charges and co-operating with the administrators in sorting out Polly Peck, Asil Nadir was also attempting to stave off personal bankruptcy. For some time he was successful and kept his creditors at bay by selling off a number of assets, including a bank in Istanbul, Impexbank, that fetched several million pounds.

But in November 1991 he was suddenly sued from an unexpected quarter. Den Norske, a small Scandinavian bank, pursued him for a guarantee that he had given on a loan to a relative. All his other creditors then followed Den Norske's example, and he was declared bankrupt.

That meant he could no longer be a director of a UK company, and he finally relinquished his title as chairman of Polly Peck – almost a year after he had first been arrested. It also meant that he had to sell his house in Aldford Street and move into the rented apartment in Eaton Square.

The trustee in bankruptcy – Neil Cooper of the accountants Robson Rhodes – continued to pursue Mr Nadir after he had been declared bankrupt, convinced that he had assets hidden away elsewhere and that he was moving his wealth around in the form of valuable paintings. After Mr Nadir secretly left England for northern Cyprus in May 1993, the contents of the Eaton Square apartment – down to his hairdryer – were auctioned for the benefit of the trustee. The contents fetched £73,000. The trustee even laid claim to the £2 million bail money that the court requested after Mr Nadir had fled the country. Here it came up against the administrators, who also laid claim to the bail money.

And what of Asil Nadir's guarantors? Ayşegül had moved out of the smart rented flat in Eaton Square where she had stayed on after Asil's arrest, and had gone back to her home town of Istanbul. She sold her admirable collection of Ottoman calligraphy to the Sultan of Brunei, reputedly for $2 million, but she had to tighten her belt considerably. She eventually moved out of the Sa'dullah Pasha *yali* and set about refurbishing a derelict small house that had once been the maid's quarters for another yali. At the end of July 1993 she was called upon to hand over within 28 days the £500,000 that she had pledged as surety for Nadir's bail. When she did not pay in time a request went out from the British government for her extradition.

Ramadan Guney, the family friend who owned one of Britain's biggest cemeteries, was ordered to pay up £650,000 of the £1 million that he had pledged to Mr Nadir's bail. Mr Guney was told by the trial judge Mr Justice Tucker that he had not taken all reasonable steps to ensure that Mr Nadir presented himself for trial, so he would have to pay within six months or go to prison for two years.

The elderly Mr Guney, awaiting heart surgery at the time, was grey-faced as he announced that he would appeal. 'As far as I can see there is no justice,' he declared. It rankled, too, that the judge had not even bothered to find out how to pronounce his name correctly.

Mr Nadir's houses in England were put up for sale. Burley on the Hill, the glorious Palladian mansion overlooking Rutland Water that cost £7 million, remained on the market for a long time. Mr Nadir had wanted to turn it into a luxury hotel, but he had run up against problems in getting planning permission for an extension. At one time Ramadan Guney was to buy Burley on the Hill for £3 million, but that deal fell through. Another country house, Baggrave Hall in Leicestershire, which Nadir bought for his own use but which he hardly ever stayed in, was sold at a considerable loss for £4 million.

The two-bedroom flat in London's Eaton Square, where Asil and Ayşegül had spent some of their most glorious times together, reverted to its freeholder, the Duke of Westminster's Grosvenor Estate, after Mr Nadir defected to Cyprus. The rent was allegedly long overdue.

Lesley Ellwood, a former mistress and mother of two of Asil Nadir's children, continued to live in Chelsea in a house bought for her by Asil. The mother of another of his children, a former hostess with Turkish Airlines, married an Englishman and settled in a house that was again paid for by Asil.

The Nadir companies and the 200-odd subsidiaries of Polly Peck suffered a similar fate to his houses – they were either sold, reorganised or closed down. South Audley Management continued in existence until May 1992 when it was liquidated for not paying its rent.

There was a minor brouhaha about the appointment of the administrators. Two of them – Michael Jordan and Richard Stone – worked for Cork Gully, a subsidiary of Coopers & Lybrand. Not only had Coopers & Lybrand done a good deal of consultancy work for Polly Peck on a number of new industrial projects (including the setting up of Vestel, the electronics company in Turkey), but it had also been Asil Nadir's personal accountant in the 1980s. At one stage the firm had threatened to cease co-operation with the Inland Revenue when it suspected that someone there was passing information about Mr Nadir's personal affairs to the SFO.

In October 1992 the ICA, the British accountancy profession's ruling body, fined the two administrators £1,000 (the maximum possible), judging that insolvency practitioners should not be appointed to a company with which their firm had a 'continuing professional relationship'.

In the hands of the administrators Polly Peck ran into hard times. The formerly gracious 42 Berkeley Square was left looking increasingly down at heel. Unoccupied for years, there was no one even to remove the dead ivy that had once looked so handsome hanging from the first-floor balconies. Polly Peck's headquarters returned to its rag-trade roots and the company's registered office reverted once again to the Commercial Road in the East End of London. The company kept a small and inconspicuous West End office in Brook's Mews, around the corner from Berkeley Square.

Of the star names in the group, Sansui continued to make losses for a while, but then began to improve. Profits at Vestel, the electronics company quoted on the Istanbul Stock Exchange, dropped sharply but remained positive. Meyna, however, the Turkish fruit and packaging business, made a loss in 1991. The *ancien régime* had maintained that it had contributed profits of £161 million to the group in 1989. If so, that was an extraordinary turnaround in its fortunes.

Del Monte was sold off, but the break up of the company after the buy-out of RJR Nabisco had dispersed the famous brand name around the world and into many different hands. It was in danger of being devalued.

The administrators had a constant tussle to get access to the books of the group's subsidiaries in northern Cyprus, where they believed there were Polly Peck assets worth many millions of pounds. On the Turkish mainland the magnificent Sheraton Voyager hotel in the southern resort of Antalya was sold to Dogus, a local construction company, at a loss believed to be in the order of $20 million. The hotel where Nadir had appeared at its glorious opening in the late summer of 1990, just as his whole empire was beginning to crumble, had been rather ignominiously advertised for sale in the press.

Initially the administrators had made the decision to co-operate with Asil Nadir since they felt that shareholders and creditors were likely to retrieve much more from Polly Peck that way than by fighting Nadir through the courts. In May 1991 they were promising creditors and shareholders, at a mass meeting held in London's Alexandra Palace, that 'everyone in this hall' could expect 52 pence back for every pound that they had lost. But it became apparent that this was wildly optimistic.

After Mr Nadir's departure from the UK in 1993 the best estimates were that creditors would be lucky if they eventually got 4 pence in the pound. The administrators got a considerably better deal. Their costs just up until 15 June 1991 amounted to £8.4 million.

At the end of the day administrators are judged by what they can retrieve for creditors and shareholders. If in Polly Peck's case this turns out to be less than they earn in fees for themselves it will not be the first time in British corporate history that the process of administration has been a complete fiasco.

As the value of what the administrators had been entrusted with diminished before their eyes, they turned to the courts in the hope of retrieving something there. In October 1991 they sued Asil Nadir, his mother, the Central Bank of Northern Cyprus and four others for £1 billion in damages. In February 1993 they sued

Citibank, Asil Nadir's private banker, for £75 million, alleging that the bank had acted as an intermediary in passing that amount from Polly Peck to Asil Nadir's personal account with a Citibank offshoot in Switzerland.

Then in April 1993 the administrators said they would sue Stoy Hayward, Polly Peck's long-time auditors, for an unspecified amount of damages – a suit which set accountant against accountant, both members of a profession that cannot be too proud of the role that it played in the Polly Peck affair.

CHAPTER FOURTEEN

THE FLIGHT TO APHRODITE'S ISLAND

ON the morning of 4 May 1993 two men arrived by car at a small airstrip near the village of Compton Abbas in southern England. One of the men was Peter Dimond, a small-time aircraft dealer well known to the owner of the airstrip. The other man, wearing sunglasses and a hat, was introduced as a friend from the industry.

The two had hired a small Piper aircraft to take them across the English Channel to Beauvais in France. With the increasing freedom of movement within the European Community there were few checks made on the passengers on such flights.

Throughout the one-hour flight the stranger sat facing backwards, unidentifiable by the pilot, who left the two men at Beauvais. There a private Cessna 500 jet, which had flown in from Hatfield in England, was waiting to take them on the next leg of their journey.

That leg took them to northern Cyprus via Istanbul, where their plane stopped to refuel. For the man in the sunglasses and hat was Asil Nadir, and he was jumping bail on the grounds, he later claimed, that the prosecution in his case was attempting to pervert the course of justice. When he arrived at Ercan airport in the Turkish quarter of Nicosia he was met by his sister Bilge Nevzat and a minister in the government of the self-declared Republic of Northern Cyprus.

His feelings of well-being and delight at being free again in the place of his birth might have been dampened somewhat had he realised that just across town, in the Greek quarter of Nicosia, was being held a Commonwealth law conference. The conference was being attended, *inter alia*, by George Staple, the director of the Serious Fraud Office; Barbara Mills, his predecessor at the

SFO when Mr Nadir had first been arrested, who had since been promoted to Director of Public Prosecutions; and Lord MacKay, the Lord Chancellor.

Peter Dimond, who had organised the details of the trip, remained in northern Cyprus with Mr Nadir. If he returned to England he was sure to face charges of aiding and abetting the ex-chairman of Polly Peck to jump bail. When subsequently describing the flight, he said that 'there was a time when it was time to go, and so his friends said "OK, let's do it". It was just an act of friendship – like giving a friend a lift in a car.'

The Turkish press got a rather different view of events – describing Mr Nadir as having been chased across the English countryside, his fingers on the trigger of a gun. Even his ex-wife Ayşegül, by now living modestly in Istanbul, enjoyed describing to friends how Asil had fled across fields towards a waiting jet, hotly pursued by the plodding British police. There was no way, however, that a plane could have taken off if the police were so hot on the heels of one of its passengers and genuinely wanted to detain him.

The British police were not, however, totally unaware that there might be an attempt by Mr Nadir to jump bail at around this time. They had been warned by the SFO on the Sunday before Mr Nadir left that he was about to flee the country. The SFO had received an anonymous phone call – the latest in a series of such tip offs. So when Mr Nadir turned up at Savile Row police station to report as usual on the Monday evening, the police dropped their guard and assumed the SFO's call had been yet another false alarm. The flight took place the very next day.

Northern Cyprus had no extradition treaty with the United Kingdom – not surprisingly since the small parcel of land was recognised as an independent territory by nobody but Turkey. Asil Nadir could be sure to be safe from prosecution there for a while. He could take stock in his modest-looking house in the village of Lapta, which he had once said was the only place he really wanted to be (together with some tomatoes and his beloved Turkish white cheese). For some days before his arrival local people had been preparing the house. Behind its walls lay a roomy internal courtyard, a terrace overlooking a mature garden and stone-walled public rooms.

When news of Nadir's flight became known the world's press

had no intention whatsoever of leaving him alone with his tomatoes and white cheese. They were on the next flight to Ercan, pronouncing local Turkish family and place names with all the subtlety of a concrete mixer.

By the evening of Wednesday 5 May Fleet Street's finest 'investigative reporters' were prowling in a convoy of taxis around the narrow silent streets of Lapta. At the sight of two black Mercedes 500s parked outside a modest villa next to the village square, the leading taxi stopped. Out jumped a diminutive reporter from the *Daily Mirror*, Britain's second-best-selling tabloid newspaper, and headed for the villa door. In the argot of the trade, Mr Nadir was about to be 'monstered'.

The reporter reached up on tiptoe and banged the heavy wooden knocker. 'Come on out, Mr Nadir,' he growled. 'We know you're there. We won't go away. You're on the run. You've got to come out and talk to us.'

Inside, Asil Nadir was spending his second evening of freedom with his mother, sister and advisers. Despite his personal bankruptcy he had still been able to retain the services of his barrister Anthony Scrivener, a Manchester firm of solicitors, Pannone & Partners, and of a public relations firm, Morgan and Rogerson. In his fastness that night he was awaiting the arrival of Christopher Morgan, the senior partner in the PR firm who had been hastily summoned from business in Singapore.

With the flower of the Turkish and British press corps encamped around his doorstep, Mr Nadir finally made an appearance the next morning. Commanding the tumultuous scrum to calm down, he promised them a press conference the next day at which he would 'answer all your questions'. Appeased, the press retired to a nearby café and local police moved in to cordon off access to the Nadir home.

The press conference was duly scheduled for 6 May at the four-star Jasmine Court hotel, suddenly enlivened by the arrival of hordes of media people and of several Nadir supporters. It was a very different atmosphere from that prevailing in the luxury hotel at the time of Nadir's arrest, when the threat of war in the Gulf had frightened away all but an intrepid few from Aphrodite's island.

Arriving to a traditional drum-beat from local admirers who offered him a sacrificial ram (which he gracefully declined), Mr

Nadir looked suave and out-of-place. He delivered a long-winded diatribe about the injustices of the British legal system to which he was, at least for the time being, joyously impervious. But he soon took fright at the aggressive questions that were shouted at him, and he fled the conference without answering a single one of them.

Two days later Christopher Morgan was persuaded that Mr Nadir should try again with an interview. But this time he wisely decided to grant it to one journalist alone, not the whole pack. The man who convinced Morgan to follow this strategy was the BBC's Iain Carson, a bearded Scot and business correspondent for the main evening news programme. Carson was rewarded with the first exclusive interview with the fugitive.

Nadir gave the interview in the citrus groves outside his house. His face looked older and heavier than when he had first appeared in Bow Street Magistrates' Court twenty-nine months earlier; his red cardigan was stretched over a paunch added to his once slim figure. His appearance had not been helped by a painful attempt to give up smoking, an attempt which he had abandoned as the pressure increased before his departure from London.

At one stage he raised his arm to pluck a blossom from a lemon tree. Rolling it gently between thumb and forefinger, he held it up to his nose. Knowing that the cameras were not yet rolling, he turned to the cameraman and said, 'This has got to be better than Wormwood Scrubs.'

When the cameras did roll, he talked about the many injustices he had suffered at the hands of the British legal system, about his hopes of getting more involved in his businesses in Cyprus and of going to Turkey to inspect his assets there, and then later to Japan.

He told the *Wall Street Journal* a few days later that he had two aims in life: 'One is to clear my name, and two is to ensure that the shareholders, who have had the rawest deal ever, are compensated.'

Then he was asked whether he would go back to England to face his trial scheduled for early October. Only, he said, if his bail conditions were relaxed. But he probably knew that was impossible, and that he would have handcuffs snapped on him as soon as he set foot on British soil.

After the initial brouhaha with the press, Nadir settled down to reinforce his image as a fugitive from injustice. The core of his case was his claim that in the six months before his departure there had been a major conspiracy by the prosecution to deny him justice and a fair trial. This hinged on an alleged attempt to intimidate the trial judge, Mr Justice Tucker, into resigning.

The origins of the plot went back to 1 October 1992, the day before Mr Nadir was due to appear at a preparatory hearing for his trial at the Old Bailey. The SFO said that on that day it had received a piece of paper, a photocopy of a contract drawn up between a David Kent on the one hand, and Asil Nadir's mother and sister on the other. The contract was apparently an agreement to pay to David Kent £3.5 million 'within seven days of my departure from the United Kingdom'. At the bottom, in crude handwriting, was added the clause 'We the above named persons sign on behalf of and for Mr Asil Nadir.' The document was then signed by Safiye Nadir and Bilge Nevzat. On the photocopy the names of the witnesses to the signatures had been purposely blocked out.

As a result of receiving this document, the SFO made a submission to the Lord Chief Justice that the trial be postponed. It was driven to such an extreme, it subsequently asserted, because 'there was in addition to the document an allegation that the sum of money was to be paid to Mr Justice Tucker following the successful application for variation of bail conditions'. As a result of the SFO's intervention, Mr Justice Tucker did not appear at the 2 October court hearing, a hearing at which the court was to decide whether to relax Mr Nadir's bail conditions sufficiently to allow him to accompany his solicitor to Cyprus in pursuit of his defence.

There were at least three possible explanations of the timing and appearance of this document:

- that it was a desperate last-minute ruse by the SFO to prevent Nadir leaving the country, since it had every reason to believe that Mr Justice Tucker would approve his application for the return of his passport on 2 October
- that it was a fabrication by Mr Nadir (or his supporters) to muddy the waters, postpone his trial (by changing the judge) and increase the chances of his case being abandoned

- that it was a genuine attempt by Mr Nadir and/or his supporters to bribe the judge and obtain his freedom, and that it was leaked to the SFO by a third party who believed that Mr Nadir was about to flee the country, and who had a vested interest in making sure that he stayed in the UK.

Mr Nadir had his own explanation of what this document was about – an explanation that was almost more incredible than anybody else's. He claimed that the document was part of a business deal that his mother and sister had been involved in. In early 1992 they had been approached by a woman called Wendy Welsher, a woman that they had never met before. Wendy Welsher had wanted to go into a joint venture with the two women – developing a holiday village in northern Cyprus.

Even though Mr Nadir was himself at this stage personally bankrupt, his two closest female relatives seem to have agreed to go ahead with the deal. Since the parties to the deal did not know each other very well, each party was to place £3.5 million in a Zurich bank account – money which could subsequently only be drawn upon when authorised jointly by both parties. An intermediary called David Kent, who was introduced to the deal by Wendy Welsher, was to oversee the monies in Zurich.

Mr Nadir even added that his ex-wife Ayşegül was so taken with the idea of this project with Wendy Welsher that she agreed to be a 'sleeping partner' in the venture. Apparently she had agreed to sell a painting of hers that was worth about £500,000 in order to obtain a stake in the development. So as far as its ownership was concerned, it was to be a ladies-only village – owned by Asil Nadir's mother, his sister, his ex-wife and the unknown Wendy Welsher.

Shortly after Mr Nadir, from his home in northern Cyprus, had made his explanation of the document known, the *Today* newspaper tracked down a woman they claimed was Wendy Welsher. *Today*'s Wendy Welsher had been in hiding for eight months, and she told the newspaper: 'I can't say a thing. Don't you know what that man will do to me? My life is in grave danger.'

She was a 42-year-old overweight and under-cared-for divorcée. Although *Today* said that she was an ordinary housewife who had 'child-like writing', she alleged that she had been used to take a painting from an address in Berkeley Square where there was a sign on the door saying Nadir Investments. She carried the painting wrapped in brown paper to Bonhams, the fine-art auctioneers. There she showed the power of attorney that she had been given authorising her to sell the picture.

Inside Bonhams she was able to get a meeting with no less a person than the director of fine art himself, according to *Today*. The article went on: 'He unwrapped the painting – and Mrs Welsher was surprised to recognise it as the highly-prized *Sisters* by Lord Frederick Leighton', a painting estimated to be worth about £500,000.

So the ordinary housewife with the child-like writing was able to recognise instantly a painting by the obscure nineteenth-century English artist Lord Frederick Leighton? And was it mere coincidence that the sum of £500,000 was exactly the same amount that Asil Nadir had said his ex-wife Ayşegül was to put into the joint venture with Wendy Welsher – an amount that was to come from her sale of a painting? What on earth were the Nadirs, those sophisticated international travellers, doing mixing with the likes of Wendy Welsher?

Certain features of the alleged contract with David Kent were peculiar. The names of Nadir's sister and mother, the parties to the contract, had been handwritten in capital letters by a Turk or Turkish Cypriot. The capital i's, including the one in Nadir, had a dot on top of them, which nobody without a decent knowledge of Turkish would ever include.

Further down the document, however, where another hand had added 'We the above-named persons sign on behalf and for Mr Asil Nadir' – again in capitals – there was no dot above the i of Nadir – i.e., the addition had been made by a non-Turk.

At one stage Bilge Nevzat agreed that the signature on the document was genuine; but then at a later stage Asil's lawyer said that the fact that it was her signature did not necessarily mean that she had signed that particular document – the implication being that maybe her signature had been taken from elsewhere and transposed onto the document, an act that might not have been revealed in a photocopy.

Then the hunt was on for the mysterious David Kent. The

police claimed that it was a codename for somebody, and that they knew who that somebody was. Nadir had become so concerned about interference with his defence that he had given everybody close to his case codenames; he was called 'Dover' – after the sole apparently, not the white cliffs that he was longing to wave goodbye to. But what could have been the point in drawing up a contract in the fictitious codename of David Kent? Could such a contract ever have been made to stand up in a court of law?

The Kent contract was not to be the last disturbance in the course of the Nadir trials. At another preliminary hearing held before Mr Justice Tucker on 8 March 1993, the lawyer for the Director of Public Prosecutions turned up unexpectedly and dropped a bombshell by telling the court that the police were looking into an alleged conspiracy to pervert the course of justice. This was not just any old conspiracy, however. It involved Mr Nadir, Anthony Scrivener, one of the leading barristers in the country, the poor long-suffering Mr Justice Tucker and an assistant commissioner of the Metropolitan police, Wyn Jones.

Wyn Jones had appeared earlier in the Nadir story. In 1991 he had been suspended for five months while his links with Nadir were investigated. His name had been found in the raid on South Audley Management in 1990. Wyn Jones was subsequently cleared of any impropriety, but why his name should have resurfaced in court in connection with Mr Nadir in 1993 is still a mystery.

The DPP's lawyer gave no indication as to the source of these allegations, saying only that 'the interests of maintaining anonymity of informants are paramount in order to prevail'. That it was the DPP's wish that the judge remove himself from the trial was left in little doubt by the lawyer saying, 'I am submitting that, on behalf of the Director of Public Prosecutions, there are serious problems foreseeable and dangers in your lordship presiding over the trial.' Because of an allegation for which the police have at no time since produced the least scrap of evidence? The Director of Public Prosecutions at the time was Barbara Mills. She had been head of the SFO when Nadir had been first arrested in December 1990.

Asil Nadir has claimed that this allegation – over which he and his sister were arrested and interrogated two days later (although none of his alleged co-conspirators have to this day been interrogated about the allegation) – was the final straw that made him decide that he was not going to get a fair trial in Britain and that he should leave the country. It would be ironic if the SFO's zealous determination to see him behind bars ultimately frustrated its own purpose.

Nadir's flight to northern Cyprus, however, was not the end of his story in the UK. He left behind a trail that threatened to damage the Conservative party that had governed the country uninterruptedly since 1979, and whose policies had made the Polly Peck story possible in the first place.

It had long been known that Nadir had received a letter from Mrs Thatcher shortly after the 1987 general election. In it she had written 'I cannot thank you enough. It was marvellous encouragement to know that you were so committed to the cause in which we all believe.' It had also been claimed that he had given the party over £1.5 million between 1986 and 1990. This had never appeared in Polly Peck's accounts – which legally it should have done if it had been a Polly Peck donation.

Soon after Asil Nadir fled from England the Conservative party revealed the precise sum that he had donated to the party: £440,000 over a period of five years, his last contribution having been made in March 1990. Most of this money had come from Unipac, a wholly owned subsidiary of Polly Peck in Cyprus. Donations from wholly owned subsidiaries, it was suggested, did not need to appear in the accounts of the parent company.

The donations embarrassed the Conservative party deeply, and the party chairman said that the money would be returned were it discovered to have been stolen. The party tried to distance itself more and more from Nadir. Lord McAlpine, the party's treasurer from 1981 to 1990, had once upon a time begun his letters to the chairman of Polly Peck 'Dear Asil'. But with the benefit of hindsight he could recall only two meetings with 'Mr Nadir', one lunch in 1988 and a visit to Mr Nadir's office in September 1991.

Gerald Malone, the party deputy chairman, had several meetings with Mr Nadir. He had been parliamentary consultant to Morgan & Rogerson, Nadir's public-relations advisers, but resigned soon after Asil fled to Cyprus. Although not denying that he had met Mr Nadir, Mr Malone did subsequently find himself denying that he had ever had dealings with the former Polly Peck chairman.

However, the party was far more embarrassed by the revelation in June that Michael Mates, a feisty former army officer and a junior minister in the Northern Ireland office, had written to the Attorney General on behalf of Asil Nadir. Mr Mates had been introduced to the case by Christopher Morgan, an old friend at whose house in the South of France he had stayed. It subsequently transpired that Mates was one of eight Conservative MPs, including Michael Heseltine, the trade and industry minister, to intercede on Asil Nadir's behalf by writing to the Attorney General.

The embarrassment was heightened by the revelation that Mates had given Nadir a watch shortly before his flight, on which was inscribed the words 'Don't let the buggers get you down'. This gift was subsequently described by the Prime Minister, John Major, as 'a misjudgement'.

Although he consistently made it clear that he was saying nothing about the guilt or innocence of Asil Nadir, Michael Mates was forced to resign. But he remained in the spotlight with a dramatic resignation speech in the House of Commons which had the speaker of the house hopping up and down with warnings about contempt of court.

In his speech Mr Mates outlined some of the history of the SFO's investigation of the Nadir case and of the alleged attempt to bribe the judge. The cumulative effect of it all was to suggest nothing so much as the growing frustration of a number of people from one culture at their inability to gather the necessary evidence to convict somebody from a completely different culture whom they had pre-judged as guilty of taking them for a ride to the tune of several hundred million pounds.

INDEX